Transboundary Marine Spatial Planning and International Law

Marine Spatial Planning (MSP) is an integrated and comprehensive approach to ocean governance and is used to establish a rational use of marine space and reconcile conflicting interests of its users. MSP allows both a high level of environmental protection and a wide range of human activities and emphasizes coordinated networks of national, regional and global institutions.

This book focuses on the framework of international law behind MSP and especially on the transboundary aspects of MSP. It first sets out a general framework for transboundary MSP and then moves on to compare and assess differences and similarities between different regions. Specific detailed case studies include the EU with the focus on the Baltic Sea and North Sea, the Bay of Bengal and the Great Barrier Reef in Australia. The authors examine the national and regional significance of MSP from an integrated and sustainable ocean governance point of view. They also show how transboundary MSP can create opportunities and positive initiatives for cross-border cooperation and contribute to the effective protection of the regional marine environment.

Daud Hassan is Director of Higher Degree Research in the School of Law at the University of Western Sydney, Australia.

Tuomas Kuokkanen is a Ministerial Adviser with the Ministry of Environment, Finland and Professor of International Environmental Law at the University of Eastern Finland.

Niko Soininen is Lecturer of Environmental Law and Jurisprudence at the University of Eastern Finland.

Earthscan Oceans

Transboundary Marine Spatial Planning and International Law
Edited by Daud Hassan, Tuomas Kuokkanen, Niko Soininen

Marine Biodiversity, Climatic Variability and Global Change
By Grégory Beaugrand

Marine Biodiversity Conservation
A Practical Approach
By Keith Hiscock

The Great Barrier Reef
An Environmental History
By Ben Daley

Governing Marine Protected Areas
Resilience through Diversity
By Peter J.S. Jones

Marine Policy
An Introduction to Governance and International Law of the Oceans
By Mark Zacharias

For further details please visit the series page on the Routledge website: http://www.routledge.com/books/series/ECOCE

Transboundary Marine Spatial Planning and International Law

Edited by Daud Hassan, Tuomas Kuokkanen and Niko Soininen

Routledge
Taylor & Francis Group
LONDON AND NEW YORK

earthscan
from Routledge

First published 2015
by Routledge

2 Park Square, Milton Park, Abingdon, Oxfordshire OX14 4RN
711 Third Avenue, New York, NY 10017

Routledge is an imprint of the Taylor & Francis Group, an informa business

First issued in paperback 2017

British Library Cataloguing-in-Publication Data
A catalogue record for this book is available from the British Library

Library of Congress Cataloging in Publication Data
Transboundary marine spatial planning and international law / edited by S.M. Daud Hassan, Tuomas Kuokkanen and Niko Soininen.
pages cm
Includes bibliographical references and index.
1. Marine resources conservation–Law and legislation. 2. Marine spatial planning. 3. Law of the sea. 4. International law. I. Hassan, S.M. Daud, editor. II. Kuokkanen, Tuomas, editor. III. Soininen, Niko, editor.
K3485.T73 2015
346.04'69164–dc23
2015005142

ISBN: 978-0-415-73970-2 (hbk)
ISBN: 978-1-138-57488-5 (pbk)

Typeset in Goudy
by Swales & Willis Ltd, Exeter, Devon, UK

Contents

Illustrations

Figures

Tables

Contributors

Hermanni Backer, MSc (Marine Biology), LLM (Public International Law), Professional Secretary, Helsinki Commission (HELCOM) responsible for groups related to environmental effects of maritime traffic, response to spills and MSP. He was the leader of the European Commission preparatory action on maritime spatial planning in the Baltic Sea 'Plan Bothnia' (2010–2012).

An Cliquet is a professor at the Department of European, Public and International Law (EPIL) of the Law School of Ghent University, and a researcher at the Maritime Institute of Ghent University. She holds a PhD in law on the subject of marine nature conservation. She was involved in the Belgian research project GAUFRE (Towards a Spatial Structure Plan for Sustainable Management of the Sea). She has done research on international, European and Belgian marine nature conservation law, integrated coastal zone management in Belgium, the process of designation of marine protected areas in the Belgian part of the North Sea, the conflict between wind farms and marine protected areas in Belgium and public participation in coastal decision making processes.

Jon C. Day, Bach. of Natural Resources (Hons IIA) was previously one of the Directors at the Great Barrier Reef Marine Park Authority; now completing a PhD at the Australian Research Council Centre of Excellence for Coral Reef Studies at James Cook University in Townsville. Jon had 39 years of professional experience as a protected area planner and manager, 28 years of which with the Great Barrier Reef Marine Park. Between 1998 and 2003, Jon was the Director responsible for commencing and coordinating the Representative Areas Program (RAP), the major rezoning program undertaken for the entire Great Barrier Reef. For his efforts with RAP, Jon was awarded an Australian Public Service Medal (PSM) and a Smithsonian-Queensland Fellowship. Jon is the primary author of ten book chapters or books (including the 'Guidelines for applying the IUCN Protected Area Management Categories to Marine Protected Areas') and has more than 40 peer-reviewed publications.

Emdadul Haque is a Joint District Judge in Bangladesh. Currently he is a Doctoral student at the School of Law, University of Western Sydney. Mr Haque is writing his PhD thesis on the Delimitation of Maritime Boundaries in the Bay of Bengal Sub-region in South Asia. Mr Haque holds a Bachelor degree with Honours as well as a Master's degree in Law. He has special interests in the law of the sea with particular reference to South Asian Seas.

Daud Hassan is the Director of Higher Degree Research at the School of Law, University of Western Sydney. He has a PhD in International Marine Environmental Law. Dr Hassan has considerable teaching, research and community service experience in marine environmental issues. He has published widely in the area of international comparative marine environmental law. Most of Dr Hassan's research was directed towards the study of the problems, prospects and issues of marine pollution and its effect on the marine environment in various parts of world's oceans. Dr Hassan's current research interests include sustainable ocean governance with particular reference to marine spatial planning. In 2003 Dr Hassan held a visiting professor position at the Graduate School of Law, Kobe University, Japan. He was the recipient of the Japan Society for the Promotion of Science (JSPS) Fellowship 2003. In 2006 he was invited as a Keynote speaker for the International Conference on Marine Waste Water Discharges and Coastal Environment held in Antalya, Turkey. In 2007 Dr Hassan was a visiting professor in International Environmental Law at the Faculty of Law, University of Bern, Switzerland. He was a visiting scholar at the David C. Lam Institute for East West Studies (LEWI), Hong Kong Baptist University and the University of Eastern Finland in 2010 and 2012 respectively.

Stephen Jay is a lecturer at the University of Liverpool, UK, specializing in marine aspects of spatial planning. He has carried out research projects into the development of offshore wind energy in the UK and other European countries, and into the emerging systems of marine spatial planning. He helps to coordinate the Marine Spatial Planning Research Network and has recently completed the EU-funded project 'Transboundary Planning in the European Atlantic'. He has published and spoken widely on these topics and has organized academic exchanges on marine planning. He is also exploring more theoretical aspects, such as tracing the conceptual origins of marine planning and the interpretation and representation of space in these initiatives.

Tuomas Kuokkanen, Doctor of Law (Helsinki University), is working as a Ministerial Adviser with the Ministry of Environment, Finland. In addition, he is a Part-time Professor of International Environmental Law at the University of Eastern Finland. Between 2004 and 2014, he has been a co-leader for the University of Eastern Finland and UNEP Course on Multilateral Environmental Agreements. Mr Kuokkanen has published a number of articles on international environmental law. He has also worked briefly as an adviser to HELCOM in transboundary MSP-related matters.

Frank Maes, who holds a PhD in Law, is a full-time Professor at the Law School of Ghent University, Head of the Department of European, Public and International

Law (EPIL) and Research Director at the Maritime Institute. Maritime spatial planning experience started with the research project GAUFRE (Towards a Spatial Structure Plan for Sustainable Management of the Sea) (2003–2005), followed by contributions to the first UNESCO International Workshop on marine spatial planning (2006), the ENCORA Paris Conference on a European Coastal Action Plan (2007), CALAMAR (on the topic of transatlantic spatial planning, 2009–2010), partner in MASPNOSE (Preparatory Action on Maritime Spatial Planning in the North Sea – EU DG MARE: 2010–2011), host institute for TransMASP (Transboundary Marine Spatial Planning – EU Marie Curie FP7: 2010–2012) and partner in MESMA (Monitoring and Evaluation of Spatially Managed Areas – EU – FP7: 2009–2013).

Tavis Potts, PhD, is a Senior Lecturer in Human Geography at the University of Aberdeen. Dr Potts has an interest in the social and political dimensions of coastal and marine systems. His research interests span the process and effectiveness of marine spatial planning and integrated coastal management; assessing cultural ecosystem services and incorporating them into policy; and the development of the low carbon blue economy. A common thread in his research is to do with understanding the complexities that face communities and institutions in driving sustainable marine systems and the role of policy, law and politics as a facilitator of change.

Betty Queffelec is a Public Law Researcher and Teacher at University of Brest (UBO), her main topics are maritime spatial planning, integrated coastal zone management, marine biodiversity, ecosystem approach and public participation from national, European and international law perspectives. After some research projects developing integrated coastal zone management from a legal perspective, she was awarded a Marie Curie EU grant to develop a post-doctoral project about transboundary aspects of maritime spatial planning at University of Ghent (Belgium). Based on this two years of research, she explored several maritime spatial planning topics, especially transboundary and land–sea aspects, links between maritime spatial planning and ecosystem approach or biodiversity.

Niko Soininen, MSc (Environmental Law), is a lecturer in Environmental Law and Jurisprudence, University of Eastern Finland. Niko Soininen is a doctoral student of environmental law and will be defending his doctoral thesis on Finnish Water Law in 2015. Expanding on his scholarly work to marine environmental law, Soininen has written about MSP from a rule of law perspective and has studied the implementation of MSP in northern Europe. Outside academia, Soininen has also worked briefly as an adviser to HELCOM in transboundary MSP-related matters.

Acknowledgements

This book has been a journey and is the product of many discussions among the present editors and authors. It assembles many renowned scholars to analyse the different legal and governance aspects of transboundary marine spatial planning (MSP). As a future-oriented process, MSP offers ways to minimize conflicting uses of marine spaces, to support blue growth and to address the most pressing marine environmental concerns, such as climate change, natural hazards, overfishing, coastal erosion, oil, gas, sand and gravel deposits and biodiversity through appropriate management strategies. With the promise of better and more effective ocean governance, it is no wonder that there has been considerable academic research and government interest towards MSP in recent years. However, to our knowledge, this is the first monograph trying to shed light on the overall legal and governance framework of transboundary MSP and it will hopefully be of use to academics, students, government officials, policy makers and practising lawyers interested in marine environmental issues.

A book such as this includes a considerable amount of effort and support. First and foremost, we would like to thank all the chapter authors, Dr Tavis Potts, Prof. Frank Maes, Prof. An Cliquet, Jon Day, Hermanni Backer, Betty Queffelec, Dr Stephen Jay and Emaduel Haque for their valuable contributions to the book. We hope to continue these discussions and collaboration in the future.

The editing work for the book and much of the research has been funded by the Academy of Finland through the 'Environmental justice and ecosystem services: Access, equity and participation in the use and management of aquatic environments in the Helsinki region' (ENJUSTESS, 263403) and 'Legal Framework to Promote Water Security' (WATSEC, 268151) project. We would especially like to thank the ENTJUSTESS-project director Dr Lasse Peltonen for facilitating many valuable and informative discussions and seminars regarding MSP. In addition, we would also like to thank the University of Eastern Finland and its Institute for Natural Resources, Environment and Society (LYY) for providing additional funding for finalizing the book.

We would also like to express our sincere appreciation to the University of Western Sydney Law School, particularly Prof. Michael Adams, Dean of UWS Law School, and Prof. Donna Craig for their support in facilitating editors' meetings in Helsinki for this project. The University of Eastern Finland Law School, the Finnish Ministry of Environment, the Finnish Environment Institute and International Union for Conservation of Nature Environmental Law Centre deserve our gratitude for providing access to facilities for the various contributors of this book to meet and work on the project.

Dr Anita Mäkinen and Dr Riku Varjopuro deserve our gratitude for many discussions regarding MSP in the Baltic Sea. We offer a special thank you to Anita for offering her valuable insights regarding the conclusions chapter. Sarah Olivier has done a remarkable job proofreading the book and putting it together. Furthermore, we are grateful to the publisher for accepting our book proposal for publication and their continuing efforts in finalizing the publication of the book.

Finally, we would like to express our sincerest gratitude to our families for their encouragement, tolerance, support and understanding. We dedicate this book to them.

Daud Hassan
Tuomas Kuokkanen
Niko Soininen

Abbreviations

ABNJ	Areas Beyond National Jurisdiction
BDC	OSPAR Biodiversity Committee
CBD	Convention on Biological Diversity
CEC	Commission of the European Communities
CFP	Common Fisheries Policy
COP	Conference of the Parties
CP	Contracting Party
EBSA	Ecologically or Biologically Significant Marine Areas
EC	European Commission
EEZ	Exclusive Economic Zone
EGTC	European Grouping of Territorial Cooperation
EIA	Environmental Impact Assessment
EIHA	Environmental Impacts of Human Activities
EMODnet	European Marine Observation and Data Network
EU	European Union
FAO	Food and Agriculture Organization
GEF	Global Environment Facility
GIS	Geographic Information System
HELCOM	Helsinki Commission
ICES	International Council for the Exploration of the Sea
ICG-MSP	Intersessional Correspondence Group on Marine Spatial Planning
ICJ	International Court of Justice
ICZM	Integrated Coastal Zone Management
IMCAM	Integrated Marine and Coastal Area Management
IMO	International Maritime Organization
ITLOS	International Tribunal for the Law of the Sea
JMM	Joint Ministerial Meeting
LOSC	Law of the Sea Convention
MASMA	Workshop on Marine Spatial Management (OSPAR)
MoU	Memorandum of understanding
MPA	Marine Protected Area

MS	Member States
MSFD	Marine Strategy Framework Directive
MSM	Marine Spatial Management
MSP	Marine Spatial Planning
NSRAC	North Sea Regional Advisory Council
OSPARCOM	Oslo and Paris Commission
SAC	Special Area for Conservation (Habitat Directive)
SBSTTA	Subsidiary Body on Scientific, Technical and Technological Advice
SEA	Strategic Environmental Assessment
SPINS	Spatial Planning in the North Sea
TBPA	Transboundary Protected Area
TPEA	Transboundary Planning in the European Atlantic
ToR	Term of Reference
UNCED	United Nations Conference on Environment and Development
UNCLOS	United Nations Convention on the Law of the Sea
UNECE	United Nations Economic Commission for Europe
UNESCO	United Nations Educational, Scientific and Cultural Organization
UNEP	United Nations Environment Programme
UNGA	United Nations General Assembly
UNICPOLOS	United Nations Open-ended Informal Consultative Process on Ocean and the Law of the Sea
VASAB	Visions and Strategies around the Baltic Sea
WG	Working Group
WSSD	World Summit on Sustainable Development

Part I

Introduction

Chapter 1

Marine spatial planning as an instrument of sustainable ocean governance

Niko Soininen and Daud Hassan

Need for new forms of governance

All living organisms, including humans, rely on the Earth's ecosystems and ecosystem services to provide such things as food, water, minerals, energy, transportation, disease management, climate regulation, spiritual fulfilment and aesthetic enjoyment.[1] The marine environment has the vital diversity of marine and estuarine animals and plants that are an integral part of the natural and cultural heritage of the earth (Kelleher and Kenchington, 1991). Oceans also present an enormous and nearly untapped reserve of genetic resources for humankind.[2] Despite the paramount importance of the marine environment, its condition is declining. A study by a group of leading scientists concluded that, 'the loss of marine biodiversity is increasingly impairing the ocean's ability to produce seafood, resist diseases, filter pollutants, maintain water quality and recover from perturbations such as over-fishing and climate change' (Worm *et al.*, 2006; United Nations Environmental Programme, 2010).

Over the past 50 years, humans have changed ecosystems, including marine ecosystems, more rapidly and extensively than in any comparable period in human history (World Resources Institute, 2005). Protection of the marine environment is increasingly becoming a problem as more and more people and industries compete for limited marine space and ecosystem services provided by the marine environment. The finite nature of resources is causing conflicts among human uses (human–human conflicts) as well as conflicts between human uses and the environment (human–environment conflicts). The conflicts are growing and will continue to accelerate in the future. These conflicts have mostly been dealt with reactively instead of proactively, and a holistic view which would take into account all the aspects and sectors of marine governance has been lacking.[3] This has led many scholars to argue that the present situation of conflicts between human uses and between humans and the environment is caused by 'a failure in the governance of the marine environment' (Crowder *et al.*, 2006; Pew Oceans Commission, 2003; U.S. Commission on Ocean Policy, 2004; Hall, 2005; Craig, 2012).[4]

Marine Spatial Planning (MSP)[5] is a relatively new instrument designed to alleviate conflicts between human uses as well as between human uses and the marine environment. According to a popular description, MSP is 'a process of analysing and allocating parts of three-dimensional marine spaces (or ecosystems) to specific uses or objectives, to achieve ecological, economic, and social objectives that are usually specified through a political process' (UNESCO, 2013). It 'allows both a high level of environmental protection and a wide range of human activities' (Day, 2008, p. 823). MSP can play a proactive role in planning, setting out a future framework and targets for spatial use. Forward-looking planning can therefore supplement or even replace the *ad hoc* systems of decision-making and regulation (Crowder and Norse, 2008, pp. 772–78; Ehler and Douvere, 2009a, p. 20). This approach is aimed 'to create and establish a more rational use of marine space and the interactions between its uses, to balance demands for development with the need to protect the environment and to achieve social and economic objectives in an open and planned way' (UNESCO, 2013). What MSP is promising, then, is a new future-oriented planning process, which takes into account all the sectors related to the governance of marine issues and allocates marine space both geographically and temporally for different purposes (interests), which are deemed politically desirable.[6]

MSP aims at identifying, allocating[7] and reconciling ecologically, economically and socially important uses of the marine space (Ehler and Douvere, 2009a, p. 21). It is commonly thought that identification of different uses of the marine environment and ecosystem services provided by the marine environment is needed in order to avoid unnecessary conflicts and in order to acquire the knowledge of what resources are to be allocated and the interests and uses that need reconciling.[8] Allocation and reconciliation are necessary because the outputs of the marine environment are limited, and the marine environment cannot usually meet all of the conflicting needs simultaneously without management (ibid., p. 18).[9] MSP can also be used to ensure more equitable access to marine resources and the benefits arising from their use. The siting of key industries could be a means for steering development, for instance in rural or structurally weak areas of coast and coastal hinterland. Indirectly, MSP can also be used to facilitate urban regeneration, such as that of former port areas (ibid., p. 5).

Currently, marine spatial planning can be described broadly as consisting of four main principles:[10] (1) the principle of fit; (2) the principle of multiple use; (3) the principle of stakeholder involvement; and (4) the principle of adaptive management.[11] The principle of fit usually means the management tools, which aim at avoiding or minimizing conflicts or mismatches between 'biophysical systems, socioeconomic activities and governance practices' (Young *et al.*, 2007, p. 27). The principle of multiple use is generally taken to mean the idea that there should be a procedure 'that can mediate among different uses of marine resources and establish priorities when conflicts are unavoidable' (ibid.). In some cases, this means solving *a priori* conflict by adjusting the activities in conflict so that they could coexist. However, in severe conflicts one has to resort to spatially separating the conflicting interests so that they do not interfere with each other (ibid., pp. 27–29). Adaptive management is usually taken to mean 'managing according to plan by which decisions are made and modified as a function of what is known and learned about the system, including information about the effect of previous management actions' (Parma, 1998, p. 26).

Marine spatial planning is most frequently presented to adopt an integrated approach to marine governance. Traditionally, the use of marine space has been planned on a single-sector basis and without considering either cross-sectoral objectives or a plan-based approach (Douvere *et al.*, 2007, pp. 182–191; Young, *et al.*, 2007, pp. 22–27; Douvere, 2008, p. 764; Ehler and Douvere, 2009a, pp.18–19).[12] This is one of the big problems that MSP tries to tackle. In order to deliver sustainable use of ecosystems, it is of primary importance that all the sectors of economic use and environmental protection as well as social issues are involved in the process (Gilliland and Laffoley, 2008, p. 788).[13] MSP places sound science and the best available information at the heart of decision-making. It brings federal, state, local, tribal and other stakeholders together to cooperatively develop marine spatial plans, and this process is designed to decrease user conflict, improve planning and regulatory efficiencies, decrease associated costs and delays, engage affected communities and stakeholders, and preserve critical ecosystem functions and services (NOAA, 2013). Consequently, one might add the principle of integration to the list of management principles within MSP.

A comprehensive marine spatial plan is usually long-term, general in nature, policy oriented and is implemented through more detailed zoning maps, zoning regulations, environmental impact assessment and a permit system. Based on an MSP, individual permit or licensing decisions can be made based on the zoning maps that in turn reflect the vision of the comprehensive marine spatial plan (Ehler and Douvere, 2009b, p. 79). MSP has also been associated with delivering better regulation, implementing multiple legal principles of international environmental law – such as the precautionary principle[14] and the polluter pays principle[15] – and enabling compliance with international, regional and national obligations (Gilliland and Laffoley, 2008, pp. 788–89). MSP is not an instrument that would replace other instruments of governance, but rather it complements and is based on them. Marine spatial planning can be legally binding or a mere policy instrument. However, other instruments of governance are needed to safeguard the sustainability of the allocated activities and the effectiveness of the plan. Allocating the space is one problem, limiting the use of that space to a sustainable level quite another (Ehler and Douvere, 2007, p. 11).

MSP brings many of the marine governance instruments together in a holistic manner and integrates different governance mechanisms related to the use of marine space with different sectors[16] and agencies (Ehler and Douvere, 2009a, pp. 18, 22–23).[17] In this way, MSP is an instrument for managing other instruments of governance. From another perspective it can be said that the more traditional instruments are vehicles of implementation for MSP. It also gives other governance instruments a more temporal dimension and a strategic, as well as an anticipatory, nature: it is not enough merely to allocate space and reconcile conflicting interests here and now – future developments and needs also have to be taken into consideration. In a long-term evaluation, it is paramount to understand how ecosystems and different human uses of the marine environment change over time (Crowder and Norse, 2008, p. 772–778; Ehler and Douvere, 2009a, p. 20). MSP provides a means of strategic conflict resolution at a regional rather than a project level. MSP has a central co-ordinating function for which it can bring disjointed decision-making regimes under one umbrella (Heinrichs, 2007, p. 4).

Mediating between different conceptions of sustainability

Marine spatial planning is connected to the emerging concept of the 'Blue Economy'.[18] From this perspective MSP can be seen as an instrument that helps to boost economic growth and prosperity of a state, and to increase the opportunity for employment (Backer and Frias, 2012, p. 16). MSP provides certainty for investors by increasing investor confidence in regulatory processes and decision-making, especially if coupled with tools such as licensing (Ehler and Douvere, 2009a, p. 5). By facilitating predictability, competitiveness, entrepreneurship and the ability to innovate, MSP provides a means of visualizing future trends and demands and provides a framework for responding to these demands. In turn, this can ensure better access to markets, for instance by providing transport connections, links to other countries, or supporting the development of ports as a key for future competitiveness. The establishment of maritime industry clusters on the mainland and on the coast is one example of this (Heinrichs, 2007, p. 6).

One of the major issues that the Blue Economy tries to untangle and emphasise is the interdependence between the 'ocean – urban coast – human settlement' nexus and its effects on the economic, social and environmental sustainability of both the ocean and the coast (Behnam, 2012, pp. 4–6). Presently, climate change highlights the importance of this nexus. It is placing increasing pressure on coastal regions, causing among other things population displacement,[19] which has been marked as a recipe for conflict and a threat to global security. This raises the question as to what extent coastal and marine areas will retain their residential and economic value in the decades and centuries to come. Seen from the Blue Economy perspective, MSP places emphasis on the *weak conception* of sustainability in saying that social and economic aspects should be emphasized when illuminating sustainability. In other words this means that human well-being is seen to be *based* on economic and social aspects of sustainability. In this line of thought, environmental sustainability is seen to a certain extent as subordinate to other aspects of sustainability.

Contrasting to a certain extent the idea of the Blue Economy, or at least Blue Economic Growth, Ecosystem-Based Management (EBM) places different emphasis on the environmental sustainability. It has been described as one of the tools for implementing the idea of sustainable development and helping to address the governance problems relating to marine issues.[20] The argument is that, in order to achieve sustainability, we need to adopt an ecosystem approach, which 'considers the entire ecosystem, including humans. The goal of ecosystem-based management is to maintain an ecosystem in a healthy, productive and resilient condition so that it can provide the goods and services humans want and need' (Ehler and Douvere, 2009a, p. 24). Within the Convention on Biological Diversity (CBD),[21] EBM is defined as a 'strategy for the integrated management of land, water and living resources that promotes conservation and sustainable use in an equitable way.'[22] For the management of sea use purposes, OSPAR[23] and HELCOM[24] have defined EBM as follows: 'The comprehensive integrated management of human activities based on the best available scientific knowledge about the ecosystem and its dynamics, in order to identify and take action on influences which are critical to the health of marine ecosystems, thereby achieving sustainable use of goods and services and maintenance of ecosystem integrity' (OSPAR-HELCOM, Statement, 2013).[25]

In these conceptions of sustainability, protection and conservation of the environment are seen as the bedrock underlining other aspects of sustainability. In other words, EBM can be seen to have adopted a strong version of sustainability on which economic and social aspects are reliant. It is a question whether human well-being is based on economy or ecology.

The discussion on different conceptions of sustainability goes to the core of marine spatial planning. Some may view MSP mainly as an instrument of environmental protection, whereas others view the primary purpose of planning instruments as being to advance economic interests (Siegel, 2010, p. 27). With regard to the aims of MSP, Ehler and Douvere (2007) have recognized that: '[a] key problem with various existing definitions on marine spatial planning is that they refer to planning and management of human activities and protection of the marine environment as if they were synonymous. They are not, however, and the lack of consistency in the use and application of both terms is one of the main reasons why fruitful discussions and interactions on the need of marine spatial planning regularly fail to go any further.'

Conceptual debate surrounding MSP is a symptom of deeper disagreements and to a certain extent misunderstandings, which can be traced back to the concept of sustainable development. Since its wider popularization in the 1980s, the idea of sustainable development has been influential and widely accepted in international environmental policy and law (Cordonier and Khalfan, 2004, pp. 15–50).[26] No doubt, a big part of this success is a result of the concept's somewhat vague formulation and simultaneous adoption of at least seemingly conflicting views in a way that environmental, social and economic development were seen as mutually reinforcing instead of conflicting aims (Bosselman, 2002, p. 87).[27] What the idea of sustainable development seems to be implicating is that it is *not impossible* to achieve a high level of social, environmental and economic conditions at the same time.[28]

The vague formulation, and adoption of aims which are at least to some extent conflicting, within the idea of sustainable development has led to a situation in which sustainability is used to justify economic growth at the same time as demanding radical changes to the current social and economic structures of societies on the basis that the carrying capacity of the earth will not sustain the present level of social and economic pressure. As Holling (2010) has noted: '[s]ustainable designs driven by conservation interests often ignore the needs for an adaptive form of economic development that emphasizes human economic enterprise and institutional flexibility. Those driven by economic and industrial interests often act as if the uncertainty of nature can be replaced with human engineering and management controls, or be ignored all together. These are not wrong, just too partial.'

Advancing only certain interests was never the idea of sustainable development. Rather, the idea of reconciliation or balancing between the environmental, social and economic aspects was and still is paramount.[29] This idea of reconciliation behind sustainability is neatly characterized by the International Court of Justice (ICJ) in the *Gabcikovo–Nagymaros* case: '[t]hroughout the ages, mankind has, for economic and other reasons, constantly interfered with nature. In the past, this was often done without consideration of the effects upon the environment. Owing to new scientific insights and to a growing awareness of the risks for mankind – for present and future generations of pursuit of such interventions at an unconsidered and unabated pace, new norms and standards have been developed, set forth in a great number of instruments during the last two decades. Such new norms have to be taken into consideration, and such new standards given proper weight, not only when States contemplate new activities but also when continuing with activities begun in the past. This need to reconcile economic development with protection of the environment is aptly expressed in the concept of sustainable development [own emphasis].'

In marine areas, the tool designed to implement sustainable development is marine spatial planning (Sivas and Caldwell, 2008, pp. 226–77). Taking into consideration the fundamental aim of reconciliation established above, it is quite clear that MSP should not be viewed purely as either an instrument of environmental protection or as an instrument advancing economic or social interests.[30] The somewhat idealistic aim of MSP is to achieve all of these objectives at the same time. The rationale of this thinking is to enable maximum utilization as well as maximum protection of biodiversity and ecosystems simultaneously.[31] According to Gilliland and Daffoley (2008, pp. 788–9): 'MSP should encompass the principles that underpin sustainable development . . . [and at the heart of this idea is providing] a balanced view between competing uses, high-lighting where one human activity might preclude another, helping avoid or minimise conflicts of interest, and, where possible, optimising the co-location of compatible activities.'[32]

It is true that many MSP systems have close (past or present) linkages to conservation (for instance, marine-protected areas), but marine zoning within any MSP can also be used for purposes opposed to this. According to Agardy (2010, p. 18): ' . . . zonation may also be based on a kind of conservation-in-reverse process, whereby areas *not* needing as much protection or management as others would be highlighted. Such high-use zones could be "sacrificial" areas, already so degraded or heavily used that massive amounts of conservation effort would not be cost-effective, or they might be areas determined to be relatively unimportant in an ecological sense.'

In conclusion, MSP is aimed at achieving sustainable development. On the whole, sustainable development is firmly based on the idea of reconciliation between environmental, social and economic development. MSP is based on implementing the Blue Economy *and* EBM, which are in their own right implementation mechanisms for sustainable development. Marine spatial planning can be seen as trying to *mediate* between different conceptions of sustainability. The emphasis on economic growth in the form of the Blue Economy and on environmental protection in the form of Ecosystem Based Management can be seen as examples containing different conceptions of sustainability, which MSP tries to reconcile. However, the requirement for sustainability is not only a substantive one but can also be seen placing certain *procedural* aims for MSP. In this line of thought, aiming at sustainability does not mean only balancing competing interests in the use and protection of the marine environment, but also reconciling social needs such as the predictable functioning of the legal system and the rule of law, with other aspects of sustainability. In other words, this means that the process of marine spatial *planning* should be sustainable as well.[33]

MSP as a transboundary process

'Water does not respect boundaries' (Backer and Frias, 2012, p. 14). This means that water, either of the river or of the seas, cannot be parted in the course of its delimitation between states. Any hazardous activities by any state affect the whole marine space of that particular or regional area. Furthermore, as the Secretary-General of the UN has rightly stated, '[m]ost of the oceans are beyond the limits of national jurisdiction. From the seabed to the surface, states benefit from these vast expanses' (United Nations, Secretary-General's remarks, 2012). The interconnectedness of marine ecosystems and activities underpin the importance of transboundary governance of marine areas. Consistent with this, MSP is not prescriptive in terms of the spatial scale it uses and can be implemented at different scales. It can be done at an international, regional, national or local level, depending on the context and needs. There is also the possibility of creating a nested approach, with different plans created for different marine areas. The advantage of this approach is that it ensures greater overall coherence of planning (Heinrichs, 2007, p. 4). A transboundary MSP can be a way forward in enhancing integration and transboundary cooperation in issues such as shipping, commercial fishing and cultural heritage.

In the last 10 years, globally about 20 countries have prepared or are preparing over 40 marine spatial plans and notably almost all plans claim to be ecosystem-based (Ehler, 2012). A study revealed that over the next 10 years at least 80 MSPs will be completed globally (ibid.). Countries that have completed MSPs include, among others, Australia (five Regional MSPs, Coral Sea MPA proposed), Canada (three Regional MSPs), Portugal, Belgium, The Netherlands, Germany (two Federal and three Länder), China (11 Provincial Level MSPs), USA (states of MA and RI) and Norway (Barents and Norwegian seas). Some countries, such as the Netherlands, Norway (Barents Sea) and Belgium, are already preparing second-generation MSPs. Other countries, such as Spain, France, Poland, Finland, Sweden, New Zealand, United Kingdom (two English MSPs and Scotland) and St Kitts and Nevis, are in the process of developing MSPs. In this regard the picture changes constantly as countries develop and tackle aforementioned problems with ocean governance (ibid.).

While many marine spatial plans have been national in character, there are already quite a few examples of transboundary MSP as well.[34] Transboundary MSP in this context means a process in which at least two states, sharing a boundary on the Territorial Sea or the Exclusive Economic Zone, jointly manage a marine area. Taking one example, the European Union (EU) is moving forward in developing regional MSP. During recent years, the need for the development of a comprehensive MSP system for European seas has become increasingly more important, as reflected in various legal and policy documents. As part of its integrated maritime policy a number of instruments have been adopted by the EU, incorporating various strategies and programmes for sustainable management of marine and coastal resources which include among others the EU Integrated Maritime Policy (IMP) 2007, the EU Marine Strategy Framework Directive (MSFD)[35] 2008 and more recently the EU Framework Directive for Maritime Spatial Planning (MSPD)[36] 2014. Although the legal and policy measures and requirements for MSP are yet to be fully developed on the EU-level, there has been some success in developing and implementing MSP in northern parts of Europe. For instance the Baltic Marine Environment Protection Commission (HELCOM) under the Convention on the Protection of the Marine Environment of the Baltic Sea Area and the Commission under the Convention for the Protection of the Marine Environment of the North-East Atlantic (OSPAR) serve as important platforms to encourage and facilitate transboundary MSP due to the importance of cross-border collaboration as well as the transboundary nature of marine resources and activities.

Procedurally, MSP has been characterized by Ehler and Douvere (2009a) in 10 stages, which include:

1. identifying need and establishing authority
2. obtaining financial support
3. organizing the process through pre-planning
4. organizing stakeholder participation
5. defining and analysing existing conditions
6. defining and analysing future conditions
7. preparing and approving the spatial management plan
8. implementing and enforcing the spatial management plan
9. monitoring and evaluating performance
10. adapting the marine spatial management process.

While many of the aspects of transboundary and national MSP process are similar, some elements of the planning process gain especial importance in transboundary MSP. A transboundary MSP requires the development of a common vision of regional actors in assessing, evaluating and monitoring marine spatial plans. As a consequence, joint governance, balancing of powers, institution and capacity building, sufficient stakeholders' participation and open and transparent dialogue in the planning process gain importance. Some of the elements listed above have a more legal character, such as stakeholder participation through Strategic Environmental Assessment (SEA). In general, all the states, organizations and groups that are affected by the MSP can be considered stakeholders in the process. However, involving too many stakeholders at the wrong stage of the process or in the wrong way can distract the process from the anticipated results and takes a lot of time. For these reasons, stakeholder participation should be assessed taking into account certain criteria which can be used to evaluate the importance of a certain stakeholder to the MSP-process. For instance, existing legal rights as well as knowledge and skills and historical and cultural relations to the resources, or the degree of economic and social reliance to the resources to be allocated in the planning-area, are criteria that should be taken into account when deciding on the extent of stakeholder participation (ibid., p. 18 and pp. 43–44). These procedural elements will be considered in more detail later on in Part 3 of the book.

Structure of the book

After the introduction, the authors of the book turn to the question of marine spatial planning as a legal instrument as well as a management and planning tool. In Chapter 2, Tuomas Kuokkanen will take a look back in the recent historical developments of international law in analysing the legal–historical context and background of MSP. In Chapter 3, Tavis Potts will first set the stage for the reality context of MSP. His analysis will provide an overview of the multitude of interests and uses of marine space that need to be considered in marine spatial planning. The chapter will also provide a more detailed analysis on the different management principles and tools of MSP. This grounding of MSP will help in providing an overview for the need for different legal instruments governing MSP. Marine spatial planning has not developed in a legal vacuum and continues to be connected to several international legal instruments that are analysed more closely in Chapters 4 and 5. In Chapter 4, Daud Hassan and Niko Soininen analyse the system of the United Nations Convention on the Law of Sea[37] from *de lege lata* and *de lege ferenda* perspective. This analysis focuses more closely on the issue of implementing MSP through UNCLOS and possibilities and shortcomings UNCLOS presents for effective implementation of MSP. After the analysis of UNCLOS, in Chapter 5, Frank Maes and An Cliquet analyse other international and regional conventions applicable to MSP.

After this general framework, the authors discuss transboundary MSP in more detailed contexts. Regional seas aspect runs through the whole of the book. Three major regional oceans are included in the discussions: the Atlantic, the Pacific and the Indian Ocean (particularly the Bay of Bengal). While there would have been other regional developments with regard to MSP, the examples selected will suffice in presenting different aspects of transboundary MSP, highlighting the problems, successes and lessons learnt from different areas.

The more detailed approach begins with Jon Day's analysis of Australia's Great Barrier Reef Marine Park (GBRMP). It can be said that the GBRMP has set the stage for the following spatial planning in marine areas, being a pioneer example for many aspects in what is presently considered marine spatial planning. Since 1975, the GBRMP has been regulated by the Great Barrier Reef Marine Park Authority (GBRMPA) in accordance with the Great Barrier Reef Marine Park Act of 1975.[38] At present a comprehensive and adaptive spatial planning and zoning system exists to manage and protect the GBRMP.

After discussing the GBRMP, the authors turn to Europe. First, Hermanni Backer analyses transboundary MSP developments in the Baltic Sea area in Northern Europe. Following this, Frank Maes and Betty Queffelec analyse transboundary MSP between Belgium and France in the North Sea. The European approach is furthermore complemented by Stephen Jay's analysis on the transboundary MSP in the Irish Sea. After these regional approaches, Niko Soininen will provide a broader view of the general framework of marine spatial planning in the European Union. This analysis will mainly focus on the aforementioned directive on marine spatial planning and its obligations on the EU member states from transboundary point of view. Finally, the contextual approach to transboundary MSP is complemented by an example from the Bay of Bengal. In Chapter 10, Daud Hassan and Emaduel Haque analyse prospects and opportunities for transboundary MSP in the Bay of Bengal sub-region of the Indian Ocean.

In the final chapter the editors make a comparative and forward-looking analysis of transboundary MSP in the regional seas addressed. This analysis will focus on the joint and differentiating forms and characteristics MSP is taking in different parts of the world. By way of doing this, transboundary MSP can be presented in a broader setting which hopefully will be of value to academics, government officials and other stakeholders.

Notes

1 Ecosystem services include 'provisioning services' such as food, fresh water, fibre, biochemicals, genetic resources; 'regulating services' such as climate regulation, disease regulation, water regulation, water purification, pollination; 'cultural services' such as recreation and tourism, as well as spiritual and religious, aesthetic, inspirational, and educational benefits; and 'supporting services' such as soil formation, nutrient cycling, and primary production. See World Resources Institute (2005) *Millennium Ecosystem Assessment Summary for Decision-Makers*, <http://www.wri.org/publication/millennium-ecosystem-assessment>, accessed on 27 December 2013.

2 The resources of the ocean may be classified into three categories: chemical (materials dissolved in the water); biological (living resources) and geological (minerals that are found on or beneath the ocean floor). See Jones (1972, p. 71).
3 See on the conflicts of interests, e.g. Douvere (2008, p. 763) and Ehler and Douvere (2009a, p. 19). See on the conflicts also Peel and Lloyd (2004, p. 366). However, Peel and Lloyd are quite critical of whether there is even a real consensus on what the nature of the marine problem is or how it should be addressed.
4 The paramount shortcomings of present ocean governance are very much echoed with the visions of Rio+20 and latest initiatives taken by the Secretary-General of United Nations under the theme of the Ocean Compact: Healthy Oceans for Prosperity. Considering the increasing dependence on the sea and its resources the Secretary General of the United Nations has taken initiatives to make a common order in ocean management by way of achieving the following three objectives: protecting people and improving the health of the oceans; protecting, recovering and sustaining the oceans' environment and natural resources and restoring their full food production and livelihoods services; and strengthening ocean knowledge and the management of oceans. See United Nations (2012, pp. 4–7).
5 Most commonly, MSP is referred to as marine spatial planning but the Commission of the European Union, for example, uses the concept of maritime spatial planning to refer to the same instrument. See, for instance, COM (2008) 791 final, p. 2: 'The term *maritime* spatial planning is favoured over *marine* spatial planning to underline the holistic cross-sectoral approach of the process.' See also European Commission, 2013. See also on the conceptual differences between the EU and other parts of the world Backer (2011, p. 280).
6 Although the history of MSP can be traced back to the 1970s, the modern era of MSP can be seen to have begun at the 2002 World Summit on Sustainable Development in Johannesburg. See Douvere, Fanny (2008) 'The Importance of Marine Spatial Planning in Advancing Ecosystem-based Sea Use Management', *Marine Policy*, vol. 32, pp. 762–71. See also Ehler and Douvere (2009, pp. 79–80) and Plan of Implementation of the World Summit on Sustainable Development, UN Doc. A/CONF.199/20 (2002), para. 31(c).
7 EC COM (2008) 791 final, p. 9: 'MSP operates within three dimensions, addressing activities: (a) on the sea bed; (b) in the water column; and (c) on the surface. This allows the same space to be used by different purposes. Time should also be taken into account as a fourth dimension, as the compatibility of uses and the "management need" of a particular maritime region might vary over time.'
8 See for instance Maes *et al.* (2005) *Towards a Spatial Structure Plan for the Sustainable Management of the Sea (GAUFRE)*, Brussels, Belgian Science Policy, where the working group first identified the present uses of the marine environment in a certain area and then analysed the impacts that each individual use has on the marine environment and also laid out different scenarios of how the competing interests relating to the use of ocean space could be reconciled and the conflicts between those interests alleviated and solved.
9 For instance, in the Belgian part of the North Sea, studies showed that the need for the marine space was almost three times larger than the available space. See Maes *et al.* (2005). See on the benefits of MSP on a general level Gilliland and Laffoley (2008, pp. 787–96); Ehler (2008, pp. 840–43).
10 A principle is understood here as meaning a *management principle*, not a legally binding principle.

11 On some occasions, marine spatial planning has also been referred to as a principle of international marine environmental law. See Oral (2008). However, this description of MSP as a principle of international marine environmental law appears confusing in two respects. Firstly, MSP is an instrument that aims at implementing several principles (such as sustainable development) and contains certain principles that operationalize this aim. MSP has close relations to multiple principles of international environmental law but it seems hard to conceive of it as a principle in its own right. Secondly, MSP is presently a collection of certain highly regarded ideas of how the governance of marine areas should be organized. However, naming the instrument as a principle may present MSP as a legally (softly) binding instrument, which it currently is not, at least in its entirety.

12 See also Slocombe (1993, pp. 612–22) and Craig (2012, p. 93) has also stated that this fragmentation in governance could potentially lead to a regulatory chaos, in which case multiple authorities regulate different aspects of the same marine space '. . . while pursuing individual and often conflicting priorities'.

13 This idea of integration is present in other instruments as well, such as Integrated Coastal Zone Management (ICZM). ICZM seeks to unify policy components across the board to achieve comprehensiveness, aggregation and consistency between sectoral policies. This improved management aims to protect the marine environment and, at the same time, help the health of coastal communities. See Hassan (2006, p. 53).

14 According to art. 15 of the Rio Declaration on Environment and Development, Rio de Janeiro, 3–14 June 1992, the precautionary principle can be taken to mean the following: 'Where there are threats of serious or irreversible damage, lack of full scientific certainty shall not be used as a reason for postponing cost effective measures to prevent environmental degradation.' However, at this point it is quite clear that the precautionary principle is not yet a binding principle of international law despite of the fact that it does enjoy some normative support from non-binding legal instruments, see de Sadeleer (2007) 'Lessons from International, EU and Nordic Legal Regimes', in Nicolas de Sadeleer (ed.) *Implementing the Precautionary Principle*, Earthscan, p. 382.

15 The 'polluter pays' principle is defined in the OECD Recommendation of the Council on the Guiding Principles concerning International Economic Aspects of Environmental Policies (26 May 1972 – C(72)128) in the following way: 'This principle means that the polluter should bear the expenses of carrying out the above-mentioned measures decided by public authorities to ensure that the environment is in an acceptable state. In other words, the cost of these measures should be reflected in the cost of goods and services which cause pollution in production and/or consumption. Such measures should not be accompanied by subsidies that would create significant distortions in international trade and investment'. Sands (1994) p. *xxxiv* has stated that the legal status of the principle in international law is somewhat unclear. However, it does enjoy some normative support in some international instruments, such as the principle 14 of the Rio Declaration and OECD Council Recommendations as cited above. Within the EU, the legal status of the principle is stronger as it is incorporated in the primary and secondary legislation of the EU. The polluter pays principle is used, for instance, in the art. 191 of the Treaty on European Union (OJ C326, 26.10.2012) and in the Directive on environmental liability with regard to the prevention and remedying of environmental damage (2004/35/EC, OJ L143, 30 April 2004).

16 By different sectors this paper means, for instance, maritime transportation, renewable energy, marine conservation and protection, seabed mining, fisheries, aquaculture and military defence. See Ehler and Douvere (2009a, p. 23).

17 Agardy (2010, p. 6): 'Ocean zoning by its very nature overcomes fragmentation – obligating the managers of all the various sectors using marine resources and ocean space to think strategically and plan for sustainable use.'

18 The Concept of the Blue Economy, which integrates and is inclusive of the Green Economy, has been introduced by Awni Behnam (President, International Ocean Institute and former UN Assistant Secretary General). The Blue economy is mainly an ocean-based economy and it approaches sustainable development from ocean to land holding the view that the land is the continuation of the sea, which is different from the traditional approach of sustainable development, a land-locked vision that looked from land to the ocean space as if it were an endless horizon. According to him 'most countries' Gross Domestic Product (GDP) is contributed largely from activities in coastal areas (shipping, tourism, fisheries, aquaculture, energy, national defence, etc.). All these factors have to be integrated into holistic and collective governance architecture just as their value added is interconnected. The Blue Economy may be characterized by the recognition of the interdependence of and the necessity for the integration of all stakeholders and actors in this area. Therefore, the Blue Economy, defined as *living with the ocean and from the ocean in a sustainable relationship*, is the transition toward a human-ocean centred relationship where humankind coexists with the ocean and from the ocean in a sustainable way. See Behnam (2007, 2012). In order to implement an ocean-based Blue Economy, ten countries of East Asia signed a joint declaration in 2012. See Changwon Declaration Towards Ocean Based Blue Economy: Moving Ahead with the Sustainable Development Strategy for the Seas of East Asia (The Fourth Ministerial Forum on the Sustainable Development Strategy for the Seas of East Asia, Changwon City, Republic of Korea, 2012), <http://www.pemsea.org/sites/default/files/changwon-declaration.pdf>, accessed 28 December 2013.

19 The World Ocean Review warns that 'without doubt sea level will rise slowly at first, speeding up and continuing beyond the 21st century. Gradually many coastal areas will become uninhabitable. People will lose their homes and part of their culture'. According to this report more than one billion people, most of them in Asia are threatened with displacement. See World Ocean Review (2010, vol. 1, p. 73), <http://worldoceanreview.com/en/>, accessed 27 December 2013.

20 See Gilliland and Laffoley (2008, pp. 787–96) and Pardy (2003, pp. 675–92) who has been quite critical of the claim that ecosystems have to be managed instead of left to their own devices. While the present authors agree with Pardy on the notion that ecosystem management is a policy choice and that not every ecosystem should be managed, the authors would like to point out that modern ecosystem management instruments are constructed in a way that allows some areas to be preserved (or maintained in a natural state of non-equilibrium) and other areas to be used more heavily for human purposes. This can be seen especially well in the place-based management instruments designed for marine areas, such as marine spatial planning. Ecosystem management can be a tool of management or non-management. Craig (2012, p. 5) has also noted that all the marine governance instruments are anthropocentric and some changes in the environment can be considered as bad from the point of view of ecological and economic productivity. For this reason, some form of management should be established in marine areas.

21 Convention on Biological Diversity, Rio de Janeiro, 5 June 1992, in force 29 December 1993, 31 *International Legal Materials* (1992) 822, <http://www.biodiv.org>.

22 See CBD, 'Ecosystem Approach', available at <http://www.cbd.int/ecosystem/>, accessed on 28 January 2013. The objectives of the Convention are presented in Article 1(1)) conservation of biological diversity; (2) sustainable use of its components; and (3) fair and equitable sharing of benefits rising out of the utilization of genetic resources.

23 Convention for the Protection of the Marine Environment of the North-East Atlantic (OSPAR).

24 The Baltic Marine Environment Protection Commission (HELCOM) under the Convention on the Protection of the Marine Environment of the Baltic Sea Area.

25 See also ICES Advisory Committee on Ecosystems, Report of the Regional Ecosystem Study Group for the North Sea 2003.

26 However, debates still remain on the legal status of sustainability. The legal conversation around sustainability focuses very often on whether sustainable development is hard law or soft law and whether the idea of sustainability has legal validity. Usually, the conversation has revolved around whether sustainable development can be seen as customary international law, since it is quite clear that it cannot be regarded as hard law on the basis of the various international agreements that refer to it.

27 Bosselman (2002) also states that the idea of sustainable development can simultaneously facilitate a view holding that sustainable development poses a threat to the on-going economic growth and prosperity and, on the other hand, a view that sustainability is just another form of 'growth-obsessed industrialism'. See also Cordonier and Khalfan (2004, p.15), Costanza and Pattern (1995), and MacDonnel (1997): '[t]he virtue of sustainability as a concept sufficiently broad to embrace contemporary thinking about human objectives becomes a curse of vagueness when the discussion shifts from general to specific'.

28 However, some scholars have been somewhat sceptical as to whether this aim can be achieved. See, for instance, Pearce and Barbier (2000). Kuokkanen (2010, p. 42) states that '[t]he new paradigm [sustainable development] was to optimize short-term economic interests and long-term environmental concerns. This did not, though, lead to a harmony of interests. Rather, the reconciliation brought the two elements under the framework [of sustainable development].'

29 See, Brundtland (1987, p. 20): 'The "environment" is where we all live; and "development" is what we all do in attempting to improve our lot within that abode. The two are inseparable.'; '2005 World Summit Outcome', UNGA Res. A/60/1, adopted by the General Assembly on 15 September 2005 para. 48: ' . . . These efforts will also promote the integration of the three components of sustainable development – economic development, social development and environmental protection – as interdependent and mutually reinforcing pillars', Bosselman (2002, p. 87). However, many scholars have emphasized that the concept of sustainability has many meanings depending on the context of its use. For instance, sustainability in social sciences and natural sciences has completely different meanings. See, for instance, Kotze (2010).

30 See EC COM (2008) 791 final, p. 2: 'Objective [of the MSP] is to balance sectoral interests and achieve sustainable use of marine resources.' The Commission of the European Union is currently preparing a directive for an EU-wide framework of the MSP. See also Agardy (2010, p. 34).

31 However, Jay (2010) has been quite critical towards the idea that MSP could rationalize the use of marine space. This view is mainly based on scepticism towards MSP's

capability of controlling the use of marine environment to the extent required and on the problems of complex objectivities and political settings.

32 Somewhat similarly Arkema *et al.* (2006, pp. 525–32) have seen MSP as a means of implementing EBM which can in turn be seen as substantiating sustainable development.

33 In this line of thought, the law is not seen purely as a means to achieve sustainability but also as an instrument that has its own valuable characteristics, such as procedural safeguards, predictability etc. These can be seen as inherent parts of the social world of sustainability. On the law as a means of achieving sustainability, see Kotze (2010, p. 19).

34 See, for instance, the Plan Bothnia project between Sweden and Finland. More information on Plan Bothnia <http://planbothnia.org/about/>, accessed on 4 February 2013). See also MASPNOSE project between the United Kingdom, the Netherlands, Germany and Denmark. More information on MASPNOSE <http://www.wageningenur.nl/en/show/Maspnose-Maritime-spatial-planning-in-the-North-Sea.htm> accessed on 13 June 2013. A multitude of legal instruments have a direct connection to the drafting and implementation of an MSP. On a regional level and with regard to transboundary issues in the EU, for instance the directive on assessment of the effects of certain plans and programmes on the environment (SEA-directive, 2001/42/EC, OJ L197, 27 June 2001) states some legal obligations with regard to access to information and consultations between countries while the MSP is being drafted, see SEA-directive, art. 7.

35 Directive 2008/56/EC establishing a framework for community action in the field of marine environmental policy. OJ L 164/19 25.6.2008.

36 Directive 2014/89/EU establishing a framework for maritime spatial planning. OJ L 257/135 28.8.2014.

37 United Nations Convention on the Law of the Sea (UNCLOS), Montego Bay, 10 December 1982, in force 16 November 1994, 21 *International Legal Materials* (1982) 1261.

38 *Great Barrier Reef Marine Park Act* 1975 (Cth), Act No. 85 of 1975 as amended up to 2011.

References

Agardy, Tundi (2010) *Ocean Zoning: Making Marine Management More Effective*, Earthscan.

Arkema, Katie K., Abramson, Sarah C. and Dewsbury, Bryan (2006) 'Marine Ecosystem-Based Management: From Characterization to Implementation', *Frontiers in Ecology and the Environment*, vol. 4.

Backer, Hermanni (2011) 'Trans-boundary Maritime Spatial Planning: a Baltic Sea Perspective', *Journal of Coastal Conservation*, vol. 15, p. 279–289.

Backer, Hermanni and Frias, Manuel (eds) (2012) *Planning the Bothnian Sea: Key findings of the Plan Bothnia Project*, Finepress Turku.

Behnam, Awni (2007) 'Biodiversity of the Ocean, A Question of Governance' (IOI Proceedings of PIM XXXII, Malta).

Behnam, Awni (2012) 'From UNCLOS to RIO+20 and the Oceans Compact', <http://www.ioinst.org/index.php?option=com_phocadownload&view=category&download=319:1012-from-unclos-to-rio-20-and-the-ocean-compact-Behnam2012&id=47:ioinforma2012&Itemid=60>, accessed 28 December 2013.

Bosselman, Klaus (2002) 'The Concept of Sustainable Development', in Klaus Bosselmann and David Grinlinton, *Environmental Law for a Sustainable Society*, New Zealand Centre for Environmental Law.

Brundtland, Gro Harlem (1987) *Our Common Future*, Oxford University Press.

Cordonier Segger, Marie Claire and Khalfan, Ashfaq (2004) *Sustainable Development Law: Principles, Practices and Prospects*, Oxford University Press, pp. 15–50.

Costanza, Robert and Pattern, Bernard C. (1995) 'Defining and Predicting Sustainability', *Ecological Economics*, vol. 15, pp. 193–96.

Craig, Robin Kundis (2012) *Comparative Ocean Governance: Place-Based Protections in an Era of Climate Change*, Edward Elgar Publishing.

Crowder, L.B., Osherenko, G., Young, O.R., Airamé, S., Norse, E.A., Baron, N., Day, J.C., Douvere, F., Ehler, C.N., Halpern, B.S, Langdon, S.J., McLeod, K.L., Ogden, J.C., Peach, R.E., Rosenberg, A.A. and Wilson, J.A. (2006) 'Resolving Mismatches in U.S. Ocean Governance', *Science*, vol. 313, pp. 617–18.

Crowder, Larry and Norse, Elliott (2008) 'Essential Ecological Insights for Marine Ecosystem-based Management and Marine Spatial Planning', *Marine Policy*, vol. 32, pp. 772–78.

Convention on Biological Diversity, Rio de Janeiro, 5 June 1992, in force 29 December 1993, 31 *International Legal Materials* (1992) 822, <http://www.biodiv.org>.

Day, Jon (2008) 'The Need and Practice of Monitoring, Evaluating and Adapting Marine Planning and Management: Lessons from the Great Barrier Reef', *Marine Policy*, vol. 32, p. 823–831.

Douvere, Fanny (2008) 'The Importance of Marine Spatial Planning in Advancing Ecosystem-based Sea Use Management', *Marine Policy*, vol. 32, p. 762–771.

Douvere, Fanny, Maes, Frank, Vanhulle, An and Schrijvers, Jessie (2007) 'The Role of Marine Spatial Planning in Sea Use Management: The Belgian Case', *Marine Policy*, vol. 31, pp. 182–91.

Ehler, C. (2008) 'Conclusions: Benefits, Lessons Learned and Future Challenges of Marine Spatial Planning' *Marine Policy*, vol. 32, no 5, pp. 840–43.

Ehler, Charles N. (2012) 'Maritime Spatial Planning: International Experience with MSP' (Conference Paper presented at SHAPE Conference, Venice, Italy, 5–6 June 2012), <http://shape.ervet.it/download/listbox/Venice%20Slides/Ehler_IOC_Unesco.PDF>, accessed 28 December 2013.

Ehler, Charles and Douvere, Fanny (2007) *The Need for a Common Vocabulary for Marine Spatial Planning in Ecosystem-based Marine Management*, p. 11. Available at <http://www.unesco-ioc-marinesp.be/uploads/documentenbank/04f55833a70d8ecb2b712f5c2d23d710.pdf>, accessed on 12 May 2013.

Ehler, Charles and Douvere, Fanny (2009a) *Marine Spatial Planning: A Step-by-Step Approach toward Ecosystem-based Management*, Manual and Guides No. 53, IOCAM Dossier No. 6, pp. 18–19. Available at <http://unesdoc.unesco.org/images/0018/001865/186559e.pdf>, accessed 12 May 2013.

Ehler, Charles and Douvere, Fanny (2009b) 'New Perspectives on Sea Use Management: Initial Findings from European Experience with Marine Spatial Planning', *Journal of Environmental Management*, vol. 90, p. 77–88.

Gabčikovo-Nagymaros Project (Hungary/Slovakia), *ICJ Reports* (1997) 7.

Gilliland, Paul M. and Laffoley, Dan (2008) 'Key Elements and Steps in the Process of Developing Ecosystem-based Marine Spatial Planning, *Marine Policy*, vol. 32, pp. 787–96.

Hall, S. J. (2005) 'U.S. Ocean Policy: A Blueprint for the Future' *Environment*, vol. 47, pp. 41–43.

Hassan, Daud (2006) *Protecting the Marine Environment from the Land-Based Sources of Pollution*, Ashgate Publishing.

Heinrichs, Bernhard (2007) 'PlanCoast-Contribution to Maritime Spatial Planning'. (Paper presented at 4th International PlanCoast Conference, Berlin, 21 November 2007.)

Holling, Crawford S. (2000) 'Theories for Sustainable Futures', *Conservation Ecology*, vol. 4, available at <http://www.consecol.org/vol4/iss2/art7/>, accessed 6 February 2013.

Jay, Stephen (2010) 'Built at Sea: Marine Management and the Construction of Marine Spatial Planning', *Town Planning Review*, vol. 81, p. 173–192.

Jones, E.B. (1972) *Law of the Sea Ocean Resources*, Southern Methodist University Press.

Kelleher, G. and Kenchington, R. (1991) *Guidelines for the Establishing Marine Protected Areas: A Marine Conservation and Development Report*, IUCN, Gland, Switzerland, 1991.

Kotze, Louis (2010) 'Towards a Tentative Legal Formulation of Environmental Governance', in Ed Couzens and Tuula Honkonen (eds), *International Environmental Lawmaking and Diplomacy Review 2009*, University of Eastern Finland, UNEP Course Series 9, p. 3–20.

Kuokkanen, Tuomas (2010) 'Perspectives within the Climate Change Regime', in Ed Couzens and Tuula Honkonen (eds), *International Environmental Law-making and Diplomacy Review* (2010), University of Eastern Finland, UNEP Course Series 10, p. 41–50.

MacDonnel, Lawrence J. (1997) 'Sustainable Use of Water Resources', *Natural Resources & Environment*, vol. 2.

Maes F., Schrijvers, J., van Lancker, V., Verfaillie, E., Degraer, S., Derous, S., De Wachter, B., Volckaert, A., Vanhulle, A., Vandenabeele, P., Cliquet, A., Douvere, F., Lambrecht, J., Makgill, R. (2005) *Towards a Spatial Structure Plan for the Sustainable Management of the Sea (GAUFRE)*.

National Oceanic and Atmospheric Administration (NOAA), 'What is Coastal and Marine Spatial Planning', United States Department of Commerce, <http://www.cmsp.noaa.gov/index.html>, accessed 28 December 2013.

Oral, Nilufer (2008) 'Integrated Coastal Zone Management and Marine Spatial Planning for Hydrocarbon Activities in the Black Sea', *International Journal of Marine and Coastal Law*, vol. 23, p. 453–476.

OSPAR-HELCOM, Statement on the Ecosystem Approach to the Management of Human Activities, First Joint Ministerial Meeting of the Helsinki and OSPAR Commissions, Bremen, Germany, 25–26 June, 2003.

Pardy, Bruce (2003) 'Changing Nature: The Myth of the Inevitability of Ecosystem Management', *Pace Environmental Law Review*, vol. 29, pp. 675–92.

Parma, Ana M. (1998) 'What Can Adaptive Management Do for Our Fish, Forests, Food and Biodiversity?' *Integrative Biology*, vol. 1, p. 16–26.

Pearce, David W. and Barbier, Edward B. (2000) *Blueprint for a Sustainable Economy*, Earthscan.

Peel, Deborah and Lloyd, Greg M. (2004) 'The Social Reconstruction of the Marine Environment: Towards Marine Spatial Planning?', *Town Planning Review*, vol. 75, pp. 359–78.

Pew Oceans Commission (2003), *America's Living Oceans: Charting a Course for Sea Change*. *Arlington*, available at <http://www.pewtrusts.org/uploadedFiles/wwwpewtrusts

org/Reports/Protecting_ocean_life/env_pew_oceans_final_report.pdf>, accessed 12 May 2013.

Sands, Philippe (1994) 'International Environmental Law: An Introductory Overview', in Philippe Sands (ed.), *Greening International Law*, The New Press.

Siegel, Charles (2010) *Unplanning: Livable Cities and Political Choices*, Preservation Institute.

Sivas, Deborah A. and Caldwell, Margaret R. (2008) 'A New Vision for California Ocean Governance: Comprehensive Ecosystem-based Marine Zoning', *Stanford Environmental Law Journal*, vol. 27, pp. 211–270.

Slocombe, Scott D. (1993) 'Implementing Ecosystem-based Management: Development of Theory, Practice, and Research for Planning and Managing a Region', *BioScience*, vol. 43, pp. 612–22.

The Secretary General of the United Nations (2012) *The Oceans Compact: Healthy Oceans for Prosperity – An Initiative of the United Nations Secretary-General*, p. 2. <https://www.un.org/Depts/los/ocean_compact/oceans_compact.htm>, accessed on 29 March 2014.

UNESCO, 'Marine Spatial Planning Initiative, Marine Spatial Planning (MSP)', available at <http://www.unesco-ioc-marinesp.be/marine_spatial_planning_msp>, accessed 5 February 2013.

United Nations, *Secretary-General's remarks at Law of Sea conference and launch of UN Oceans Compact* (Yeosu International Conference, Yeosu, Republic of Korea, 12 August 2012). <http://www.un.org/sg/statements/index.asp?nid=6239>, accessed 27 December 2013.

United Nations (2012) *The Oceans Compact: Healthy Oceans for Prosperity-An Initiative of the United Nations Secretary-General*. <https://www.un.org/Depts/los/ocean_compact/oceans_compact.htm>, accessed 29 March 2014.

United Nations Environmental Programme (2010) *Global Synthesis: A report from the Regional Seas Conventions and Action Plans for the Marine Biodiversity Assessment and Outlook Series*.

U.S. Commission on Ocean Policy (2004), *An Ocean Blueprint for the 21st Century*, Final Report of the U.S. Commission on Ocean Policy to the President and Congress.

World Resources Institute (2005) 'Millennium Ecosystem Assessment: Summary for Decision-Makers'. <http://www.wri.org/publication/millennium-ecosystem-assessment>, accessed 27 December 2013. See also The Secretary General of the United Nations (2012) *The Oceans Compact: Healthy Oceans for Prosperity – An Initiative of the United Nations Secretary-General*, p. 2. <https://www.un.org/Depts/los/ocean_compact/oceans_compact.htm>, accessed 29 March 2014.

Worm, Boris, Barbier, Edward B., Beaumont, Nicola J., Duffy, Emmett, Folke, Carl, Halpern, Benjamin S., Jackson, Jeremy B.C., Lotze, Heike K., Micheli, Fiorenza, Palumbi, Stephen R., Sala, Enric, Selkoe, Kimberley A., Stachowicz, John J., Watson, Reg (2006) 'Impacts of biodiversity loss on ocean ecosystem services', *Science*, vol. 314, no. 5800, pp. 787–90.

Young, Oran R., Osherenko, Gail, Ekstrom, Julia, Crowder, Larry B., Ogden, John, Wilson, James A., Day, Jon C., Douvere, Fanny, Ehler, Charles N., McLeod, Karen L., Halpern, Benjamin S. and Peach, Robbin (2007) 'Solving the Crisis in Ocean Governance: Place-Based Management of Marine Ecosystems', *Environment*, vol. 49, pp. 20–32.

Part II

Marine spatial planning in a general framework

Chapter 2

Marine spatial planning in international law before MSP

Tuomas Kuokkanen[1]

Introduction

Even though marine spatial planning (MSP) is a relatively new instrument, its concept was established under international law. Indeed, the law of the sea has been based throughout history on different spatial zones where states have had various rights and obligations.

Describing the development of the law of the sea, René Dupuy notes that '[t]he sea has always been lashed by two major contrary winds: the wind from the high seas towards the land is the wind of freedom; the wind from the land toward the high seas is the bearer of sovereignties' (Dupuy, 1991, p. 247). The law of the sea, according to him, has been in the middle between these conflicting forces (ibid.). This dichotomy is still reflected in the broad categories of marine spaces: marine spaces under national jurisdiction and marine spaces beyond national jurisdiction. The first category can be divided into marine spaces under complete territorial jurisdiction including internal waters, the territorial sea, international straits and archipelagic waters and to marine spaces under limited spatial jurisdiction, including the contiguous zone, the exclusive economic zone (EEZ) and the continental shelf. The second category consists of the high seas and the deep seabed (the Area) (Tanaka, 2012, pp. 6–8).

In addition to the above 'spatial distribution of jurisdiction' (ibid., p. 4), the proper function of the international sea regime requires international cooperation between states. Such cooperation may involve both elaboration of substantive regulations and management actions.

Spatial distribution allocation and international cooperation also form the basis for MSP. While the spatial element refers to the allocation of jurisdiction, international cooperation refers to substantive regulations on and managerial reconciliation of different uses of marine space. These three aspects will be discussed in the following chapters.

Spatial jurisdiction

Early cases of spatial jurisdiction

Two classical marine-related disputes – the *North Atlantic Coast Fisheries* case[2] and the *Bering Sea Seals* case[3] – reflect aspects of marine spatial planning.

While the former concerned the right to fish and the right to issue protection measures the latter related to the utilization and to the protection of seals. Yet the arbitral tribunals in both cases managed to settle the disputes by applying jurisdictional principles rather than substantive rules.

The background to the *North Atlantic Coast Fisheries* case dates back to the War of 1812 between the United States and Great Britain. The American privileges along parts of the North Atlantic coast were later redefined by the treaty of 1818.[4] A few years after the conclusion of the treaty, circumstances in the treaty area started to change as the local authorities discovered the economic value of fisheries and consequently recognized a need to restrict fishing activities. From the 1830s, the Province of Nova Scotia and the Self-Government of Newfoundland started to issue fishing regulations. The United States, however, argued that many such regulations were given in the interest of local fishermen with increasing disfavour towards American fishermen. Subsequently, the United States and Great Britain engaged in a number of conflicts between the 1830s and the beginning of the twentieth century concerning the scope of the American privileges and the right of Great Britain to issue regulations applicable to the United States' fishermen.

As Great Britain and the United States were not able to settle the dispute,[5] the two countries finally signed a *compromis* on 27 January 1909 submitting the issue, comprising of seven questions, to the Permanent Court of Arbitration. The first question concerned the right, if any, of Great Britain to regulate the liberties provided by the 1818 treaty to United States nationals, and in case such a right existed, whether exercise of the right required consent by the United States.[6] The arbitral tribunal gave its decision on 7 September 1910 (*North Atlantic Coast Fisheries* case pp. 173–226).[7] With regard to the first question, the tribunal at the outset noted that as follows: 'Considering that the right to regulate the liberties conferred by the Treaty of 1818 is an attribute of sovereignty, and as such must be held to reside in the territorial sovereign, unless the contrary be provided; and considering that one of the essential elements of sovereignty is that it is to be exercised within territorial limits, and that, failing proof to the contrary, the territory is co-terminous with the Sovereignty, it follows that the burden of the assertion involved in the contention of the United States (viz. that the right to regulate does not reside independently in Great Britain, the territorial Sovereign) must fall on the United States.' (*North Atlantic Coast Fisheries* case p. 180.)[8]

Having confirmed the right of Great Britain to regulate, the tribunal next specified that the exercise of such right was limited by the 1818 Treaty (ibid., p. 187). The arbitral tribunal specified that sovereignty meant, in that particular instance, jurisdiction to legislate (ibid., p. 180)[9]. Furthermore, the arbitral tribunal noted that sovereignty was subject to limitations based on international law or limitations agreed to in a treaty (ibid., p. 187).[10] Hence, the tribunal separated form and substance by treating sovereignty as a jurisdictional rather than as a substantive category.

Turning to the classical *Bering Sea Fur Seals* arbitration between the United States and Great Britain it can be noted that the background of the dispute dates back to the fact that the United States adopted a series of acts between 1868 and 1873 in order to control over-exploitation of Bering Sea fur seals.[11] That legislation applied 'within the limits of Alaska territory or within the waters thereof'.[12] The United States was, at that time, a supporter of the three-mile limit with regard to territorial sea. As pelagic sealing by foreigners took place outside this ordinary three-mile limit, the legal issue for the United States was whether it would be entitled to exercise its jurisdiction in order to control pelagic sealing.[13]

On 1 August 1886, the United States seized three British Columbian sealing schooners in the high seas of Bering Sea for the offence of hunting and killing seals (Moore, 1898, p. 954). Great Britain protested against the seizures, arguing that such measures were unjustified under international law. As the two governments were not able to settle the case through diplomacy, in 1892 they signed a treaty of arbitration between them. The main issue submitted to arbitration was whether the United States was allowed to exercise its jurisdiction on the high seas. The tribunal gave its award on 15 August 1893. With regard to the fifth question, the tribunal decided that: 'the United States ha[d] [no] right of protection or property in the fur-seals frequenting the islands of the United States in [the Bering Sea], when such seals are found outside the ordinary three-mile limit.' (ibid., p. 949)

The main focus of the *Bering Sea Fur Seals* arbitration was on the limits of a state's jurisdiction rather than on the limits of the freedom of the high seas. The award introduced a limitation on state sovereignty based on international law: a state is not allowed to extend its legislative or its enforcement jurisdiction to the high seas, which are open to all states, and thus beyond the limits of national jurisdiction. The United States obviously had a substantive interest in attempting to exercise protective jurisdiction. However, the jurisdictional limitations introduced by the rulings were formal in the sense that they were laid down notwithstanding the substantive interests involved. The award conveyed the message that general international law imposes limitations upon a state's right to exercise legislative, judicial and enforcement jurisdiction.

While the *Bering Sea Fur Seals* arbitration concerned limits of state jurisdiction with regard to the areas beyond a state's jurisdiction, the *North Atlantic Coast Fisheries* case specified that territorial sovereignty is presumed so that limitations on state sovereignty are to be proved, not presumed. The arbitral tribunal also noted in the *North Atlantic Coast Fisheries* case that even though jurisdiction to legislate was inherent in territorial sovereignty, that right was not absolute but subject to limitations based on international law and limitations agreed upon in a treaty. The two awards established a limitation upon state sovereignty based on international law: a state is not allowed to extend its legislative or its enforcement jurisdiction to the high seas which are, by definition, open to all states and thus beyond the reach of national jurisdiction. However, in the *Bering Sea* award, the jurisdictional aspect of state sovereignty was overlegitimized with the result that the protective side was underlegitimized. This imbalance showed the insufficiency of the pure spatial jurisdictional approach.

Inadequacy of pure spatial jurisdiction

The *Bering Sea Fur Seals* award revealed the blindness of pure spatial jurisdiction to the substantive issues. Lauterpacht (1970) attacked the award in many of his writings.[14] The main object of his criticism was the arbitral tribunal's conclusion on the freedom of high seas. The limits of the freedom of high seas have been addressed in general by others as well. For example, Oppenheim (2008, p. 727) notes:

> But although the open sea is not the territory of any state, it is nevertheless an object of the law of nations. The mere fact that there is a rule examining the open sea from the sovereignty of any state whatever shows this. But there are other reasons. For if the law of nations were to content itself with the rule which excludes the open sea from possible state property, the consequence would be a condition of lawlessness and anarchy on the open sea. To obviate such lawlessness, customary international law contains some rules which guarantee a certain legal order on the open sea, in spite of the fact that it is not the territory of any state; and important international conventions have been concluded with the same object.

The need for international regulations was recognized gradually. In 1924, the Assembly of the League of Nations appointed a Committee of Experts for the Progressive Codification of International Law to report on the questions, which appeared ripe for international regulation (Committee of Experts, edited by Rosenne, 1972, pp. 31–308) The exploitation of the products of sea was one of the subjects that the Committee explored. Mr José León Suárez, the rapporteur for the subject, pointed out that animals 'are ignorant of jurisdictions and national frontiers and observe not international law' (ibid., p. 148), and that '[t]he marine species of use to man will become extinct unless their exploitation is subject to international regulation' (ibid., p. 147). The committee concluded, on the basis of Mr. Suárez's report, that it would be desirable to regulate the subject of the exploitation of the products of the sea (ibid., pp. 315–16).[15]

Substantive regulations

While the Committee of the League of Nations highlighted the need for international regulations on marine living resources, substantive marine regulations had begun to develop, albeit in a limited form, even earlier. For example, in the beginning of the nineteenth century, a number of disputes between English and French fishermen on fishing in the English Channel took place. In 1837, the French and British governments appointed a mixed commission to define limits within which the French and English fishermen would have a right to fish. On the basis of the arrangements proposed by the mixed commission, the two governments concluded a bilateral agreement in 1839.[16] The main purpose of that convention was to prevent collisions between the fishing boats of the two countries.[17] However, as fishermen from a number of countries were present in the North Sea, it became apparent that the bilateral arrangement was not sufficient, but that a multilateral convention was needed.[18] In 1882, the International Convention for the Purpose of Regulating the Police of the Fisheries in the North Sea outside Territorial Waters was concluded between Great Britain, Germany, France, Belgium, Denmark and the Netherlands.[19] The objective of the 1882 convention was the same as that of the 1839 convention: to prevent disputes and maintain order on the high seas.[20]

As scientific studies began to gradually support the establishment of conservation regulations, the objective of the regulations shifted from dispute and collision prevention to avoiding overfishing. For example, the International Council for the Exploration of the Seas (ICES) was established in 1902[21] and the North American Commission for Fishery Research in 1921. Furthermore, states began to elaborate international regulations based on scientific expertise. For example, in 1923 the United States and Canada concluded an agreement for the preservation of the halibut fisheries of the Northern Pacific Ocean.[22] Later on, several other regional fishery agreements were concluded.[23]

In the same vein, international regulations were agreed in relation to sealing and whaling in order to avoid overexploitation. For example, a multilateral convention to protect the Bering Sea seals was concluded between Russia, the United States, Great Britain and Japan in 1911.[24] The Convention established a protected area, north of the 30th parallel of north latitude, where all pelagic sealing was prohibited.[25] With regard to whaling, the Convention for the Regulation of Whaling was adopted in 1931[26] on the basis of the preparatory work by the League of Nations Committee of Experts for the Progressive Codification of International Law.[27] Although its scope was limited, the Convention, nevertheless, included certain conservation measures.[28] Moreover, the Convention's jurisdictional scope was determined to cover 'all waters of the world' including both the high seas and territorial seas. After the Second World War, a new whaling convention replacing the earlier arrangements was concluded in 1946[29] to 'establish a system of international regulation for the whale fisheries to ensure proper and effective conservation and development of whale stocks'.[30]

Consequently, the regulatory development expanded gradually in relation to marine living resources. At first the objects of regulations were fish, seals and whales, but finally marine living resources in general were also included. The jurisdictional scope of the regulations was designed to cover in particular the high seas and, as appropriate, also territorial waters. The purpose of the regulations was to avoid overexploitation based primarily on economic grounds. The purpose was further extended by the conclusion of the Convention on Fishing and Conservation of the Living Resources of the High Seas in the United Nations

Conference of the Law of the Sea in 1958.[31] The Convention applied generally to marine living resources, and not only to a particular fish or a particular species.

In the same vein, a gradual expansion of international substantive regulations took place in connection with the protection of the marine environment.[32] It was recognized that there was a need to regulate various activities in order to protect both the marine environment and legitimate uses of the sea. Therefore, in 1954, the International Convention for the Prevention of Pollution of the Sea by Oil was concluded.[33] The convention originally provided for a zone of 50 miles from any coastline, where it was prohibited to discharge oil. Later on, the system of the prohibited zone was first further extended and then replaced by emission standard regulations.[34]

Along with marine pollution, states recognized that they had a common interest in taking international action to prevent and control all sources of pollution both globally and regionally.[35] It was noted that in addition to their ecological value, the seas have also economic, social and cultural value.[36] As marine pollution was threatening both the ecological equilibrium and the legitimate uses of the sea,[37] states agreed on regulation to protect the marine environment.[38] Because many marine pollution problems were regional, it was necessary to introduce regional regulations.[39] Moreover, global treaties were also needed to regulate various activities and to provide a framework for regional regulations.[40] The international regulations were imposed to prevent, for instance, the following causes of pollution: vessel-based pollution,[41] pollution by dumping,[42] air-based pollution,[43] land-based pollution[44] and pollution from the exploration and exploitation of the seabed.[45] Furthermore, in order to prevent adverse effects arising from pollution incidents, regulations were laid down to combat such incidents.[46] These regulations set limitations for states and through their implementing actions also to private operators, concerning different uses of the sea.

Managerial approach

Along with the development of substantive marine regulations, a managerial approach began to develop, in a limited form, in connection with early treaties on the conservation of marine living resources. The purpose of that approach was to coordinate, reconcile and optimize short-term interests and long-term concerns through technically oriented management. Currently, the doctrine of sustainable development represents, albeit in a broader form, essentially the same approach.

The early treaties on marine living resources aimed to adjust the harvesting of marine resources to a level of avoiding overcatching while allowing rational exploitation. The 1911 Convention for the protection of Bering Sea fur seals[47] aimed, in fact, at reconciliation between economic and conservation interests. Although unrestricted sealing in the short-term represented a profitable business, it was leading in the long-term to the extinction of the fur seals. Therefore, it was in the states' common interest[48] to find a solution by limiting the sealing to an optimized level.[49] Once sealing was rationalized in this way, the seal herd began to recover.[50] Subsequently, the optimizing approach was extended from seals to whales. The purpose of the early whaling regulations adopted in the 1930s[51] was to maintain the whale stocks in order to secure the prosperity of the whaling industry. The optimizing approach was further elaborated under the 1946 International Convention for the Regulation of Whaling.[52] Rational exploitation was elaborated further in connection with fishery agreements. [53] At the global level, the concept of optimum utilization was incorporated into the 1958 Convention on the Living Resources of the High Seas to be applied with regard to the exploitation of marine resources in general.[54]

Later on, the optimal utilization approach was adopted under various regional conventions.[55] The method was also confirmed in the 1982 United Nations Convention on the Law of the Sea and in the 1995 Convention on Straddling and Highly Migratory Fish Stocks.[56] In addition, the ecosystem considerations were first incorporated into the determination of rational utilization in connection with the protection of Antarctic marine living resources.[57] The ecosystem approach was reflected also in the Law of the Sea Convention.[58]

The purpose of the objective of optimum utilization was to ensure the long-term sustainability[59] of stocks while also taking into account short-term needs. By integrating conservation interests with other interests it was no longer possible to consider the exploitation of marine living resources in isolation from conservation. The optimization of utilization and conservation interests gradually started to replace the classical principle of the freedom of exploitation.[60]

Conclusions

This chapter has sought to demonstrate that MSP has neither developed nor that it operates in a legal vacuum. International law has for long allocated various rights and obligations to states in relation to usages of seas. This legal background illustrates that there was marine spatial planning prior to MSP. Moreover, despite the introduction of MSP, international law and various legal instruments still continue to be applicable. MSP cannot, thus, be applied as *tabula rasa* but rather it should be placed in the context of a web made up of a number of international instruments.

More specifically, the article suggests that the three approaches discussed above – spatial jurisdiction, substantive regulations and managerial approach – appear to reflect a similar approach to MSP. Even though these approaches have been dealt with separately, this does not mean that they have been or are functionally separate. On the contrary, in many instances they are interlinked. The Convention on the Law of the Sea, for example, represents all three approaches.[61] First, the Law of the Sea allocates spatial jurisdiction on the basis of different marine zones. Secondly, it also includes substantive principles and regulations, for instance, on the right of innocent passage. Thirdly, by way of managerial approach, the Convention provides a framework which seeks reconciliation between individualistic and communal, conservation and utilization, protection and exploitation and other conflicting interests.

Notes

1 Professor of International Environmental Law (part-time), University of Eastern Finland; Counsellor, Ministry of the Environment of Finland; e-mail: Tuomas.Kuokkanen@uef.fi. The author has participated in the research projects 'Legal framework to promote water security' (WATSEC) and 'Environmental justice and ecosystems services: Access, equity and participation in the use and management of aquatic environments in the Helsinki region' (ENJUSTESS), financed by the Academy of Finland. The paper is partly based on the work of Kuokkanen (2002).

2 *North Atlantic Coast Fisheries* case, p. 68.

3 *Bering Fur Seals* arbitration, pp. 910–19.

4 Article 1 of the Convention between Great Britain and the United States, signed in London on 20 October 1818. See the *North Atlantic Coast Fisheries* case, pp. 173–4.

5 The confrontations strained the friendly relations of the two countries and even led to armed conflict. See Anderson (1913) p. 1; Lansing (1911) p. 5; Leonard (1944) p. 17.

6 The other six questions concerned more technical issues.

7 *North Atlantic Coast Fisheries* case, pp. 173–226. For discussion, see Anderson (1913) pp. 1–16; Basdevant (1912) pp. 421–582; Borchardt (1911) pp. 1–23; Hackworth (1940) pp. 783–92; Johnston (1965) pp. 261–64; Lammasch (1912) pp. 178–80; Lansing (1911) pp. 1–31.

8 The tribunal stated as follows: 'In any event, Great Britain, as the local sovereign, has the duty of preserving and protecting the fisheries. In so far as it is necessary for that purpose, Great Britain is not only entitled, but obliged, to provide for the protection and preservation of the fisheries; always remembering that the exercise of this right of legislation is limited by the obligation to execute the Treaty in good faith.' See *North Atlantic Coast Fisheries* case, p. 180.

9 See ibid., p. 180 ('Considering that the right to regulate the liberties conferred by the Treaty of 1818 is an attribute of sovereignty . . . ').

10 See ibid., p. 187 ('[E]xercise of this right of legislation is limited by the obligation to execute the Treaty in good faith.'); p. 188 ('But from the Treaty results an obligatory relation whereby the right of Great Britain to exercise its right of sovereignty by making regulations is limited to such regulations as are made in good faith, and are not in violation of the Treaty.'); p. 188–9 ('The right of Great Britain to make regulations . . . is inherent to the sovereignty of Great Britain . . . The exercise of that right by Great Britain is, however, limited by the said Treaty in respect of the said liberties therein granted to the inhabitants of the United States in that such regulations must be made *bona fide* and must not be in violation of the said Treaty.').

11 Acts of 27 July 1868, 3 March 1869, 1 July 1870 and 3 March 1873. By these acts several prohibitions were made and special reservation areas were established. Under the Act of 1 July 1870, the right to take fur seals on the Pribilof Islands could be leased for a twenty-year period. In August 1870 the sealing privileges were leased to the Alaska Commercial Company. See John Bassett Moore, *History and Digest of the International Arbitrations to which the United States has been a Party*, (1898) Vol. I, pp. 763–4; Leonard (1944) p. 56; Gay (1987) pp. 21–4.

12 See the Act of 27 July 1868, quoted in Moore (1898) Vol. I, p. 763–4.

13 The phrase 'within the waters thereof' was subject to different interpretations. Initially, the United States Treasury Department construed the phrase to refer to ordinary territorial waters. See Moore (1898) Vol. I, p. 767–8. However, in 1876 the American

schooner *San Diego* was seized twenty miles from land because it was sealing within the limits of the Alaska Territory, or in the waters thereof. See Gay (1987) pp. 24–5. In 1881, the Department explicitly held that jurisdiction could be exercised beyond the three-mile limit. See Moore (1898) Vol. I, p. 769. The State Department, however, stuck to the three-mile zone. In his memorandum of 28 May 1886 to Secretary of the Treasury Manning, Secretary of State Bayard stated that the United States denied Russia's jurisdiction beyond three miles, and that therefore the United States could not claim greater jurisdiction against other nations than what was derived from Russia. See Leonard (1944) p. 57.

14 See, for example, Lauterpacht (1970) pp. 384–5 ('On occasions, international tribunals have gone far towards asserting complete freedom of action regardless of the interests of other States. The *Behring Sea Arbitration*, in which the State's right to claim all the advantages resulting from the principle of the freedom of the seas was upheld by the Tribunal, is an instructive example.').

15 The Committee proposed that an international conference should be convened with participants such as experts in applied maritime zoology, representatives of marine product industries and jurists, and also representatives of international organizations.

16 Convention between France and Great Britain for Defining the Limits of Exclusive Fishing Rights, 1839, Preamble ('And whereas the Commissioners so appointed have agreed upon certain lines, as marked in a chart hereinafter referred to, as the limits above-mentioned, and have also agreed upon certain arrangements which they conceive to be calculated to prevent the recurrence of disputes, which have at various times arisen between the fishermen of the 2 countries.').

17 A mixed commission was established pursuant to Article XI of the 1839 convention. In 1843, the commission drafted regulations for the guidance of fishermen. The regulations were adopted by the two governments on 23 June 1843. The regulations also contained provisions applicable on the high seas. The provisions related to the size of mesh and fitting of nets, the season for oyster fishing and the size of the oysters taken (Articles 16–23, 28, 37, 41–43, 45 and 48). See also Fulton (1911) pp. 614 and Dagget (1934) footnote 133, pp. 713–4.

18 France and Great Britain concluded in 1867 a new bilateral convention: Convention between France and Great Britain relative to Fisheries, Paris, 11 November 1867. However, France failed to adopt the necessary implementing legislation to enforce the regulations of the new treaty. See Johnston (1965) p. 254 and Fulton (1911) p. 619.

19 For more details, see Fulton (1911) p. 637–9.

20 Convention between Belgium, Denmark, France, Germany, Great Britain and the Netherlands for Regulating the Police of the North Sea Fisheries, 1882. The Convention aimed at establishing fishery police outside territorial waters. The provisions of the convention related, for instance, to the registration and the numeration of boats as well as the malicious use of instruments for cutting nets.

21 Already in 1899 the Stockholm International Conference recommended a research programme to serve as the basis to subsequent international legislation. See Colombos (1967) p. 424. The ICES was founded informally in 1902 and formally in 1964 when the Council was established by an international convention. See Convention for the International Council for the Exploration of the Sea, Copenhagen, 1964. See also the 1926 reply by Sweden to the questionnaire by the League of Nations Codification Committee C.49.M.26.1926.V, p. 265 ('This Council was created on the assumption that it would be impossible to establish international rules for the fishing or catching

of certain maritime species until careful scientific research had shown that fishing or catching so seriously affected the existence of these species as to warrant their protection by international measures.').

22 Convention between the United States of America and Canada for the Preservation of the Halibut Fisheries of the Northern Pacific Ocean, 1923. Article 1 of the convention established a three-month closed winter season when it was prohibited to fish for halibut based on scientific findings on spawning seasons. Furthermore, the International Fisheries Commission was established pursuant to the Convention, to investigate the halibut fishery and recommend regulations for its preservation. A new convention was concluded in 1930 in which the powers of the Commission were further extended. See the Convention between the United States of America and Canada for the Preservation of the Halibut Fishery of the Northern Pacific Ocean and Bering Sea, 1930. See also Johnston (1965) p. 372–4.

23 Överenskommelse angående regleringen av fisket efter rödspätta (pleuronectes platessa) och skrubba (pleuronectes flesus) i Östersjön, Berlin, 1929. The agreement was concluded by Denmark, the Free City of Danzig, Germany, Poland and Sweden. In the preamble of the convention the contracting parties declared being desirous of taking measures to prevent the great decrease in catches of fish in the Baltic Sea. The convention provided *inter alia* regulations on minimum sizes and closed seasons. After the International Overfishing Conference, which was held in 1946, a convention was signed to regulate fisheries in the Atlantic and Arctic oceans. See, Convention with annexes for the Regulation of the Meshes of Fishing Nets and the Size Limits of Fish, London, 1946. The 1946 Convention was superseded by the North-East Atlantic Fisheries Convention, 1959. Regulations on research and conservation measures were adopted also for other seas. See, for example, Convention for the Establishment of an Inter-American Tropical Tuna Commission, 1949; Agreement for the Establishment of a General Fisheries Council for the Mediterranean, 1949; International Convention for the High Seas Fisheries of the North Pacific Ocean, 1952; Convention Concerning Fishing in the Black Sea, 1959.

24 The Convention for the Preservation and Protection of Fur Seals was adopted on 7 July 1911 between the four countries after a conference held in Washington, D.C. Prior to the Convention, the two countries had concluded a Treaty between Great Britain and the United States for the Protection of Fur Seals. The bilateral treaty was superseded by the Convention of 7 July 1911. The Washington Conference began on 11 May 1911. After a month of negotiations, the Conference appeared deadlocked. President Taft made a personal appeal to the Emperor of Japan in which he stated as follows: '[A]n agreement in this case will open the way for a general international game law for the protection of other mammals of the sea, the preservation of which is of importance to all the nations of the world. On the other hand a failure to reach an agreement in this case will inevitably result in the extermination of the fur seals . . . ', quoted in Gay (1987) p. 127.

25 The 1911 Convention also included provisions on port control (Article II), import restrictions (Article III), implementation and enforcement of the provisions (Articles VI and VII). See Article VI ('Each of the High Contracting Parties agrees to enact and enforce such legislation as may be necessary to make effective the foregoing provisions with appropriate penalties for violations thereof') and Article VII ('It is agreed on the part of the United States, Japan, and Russia that each respectively will maintain a guard or patrol in the waters frequented by the seal herd in the protection of which it

is especially interested, so far as may be necessary for the enforcement of the foregoing provisions.').

26 Convention for the Regulation of Whaling, 1931.

27 In its 1930 report the experts recommended the draft of a general convention, or a series of conventions, to regulate the exploitation of the products of the sea. Instead of a comprehensive convention, the League of Council, nevertheless, referred to the Economic Committee the question of preparing a convention for the regulation of whaling. After having examined the issue in consultation with the International Council for the Exploration of the Seas (ICES), the Committee concluded that overfishing had led to a risk of commercial extinction, and that, therefore, a convention was justified. See Report to the Council of the Economic Committee of the League of Nations, League Doc. C. 353, M. 146, 1930, II. See also Birnie (1985).

28 For instance, the convention prohibited the taking and killing of right whales, of calves or suckling whales, of immature whales and of female whales which were accompanied by calves.

29 International Convention for the Regulation of Whaling, (1946).

30 See the preamble to the 1946 Whaling Convention.

31 Convention on Fishing and Conservation of the Living Resources of the High Seas (1958). Three other conventions signed in Geneva on the same occasion were: Convention on the Continental Shelf; Convention on the High Seas; Convention on the Territorial Sea and the Contiguous Zone.

32 In the 1920s and 1930s there were attempts to agree internationally on the prevention of oil pollution. A conference on oil pollution of navigable waters was convened in 1926 in Washington, D.C. Later on, the issue of oil pollution was discussed at the League of Nations.

33 International Convention for the Prevention of Pollution of the Sea by Oil, London (1954).

34 The Convention was replaced by the MARPOL 73/78 Convention, which provided a more comprehensive approach. See, International Convention for the Prevention of Pollution from Ships (1973) and Protocol of 1978 Relating to the International Convention for the Prevention of Pollution from Ships (1978).

35 See Convention for the Prevention of Marine Pollution by Dumping from Ships and Aircraft, Oslo (1972) preamble ('Recognizing that concerted action by Governments at national, regional and global levels is essential to prevent and combat marine pollution'); 1972 London Convention, preamble ('Being convinced that international action to control the pollution of the sea by dumping can and must be taken without delay'); Convention on the Protection of the Marine Environment of the Baltic Sea Area (1974) preamble ('Recognizing that the protection and enhancement of the marine environment of the Baltic Sea Area are tasks that cannot effectively be accomplished by national efforts only but that also close regional co-operation and other appropriate international measures aiming at fulfilling these tasks are urgently needed'); the Preamble of the 1976 Barcelona Convention ('Recognizing fully the need for close co-operation among the States and international organizations concerned in a co-ordinated and comprehensive regional approach for the protection and enhancement of the marine environment in the Mediterranean Sea Area').

36 See the preamble of the 1974 Helsinki Convention ('Conscious of the indispensable economic, social and cultural values of the marine environment of the Baltic Sea Area and

its living resources for the peoples of the Contracting States'); the preamble of the 1976 Barcelona Convention ('Conscious of the economic, social, health and cultural value of the marine environment of the Mediterranean Sea'); Convention for the Protection of the Marine Environment of the North-East Atlantic (1992) preamble ('Recognizing the inherent worth of the marine environment of the North-East Atlantic.').

37 See, e.g., 1974 Paris Convention, article 1(1); the preamble of the 1976 Barcelona Convention ('Recognizing the threat posed by pollution to the marine environment, its ecological equilibrium, resources and legitimate uses').

38 See, e.g., Principle 7 of the Stockholm Conference; 1972 London Convention, Article 1 ('Contracting Parties . . . pledge themselves especially to take all practicable steps to prevent the pollution of the sea by dumping . . . '); 1976 Barcelona Convention, Article 4 (1) 1982 UNCLOS, Article 194 (1) ('States shall take, individually or jointly as appropriate, all measures consistent with this Convention that are necessary to prevent, reduce and control pollution of the marine environment from any source, using for this purpose the best practicable means at their disposal . . . ').

39 The 1974 Helsinki Convention was the first comprehensive regional convention. The convention was superseded by the 1992 Convention. In 1974, the Regional Seas Programme was initiated by UNEP as a global programme implemented through regional components. In 2015, the programme included 13 regions and has over 140 coastal states participating in it. For more details, see http://www.unep.org/regionalseas.

40 Environmental issues did not receive much attention in the First United Nations Conference on the Law of the Sea, convened in 1958. Only a few provisions on the protection of the marine environment were included in the Convention on the High Seas and in the Convention on the Continental Shelf. See 1958 High Seas Convention, Articles 24 and 25; 1958 Continental Shelf Convention, Article 5(1) and 5(7). The 1958 Convention on the High Seas obliged parties to take measures to prevent pollution from the discharge of oil and from the dumping of radio-active waste. However, during the Third United Nations Conference on the Law of the Sea, environmental issues played an important role. Regulations on the protection and preservation of the marine environment are laid down in Part XII (Articles 192–237) of 1982 UNCLOS.

41 See, e.g., MARPOL 73/78 Convention.

42 See, e.g., 1972 Oslo Convention; 1972 London Convention; Protocol Concerning Co-operation in Combating Pollution of the Mediterranean Sea by Oil and Other Harmful Substances in Cases of Emergency, Barcelona, 15 ILM (1976) p. 285; Protocol for the Prevention of Pollution of the South Pacific Region by Dumping (1986).

43 See, e.g., Article 212 of the 1982 UNCLOS ('1. States shall adopt laws and regulations to prevent, reduce and control pollution of the marine environment through the atmosphere . . . 2. States shall take other measures as may be necessary to prevent, reduce and control such pollution. 3. States, acting especially through competent international organizations or diplomatic conferences, shall endeavour to establish global and regional rules, standards and recommended practices and procedures to prevent, reduce and control such pollution.').

44 See, e.g., Protocol for the Protection of the Mediterranean Sea against Pollution from Land-Based Sources, Athens, 17 May 1980, 19 ILM (1980) p. 869.

45 Pursuant to the 1982 UNCLOS, the so-called Area, meaning the sea-bed and ocean floor and subsoil thereof beyond the limits of national jurisdiction, was established. In

accordance with Article 145 of the Convention, the International Sea-Bed Authority should adopt appropriate rules, regulations and procedures with respect to activities in the Area to ensure effective protection of the marine environment from harmful effects which may arise from such activities. Furthermore, in accordance with Paragraph 2 of Article 209, subject to the relevant provision of Section 3 of Part XII, states should adopt laws and regulations to prevent, reduce and control pollution of the marine environment from activities in the Area undertaken by vessels, installations and other devices flying their flag or their registry or operating under their authority.

46 See, e.g., Agreement Concerning Co-operation in Taking Measures Against Pollution of Sea by Oil, Copenhagen, 16 September 1971, 822 UNTS, p. 311; Protocol Concerning Co-operation in Combating Pollution of the Mediterranean Sea by Oil and other Harmful Substances in Cases of Emergency, Barcelona, 16 February 1976, 15 ILM (1976) p. 285; Protocol Concerning Regional Co-operation in Combating Pollution by Oil and Other Harmful Substances in Cases of Emergency (1978); Agreement on Regional Cooperation in Combating Pollution of the South-East Pacific by Hydrocarbons and Other Harmful Substances in Cases of Emergency (1981); Protocol Concerning Regional Cooperation in Combating Pollution by Oil and Other Harmful Substances in Cases of Emergency (1982); Agreement for Co-operation in Dealing with Pollution of the North Sea by Oil and Other Harmful Substances (1983); Protocol Concerning Cooperation in Combating Oil Spills in the Wider Caribbean Region (1983); Protocol to the Nairobi Convention Concerning Cooperation in Combatting Marine Pollution in Cases of Emergency in the Eastern African Region (1985); International Convention on Oil Pollution Preparedness, Response and Co-operation (1990).

47 In the late 1800s, pelagic sealing of the Bering fur seals began to create a threat to the seal herd. Because most of the catches of sealing on the open sea consisted of females, pelagic sealing was unsustainable compared to sealing on land which it was possible to limit, without affecting the stock, to nonbreeding males. As it was not allowed to extend national legislation to the high seas which was open to all states, the only option to prevent a destruction of the seals was to have recourse to international cooperation. Consequently, states exercising sealing of Bering Sea fur seals concluded the 1911 Fur Seals Convention.

48 Pursuant to the convention, Japan and Great Britain agreed to refrain from pelagic sealing, provided that the United States and Russia paid compensation for seals harvested on land. See Articles X–XIV of the 1911 Fur Seals Convention. Lynton Keith Caldwell (p. 37) notes that '[e]ach of the four treaty states benefited more from long-term conservation than from short-term exploitation'.

49 The introduction in the United States Congress of a bill to enforce the 1911 convention raised a discussion on a matter of principle. See Hayden (1942) pp. 128–9 ('The initial obligation of $200,000 to Great Britain and to Japan was pointed out, and the Congress reminded that for twenty-five years we had been telling the world that land killing was legitimate and pelagic sealing the sole evil, that our fellow signers had reluctantly yielded and surrendered their right to the latter for the sake of a share in the proceeds of the former . . . ').

50 See the figures reproduced in ibid., p. 132.

51 1931 Whaling Convention; 1937 Whaling Agreement; 1938 Whaling Protocol. Regulations contained *inter alia* provisions on the efficient use of the carcasses of the whales taken

52 In the Preamble of the 1946 Whaling Convention the parties recognized the need to balance conservation, economic and nutritional interests by stating that: 'it is in the common interest to achieve the optimum level of whale stocks as rapidly as possible without causing wide-spread economic and nutritional distress'. The role of scientific advice was also strengthened in the Convention. Parties recognized that continuous collection and analysis of biological data was indispensable for the sound and constructive management of the whale fisheries, and that whaling regulations should be based on scientific findings.

53 See, e.g., Agreement for the Establishment of a General Fisheries Council for the Mediterranean, (1949) preamble ('*Contracting Governments* having a mutual interest in the development and proper utilization of the resources of the Mediterranean and contiguous waters . . . '); Convention on the Conservation of the Living Resources of the South-East Atlantic, (1969) preamble (' . . . desiring to co-operate in the conservation and rational exploitation of [the living resources of the Southeast Atlantic] . . . '); International Convention for the High Seas Fisheries of the North Pacific Ocean (1952), Article IV (bii) (' . . . for the purpose of maintaining or increasing its maximum sustained productivity'). See Convention for the Establishment of an Inter-American Tropical Tuna Commission (1949) preamble.

54 According to Article 2 of the convention, conservation means 'the aggregate of the measures rendering possible the optimum sustainable yield from those resources so as to secure a maximum supply of food and other marine products'.

55 For example conventions referred to 'the maximum sustainable catch', 'the optimum sustainable yield' and 'the optimum yield'. See the International Convention for the Conservation of Atlantic Tunas (1966) Article IV (2b) (' . . . to ensure maintenance of the populations of tuna and tuna-like fishes in the Convention area at levels which will permit the maximum sustainable catch.'); 1972 Antarctic Seals Convention, Preamble ('Recognizing that [the stocks of Antarctic seals] should not be depleted by over-exploitation, and hence that any harvesting should be regulated so as not to exceed the levels of the optimum sustainable yield'); Convention on Fishing and Conservation of the Living Resources in the Baltic Sea and the Belts, Gdansk (1973) Article 1 (' . . . co-operate with a view to preserving and increasing the living resources of the Baltic Sea and the Belts and obtaining the optimum yield . . . ').

56 See Article 61(3) of the 1982 UNCLOS Law of the Sea and Article 5(b) of the 1994 Fish Stocks Agreement. Both Conventions specify that the concept of a maximum sustainable yield is qualified by relevant environmental and economic factors. See Article 61(3) of the 1982 UNLOS and Article 5(b) of the 1994 Fish Stocks Agreement.

57 The new method meant that when the Commission for the Conservation of Antarctic Marine Living Resources set catch limits on krill fishing, it also considered the impact on whales and penguins which depend upon krill for food. See 1980 CCAMLR Convention, Article II. See Lyster (1985) p. 158 ('The traditional approach of fisheries treaties is to consider only the stock being fished when setting harvest levels. If strictly applied, an ecosystem approach is likely to mean much lower harvest levels than would result from the traditional approach since substantial krill harvesting may affect the recovery of the already depleted populations of large baleen whales in Antarctica.'). See also Kimball (1996) p. 71 ('During the 1980s and 1990s, increasingly sophisticated ecosystem models have been applied to Antarctic and other fisheries to help determine a ceiling on harvests, based on an understanding of predator/prey relationships and ecosystem dynamics . . . '). See also 1991 Madrid Protocol, Article 2 ('The Parties

commit themselves to the comprehensive protection of the Antarctic environment and dependent and associated ecosystem . . . ').

58 See 1982 UNCLOS, Article 61 (2), Article 119; 1994 Fish Stocks Agreement, Article 5(e) ('adopt, where necessary, conservation and management measures for species belonging to the same ecosystem or associated with or dependent upon the target stocks, with a view to maintaining or restoring populations of such species above levels at which their reproduction may become seriously threatened.'). See also 1982 UNCLOS, Article 61(4) ('In taking such measures the coastal State shall take into consideration the effects on species associated with or dependent upon harvested species with a view to maintaining or restoring populations of such associated or dependent species above levels at which their reproduction may become seriously threatened.').

59 1994 Fish Stocks Agreement Article 5a ('Adopt measures to ensure long-term sustainability of straddling fish stocks and highly migratory fish stocks and promote the objective of their optimum utilization.').

60 Referring to this development, the International Court of Justice noted in the *Fisheries Jurisdiction* cases as follows: 'the former *laissez faire* treatment of the living resources of the sea in the high seas has been replaced by a recognition of a duty to have due regard to the rights of other states and the needs of conservation for the benefits of all'. See *Fisheries Jurisdiction Case* (United Kingdom v. Iceland) para. 72 at p. 31, *Fisheries Jurisdiction Case* (Federal Republic of Germany v. Iceland) para. 64, at p. 200.

61 In order to produce an overall package, the negotiations dealt with various interrelated problems and competing interests as a whole. See Resolution 3067 (XXVIII) of the General Assembly of the United Nations Convening the Conference, 2169th plenary meeting, 16 November 1973 ('*Decides* that the mandate of the Conference shall be to adopt a convention dealing with all matters to the law of the sea . . . and bearing in mind that the problems of ocean space are closely interrelated and need to be considered as a whole').

References

Agreement Concerning Co-operation in Taking Measures Against Pollution of the Sea by Oil, Copenhagen, 16 September 1971, 822 *United Nations Treaty Series* p. 311.

Agreement for Co-operation in Dealing with Pollution of the North Sea by Oil and Other Harmful Substances, Bonn, 13 September 1983, *Selected Multilateral Treaties on the Environment*, Vol. 2, edited by I. Rummel-Bulska and S. Osafa p. 268.

Agreement for the Establishment of a General Fisheries Council for the Mediterranean, Rome, 24 September 1949, 126 *United Nations Treaty Series* p. 237.

Agreement for the Implementation of the Provisions of the United Nations Convention on the Law of the Sea of 10 December 1982 Relating to the Conservation and Management of Straddling Fish Stocks and Highly Migratory Fish Stocks, New York, 4 December 1994, 6 *Yearbook of International Environmental Law* (1995) p. 841.

Agreement on Regional Cooperation in Combating Pollution of the South-East Pacific by Hydrocarbons and Other Harmful Substances in Cases of Emergency, Lima, 12 November 1981, *Selected Multilateral Treaties on the Environment*, edited by Vol. 2, edited by I. Rummel-Bulska and S. Osafa p. 134.

Anderson, Chandler P. 'The Final Outcome of the Fisheries Arbitration', 7 *American Journal of International Law* (1913) pp. 1–16.

Basdevant, Jules, 'L'affaire des pêcheries des côtes septentrionales de l'Atlantique entre les Etats-Units d'Amérique et la Grande-Bretagne devant la Cour de La Haye', XIX *Revue générale de droit international public* (1912) pp. 421–582.

'Bering Fur Seals Arbitration', in John Basset Moore, *A Digest of International Law* (1906), Vol. I, pp. 910–19.

Birnie, Patricia W. (1985) *The International Regulation of Whaling*, 2 vols., Oceana Publications.

Borchard, Edwin M. (1911) 'The North Atlantic Coast Fisheries Arbitration', XI *Columbia Law Review* pp. 1–23.

Caldwell Lynton K. (1990) *International Environmental Policy*, Durham, NC: Duke University Press.

Colombos, C.J. (1967) *The International Law of the Sea* (6th ed.), London: Longman.

Committee of Experts for the Progressive Codification of International Law, 'Report to the Council of the League of Nations on the Questions which Appear Ripe for International Regulation', C.196.M.70.1927.V. The report has been reproduced in *League of Nations Committee of Experts for the Progressive Codification of International Law [1925–1928]*, edited by Shabtai Rosenne Vol. 2 (1972).

Convention between Belgium, Denmark, France, Germany, Great Britain and the Netherlands for Regulating the Police of the North Sea Fisheries, The Hague, 6 May 1882, 160 *Consolidated Treaty Series* p. 219.

Convention between Great Britain, Japan, Russia and the United States Respecting Measures for the Preservation and Protection of Fur Seals in the North Pacific Ocean, Washington, D.C., 7 July 1911, 214 *Consolidated Treaty Series* p. 80.

Convention between France and Great Britain for Defining the Limits of Exclusive Fishing Rights, Paris, 2 August 1839, 89, *Consolidated Treaty Series* p. 221.

Convention between the United States of America and Canada for the Preservation of the Halibut Fisheries of the Northern Pacific Ocean, Washington, D.C., 2 March 1923, 32, *League of Nations Treaty Series* p. 94.

Convention between the United States of America and Canada for the Preservation of the Halibut Fishery of the Northern Pacific Ocean and Bering Sea, Ottawa, 9 May 1930, 21, *League of Nations Treaty Series* p. 46.

Convention Concerning Fishing in the Black Sea, Varna, 7 July 1959, 377, *United Nations Treaty Series* p. 203.

Convention for the Conservation of Antarctic Seals, London, 1 June 1972, 11 *International Legal Materials* (1972) p. 251.

Convention for the Establishment of an Inter-American Tropical Tuna Commission, Washington, D.C., 30 May 1949, 80, *United Nations Treaty Series* p. 3.

Convention for the International Council for the Exploration of the Sea, Copenhagen, 12 September 1964, 652, *United Nations Treaty Series* p. 237.

Convention for the Prevention of Marine Pollution by Dumping from Ships and Aircraft, Oslo, 15 February 1972, 932, *United Nations Treaty Series* p. 3.

Convention for the Prevention of Marine Pollution from Land-based Sources, Paris, 4 June 1974, 13, *International Legal Materials* (1974) p. 352.

Convention for the Protection of the Marine Environment of the North-East Atlantic, Paris, 22, September 1992, 32 ILM (1993) p. 1069.

Convention for the Protection of the Mediterranean Sea Against Pollution, Barcelona, 16 February 1976, 15, *International Legal Materials* (1976) p. 290.

Convention for the Regulation of the Meshes of Fishing Nets and the Size Limits of Fish, London, 5 April 1946, 231, *United Nations Treaty Series* p. 200.

Convention for the Regulation of Whaling, Geneva, 24 September 1931, 155, *League of Nations Treaty Series* p. 349.

Convention on Fishing and Conservation of the Living Resources in the Baltic Sea and the Belts, Gdansk, 13 September 1973, 12, *International Legal Materials* (1973) p. 1291.

Convention on Fishing and Conservation of the Living Resources of the High Seas, Geneva, 29 April 1958, 559, *United Nations Treaty Series* p. 285.

Convention on the Conservation of Antarctic Marine Living Resources, Canberra, 20 May 1980, 19 *International Legal Materials* (1980) p. 841.

Convention on the Continental Shelf, Geneva, 29 April 1958, 499, *United Nations Treaty Series* p. 311.

Convention on the Prevention of Marine Pollution by Dumping of Wastes and Other Matter, London, 29 November 1972, 1046, *United Nations Treaty Series* p. 120

Convention on the Protection of the Marine Environment of the Baltic Sea Area, Helsinki, 22 March 1974, 13, *International Legal Materials* (1974) p. 546

Convention on the Protection of the Marine Environment of the Baltic Sea Area, 1992, Helsinki, 9 April 1992, <http://www.helcom.fi>.

Convention on the Territorial Sea and the Contiguous Zone, Geneva, 29 April 1958, 516, *United Nations Treaty Series* p. 205.

Dagget, A.P., The Regulation of Maritime Fisheries by Treaty, 28, *American Journal of International Law* (1934) p. 693–717.

Dupuy, R-J. 'The Sea under National Competence' in R.-J. Dupuy and D. Vignes, A *Handbook on the New Law of the Sea*, Vol. I (Dordrecht, Nijhoff, 1991) p. 247.

Fisheries Jurisdiction Case (Federal Republic of Germany *v.* Iceland), Judgement of 25 July 1974, International Court of Justice Reports (1974) p. 175.

Fisheries Jurisdiction Case (United Kingdom *v.* Iceland), Judgement of 25 July 1974, International Court of Justice Reports (1974) p. 3.

Fulton, Thomas Wemyss (1911) *The Sovereignty of the Sea. An Historical Account of the Claims of England to the Dominion of the British Seas, and of the Evolution of the Territorial Waters: with Special Reference to the Rights of Fishing and the Naval Salute*, Edinburgh: W. Blackwood.

Hackworth, Green Haywood, (1940) *Digest of International Law*, Vol. I.

Hayden, Sherman Strong (1942) The International Protection of Wild Life. An Examination of Treaties and Other Agreements for the Preservation of Birds and Mammals.

Gay, James Thomas (1987) *American Fur Seal Diplomacy: The Alaskan Fur Seal Controversy*, New York: Peter Lang.

International Agreement for the Regulation of Whaling, London, 8 June 1937, 190, *League of Nations Treaty Series* p. 70.

International Convention for the Conservation of Atlantic Tunas, Rio de Janeiro, 14 May 1966, 37 *United Nations Treaty Series* p. 63.

International Convention for the High Seas Fisheries of the North Pacific Ocean, Tokyo, 9 May 1952, 205 *United Nations Treaty Series* p. 65.

International Convention for the Prevention of Pollution from Ships, London, 2 November 1973, 12 *International Legal Materials* (1973) p. 1319.

International Convention for the Prevention of Pollution of the Sea by Oil, London, 12 May 1954, 327 *United Nations Treaty Series* p. 3.

International Convention for the Regulation of Whaling, Washington, D.C., 2 December 1946, 161 *United Nations Treaty Series*, p. 72.

International Convention on Oil Pollution Preparedness, Response and Co-operation, London, 30 November 1990, 30 *International Legal Materials* (1991) p. 735.

Johnston, Douglas M. (1965) *The International Law of Fisheries: A Framework for Policy-Oriented Inquiries*, Yale University Press, p. 254.

Kimball, Lee A. (1996) *Treaty Implementation: Scientific and Technical Advice Enters a New Stage*, ASIL, Washington.

Kuokkanen, Tuomas (2002) *International Law and the Environment: Variations on a Theme*, Kluwer Law International.

Lammasch, H., 'Was the Award in the North Atlantic Fisheries Case a Compromise?', 6 *American Journal of International Law* (1912) pp. 178–180.

Lansing, Robert (1911) The North Atlantic Coast Fisheries Arbitration, 5 *American Journal of International Law* pp. 1–31.

Leonard, L. Larry (1944) *International Regulation of Fisheries*, Columbia University Press.

Lauterpacht, Hersch (1970) *International Law. Being the Collected Papers of Hersch Lauterpacht*, systematically arranged and edited by E. Lauterpacht, Vol. II, pp. 384–85.

Lyster, Simon (1985) *International Wildlife*, Grotius Publications.

Moore, John Basset, *History and Digest of the International Arbitrations to which the United States has been a Party*, Vol. 1, 1898.

North Atlantic Coast Fisheries Case, XI United Nations Reports of International Arbitral Awards, p. 68.

North-East Atlantic Fisheries Convention, London, 24 January 1959, 486 *United Nations Treaty Series* p. 157.

Oppenheim's International Law (2008) Volume I, Peace, Parts 2 to 4, p. 727 (9th edition), Oxford University Press.

Protocol Amending the International Whaling Agreement, London, 24 June 1938, 196 *League of Nations Treaty Series* p. 131.

Protocol Concerning Cooperation in Combating Oil Spills in the Wider Caribbean Region, Cartagena de Indias, 24 March 1983, 22 *International Legal Materials* (1983) p. 240.

Protocol Concerning Co-operation in Combating Pollution of the Mediterranean Sea by Oil and Other Harmful Substances in Cases of Emergency, Barcelona, 16 February 1976, 15 *International Legal Materials* (1976) p. 285.

Protocol Concerning Regional Co-operation in Combating Pollution by Oil and Other Harmful Substances in Cases of Emergency, Kuwait, 24 April 1978, 17 *International Legal Materials* (1978) p. 526.

Protocol Concerning Regional Cooperation in Combating Pollution by Oil and Other Harmful Substances in Cases of Emergency, Jeddah, 14 February 1982, SMTE Vol. II p. 154.

Protocol for the Prevention of Pollution of the South Pacific Region by Dumping, Noumea, 25 November 1986, 26 *International Legal Materials* (1987) p. 38.

Protocol for the Protection of the Mediterranean Sea against Pollution from Land-Based Sources, Athens, 17 May 1980, 19 *International Legal Materials* (1980) p. 869.

Protocol on Environmental Protection to the Antarctic Treaty, Madrid, 4 October 1991, 30 ILM (1991) p. 1461.

Protocol Relating to the Convention for the Prevention of Pollution from Ships, London, 17 February 1978, 17 *International Legal Materials* (1978) p. 546.

Protocol to the Nairobi Convention Concerning Cooperation in Combatting Marine Pollution in Cases of Emergency in the Eastern African Region, Nairobi 21 June 1985, SMTE, Vol. II, p. 337.

Stockholm Declaration of the United Nations Conference on the Human Environment (Stockholm, 16 June 1972, UN Doc. A/CONF.48/14/Rev.1 (1973), 11 *International Legal Materials* (1972) 1416).

Tanaka, Yoshifumi (2012) *The International Law of the Sea*, Cambridge University Press, Cambridge.

Treaty between Great Britain and the United States for the Protection of Fur Seals, Washington, D.C., 7 February 1911, 213 *Consolidated Treaty Series* p. 73.

United Nations Conventions on the Law of the Sea, Montego Bay, 10 December 1982, 21 *International Legal Materials* (1982) p. 1261.

Överenskommelse angående regleringen av fisket efter rödspätta (pleuronectes platessa) och skrubba (pleuronectes flesus) i Östersjön, Berlin, 17 December 1929, 115 *League of Nations Treaty Series* p. 94.

Chapter 3

Marine spatial planning and various uses and interests relating to the marine environment

Tavis Potts

Introduction

The oceans are increasingly busy spaces that provide a cornucopia of goods and services for society. These ecosystem services include a range of living and non-living resources for consumption, including fisheries or minerals; waste and carbon assimilation; coastal protection; and spaces for recreation, introspection and cultural importance (Potts *et al.*, 2014). With increasing demands for resources and use of marine space, conflicts are emerging between existing and ancient practices such as fishing and shipping and the innovative forms of development such as marine renewable energy and ecotourism. When practices interact, and increasingly collide, conflict between users can emerge and reduce the effectiveness of economic development and environmental protection by the fragmentation or ineffective delivery of policy.

Traditionally areas of the ocean have been designated for certain activities and the development process (if it exists at all) tends to consider the objectives within that sector, without an overall vision for ocean space or how uses interrelate. This approach fails to put the 'pieces of the puzzle together' and often misses important complexities, interactions, conflicts and trade-offs between sectors (Plasman, 2008). It also fails to identify opportunities for co-location and development between sectors. While the conventional approach has been adequate for the management of single sector activities (e.g. fishing), the oceans of today and tomorrow are increasingly busy spaces of multiple activities with cumulative impacts increasing over time. Marine spatial planning (MSP) has emerged as a tool that attempts to rationalize the use of marine space and improve decision making in marine systems (European Commission and DG-Maritime Affairs and Fisheries, 2011b). It aims to assist the planning of human activities with the protection of the marine environment. It considers the region as a whole and integrates policies and objectives across different sectors, addressing the multiple and potentially conflicting uses of the sea while reconciling economic, ecological and social objectives (Gilliland and Laffoley, 2008).

MSP has not evolved in a vacuum; it has emerged from decades of debate, theory and practice concerning the integration of marine governance (Haward and Vince, 2008) particularly around the context of integrated coastal zone management (ICZM). ICZM and other integrated approaches engaged and championed strategic and non-spatial approaches that emphasize communication and cooperation between coastal stakeholders, while MSP has embraced a more spatial approach including the delivery of zoning of marine space. This has been a process deemed full of potential but fraught with difficulty (Agardy, 2010). While the concept of spatial allocation of the uses of marine space has intrinsic appeal to legislators, a focus on rational allocation of marine space has meant its practice is often patchy, contested and usually feared (Agardy, 2010). Despite the challenges, MSP is increasingly experimented with and adopted across the international context including Australia, the EU, Norway, Canada, China and the USA (Zacharias, 2014). This chapter explores the development of MSP in parallel with the governance of key marine sectors and drawn upon a number of case studies from the international context with a focus on the North East Atlantic.

An underlying question concerning the effectiveness of MSP is how it relates to sector activity and if it is able to add value to existing arrangements through the rationalization of space, the identification of environmental and socio-economic objectives, reducing conflict and increasing co-locational opportunities. As sectors evolve, so do their respective objectives and desire for expansion, and increasingly in the marine sphere these objectives are interacting and driving conflict. A conflict is defined as a situation in which multiple activities (e.g. fishing and renewable energy) are incompatible and compete for the right to exist in a certain location (European Commission and DG-Maritime Affairs and Fisheries, 2011b). In addition to sector interactions, activities are increasingly coming up against broad environmental protection designations that cover multiple uses of the marine domain and aim to restore or maintain environmental quality. A recent example from Europe is the emergence of the Marine Strategy Framework Directive (MSFD) (European Parliament and European Council, 2008) that attempts to chart a course between managing maritime activity and environmental quality. This Directive instructs European Member States with coastal territory to give priority to achieving or maintaining 'good environmental status' by 2020 by applying an ecosystem approach to the management of human activities at the regional sea scale. The Directive obliges each member state to achieve Good Environmental Status (GEnS) within their Exclusive Economic Zone by 2020 based on eleven environmental descriptors covering differing aspects of environmental health as well as addressing anthropogenic concerns (Bainbridge *et al.*, 2011). Targets for these descriptors were established in 2012 and a programme of measures to achieve these targets must be in place in each EU member state by 2016. The MSFD mandates cooperation on a regional seas basis between EU member states as well as non-EU countries principally through the use of existing institutions, such as the regional seas commissions (e.g. HELCOM, the Barcelona Convention, OSPAR and the Black Sea Commission).

Principles of MSP

In the marine environment, decisions in one sector can have an impact on another as one sector expands and encroaches spatially on the activities of others. Sectors such as marine renewable energy and marine protected areas are recent newcomers to the marine estate and are expanding in coastal jurisdictions of States and coming up against more traditional uses of the marine environment such as fishing and shipping (Alexander *et al.*, 2013). While not all interactions are negative, processes of screening and exploration of different spatial uses have been *ad hoc* and in many instances failed to deliver an integrated approach. The usual (and safer) option has been in the form of non-spatial strategic assessments akin to the practice of ICZM where consensus of the use of coastal regions is established through consultative approaches but is essentially undermined by a lack of regulatory authority. Authors such as Agardy (2010) go further to separate the process of MSP from ocean zoning. MSP is seen as a political and social-ecological process that enables zoning to occur. Zoning, in itself, is a relatively recent phenomenon in the maritime sector and refers to rationally identifying and allocating spatial uses of the marine environment among user groups. Agardy (2010) argues that MSP without zoning is incomplete or is not taking advantage of the power of zoning as a tool for the sustainable management of the oceans. A similar idea was carried forward by the late Professor Laurence Mee, Director of the Scottish Association for Marine Science,[1] who elaborated on the concept of 'designer seas' where current and future use of the oceans should be taken forward through a participatory, democratic and planned process that sets a common vision for marine environments and articulates pathways through rational planning. Such processes inevitably tread upon the values of those who subscribe to the belief of the inexhaustible bounty of the oceans and unlimited use (Agardy, 2010; Potts *et al.*, 2012). A process such as MSP can clash with existing or perceived user rights for marine resources and inevitably comes into contact with existing power relations in ocean use, a topic rarely explored in marine policy (Bainbridge *et al.*, 2011).

MSP does not seek to plan every square mile of ocean, but the process does progress the identification of areas of strategic importance, addresses cumulative impacts, maximizes and conserves ecosystem services and moves from piecemeal to integrated management across sectors. While a number of views exist over the process of delivering MSP, all converge on a consensus around transparent and meaningful engagement, data collection, mapping and analysing existing uses, identifying alternative use patterns, monitoring and enforcement. Figure 3.1 identifies two similar processes for operationally delivering MSP. The process articulated by the IOC (Ehler and Douvere, 2009) highlights the importance of pre-planning processes to build trust and capacity. The step of identifying and establishing authority is critical from the perspective of who will plan for MSP, who will be 'at the table' and who will be the implementation agency. The IOC notes that often MSP initiatives establish a single body for the planning function (for example the UK Marine Management Organisation) while the delivery

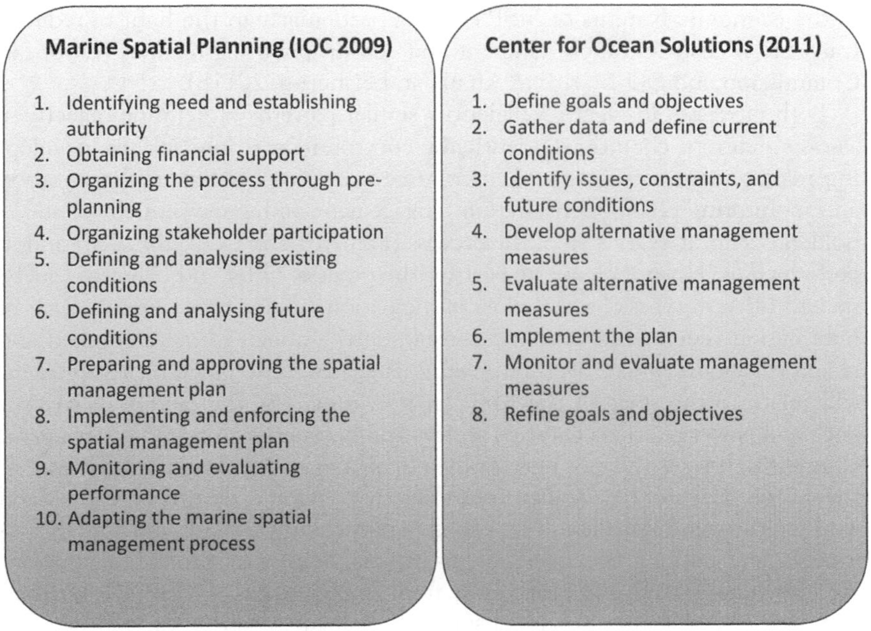

Figure 3.1 Stages in MSP.

function is pushed out through existing authorities (Ehler and Douvere, 2009). This is an important distinction. Planning can often occur in a 'bubble' that is sometimes separated from the reality on the water where users and uses interact in space and time. Achieving effective marine governance through MSP will often take both government support and the support of the managed sectors and the communities in which they operate. Often, and particularly in Europe, planning outputs will need to be joined up from local to national and international scales to reflect the nature of maritime sectors, such as fisheries and shipping. The emergence of regional sea scale strategies in the EU, for example the Maritime Strategy for the Atlantic Ocean (European Commission Maritime Affairs and Fisheries, 2011a) within the context of the EU Blue Growth Strategy (European Commission Maritime Affairs and Fisheries, 2012) compel European states to coordinate their MSP planning and delivery strategies.

The IOC identified another critical stage for the MSP process – that of financing and resources. While financing MSP is a matter of government budgetary concerns and subject to policy priorities, it is important to acknowledge the significant role that maritime sectors and research providers can play. Ehler and Douvere (2009) note the opportunity to levy finance directly from affected sectors; for example, from tourism, energy, mining and fishing revenues. Naturally, allocating expenditure could potentially be resisted by sectors acting in their individual interests, but support may improve over time as the economic benefits of MSP emerge, particularly in the light of reduced transaction costs and more efficient and certain planning regimes (European Commission and DG-Maritime Affairs and Fisheries, 2011b).

Both processes in Figure 3.1 identify similar patterns of defining objectives, assessing current conditions, identifying constraints and interactions, developing management measures and alternative scenarios and an implementation and monitoring phase. Consultation, engagement and empowerment of stakeholders occurs at every step of the process (Pomeroy and Douvere, 2008) and, if performed well, can increase support for the process. Ehler and Douvere (2009) specify different types of stakeholder participation ranging from one-way flows of information (communication and consultation) through to more engaged and reciprocal modes where decision making is shared. The mode of involvement will relate to the stage of the MSP process, resources, the culture of governance and power relations between sectors and between sectors and government. Consensus, however, is not necessarily a final goal or objective for MSP and, in some cases, may not be a realistic or productive outcome. Setting objectives and working through implementation can be a particularly difficult and contentious process, and pushing for consensus in artificial 'win-win' scenarios may alienate individual sectors and move away from the objective of MSP. Rather than consensus, MSP should provide a stage for dialogue, cooperation and negotiation over integrated management and co-location in the marine sphere and a means to explore and evaluate alternative management measures that are spatial in nature and are adaptive (The Center for Ocean Solutions, 2011).

The drive for integration and zoning in marine governance

Marine spatial planning strives for integration. Integration has long had a place among the principles of good environmental governance and includes identifying common goals, coordination among sectors, trade-offs and accountability. In coastal and marine policy, management has developed in a fragmented manner and integrated oceans management has been the 'catch call' for improved processes since the 1970s (Haward and Vince, 2008). The emergence of Marine Spatial Planning has been, in part, a response to this fragmentation and uncertainty. Potts, O'Higgins and Hastings (Potts *et al.*, 2012) highlighted a typology of integration based on sector activity, spatial and temporal scales and the broader principle of the ecosystem approach to management. We will use this typology to explore the evolution of sector-based approaches and integrated marine planning.

First order integration

First order integration refers to the operational dimensions of integration and is that which is currently pursued across national and regional systems. These

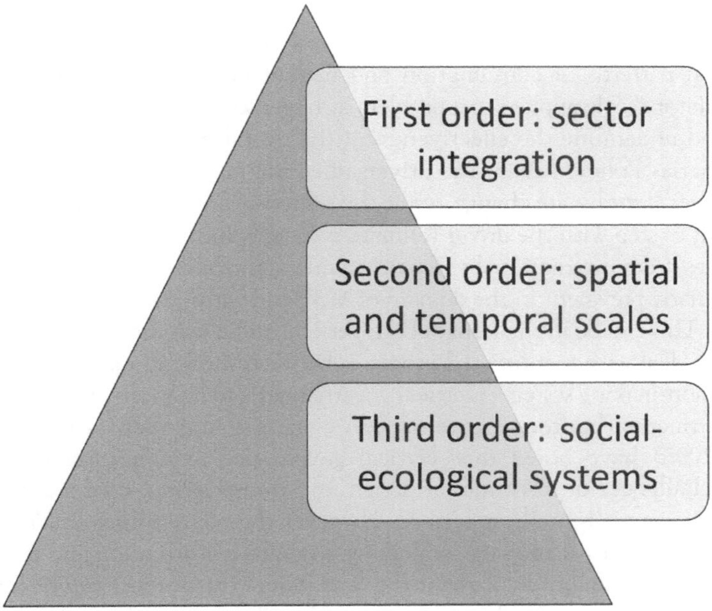

Figure 3.2 Conceptual view of the tiers of integration activity (adapted from Potts *et al.*, 2012).

mechanisms, which are regulatory, policy and civil, aim to encourage or promote both the maritime industries and their users to work together to reduce conflict and to explore co-locational activities (e.g. aquaculture within a site for offshore wind energy). It implies building upon the existing sector approach and focusing on the articulation of common goals, objectives and activities through coordination mechanisms such as MSP. Within sector-based approaches, sectors generally remain managed by their existing mechanisms (e.g. fisheries management, energy regulations, marine conservation) but the existence of a marine planning process calls for recognition and resolution of overlaps, particularly where conflicts occur. If there is a lack of conflict, MSP measures are likely to be relatively passive, identifying areas for future development or firming up existing property rights, particularly if the users are offshore-based industries such as oil and gas.

Second order integration

Second order integration emphasizes the integration of scales (e.g. international to local) and jurisdictions into the planning systems of oceans governance and MSP. Costanza *et al.* (1998) notes in the Lisbon Principles of Sustainable Oceans Governance (Principle 2: Scale Matching) that incorporating and harmonizing scales to ensure effective decision making is a key element of marine governance. It is also one of the most intractable issues due to inefficiencies in decision making across multiple jurisdictions and political contexts. Often the nature of problems in the marine environment and their respective solutions occur at different scales; for example, impacts from local fisheries may occur as a result of larger global patterns of consumption and market preference. Conversely, often the regulatory scale applied to a problem at larger scales might not fit local preferences and undermine the effectiveness of the overall regime (e.g. the EU Common Fisheries Policy). Often the drivers affecting marine space are large-scale global issues, e.g. climate change, while the responses are limited to multiple small scales out of step with the driver (climate change being a case in point).

Spatial scales, from international to local, interact with scales of policy making and are particularly prevalent in the domain of MSP and within the second order of integration. This can be in the form of both vertical and horizontal governance relations which deal with institutional processes between international, national and local decision-making systems (vertical governance) and relations across government departments (horizontal governance). Commentators such as Haward and Vince (2008) have noted that vertical governance relationships, while fraught with challenges of institutional design and transposition, coordination and delivery are generally well established. However the relationships *within or across* government bodies at the same scale have received less attention and raise challenges for integration, particularly at the operational (first order) end of the spectrum. Haward and Vince (2008, p. 24) refer to the concept of 'rods of iron' and 'threads of gossamer' when referring to vertical and horizontal relationships, with the weaker set of relationships between agencies of the same government. Finding agreement across government agencies with competing and sector-driven views on the marine domain may be more difficult than finding agreements between governments at different scales. For instance, while procedural rules form the basis of institutional arrangements between national and regional governments, the processes between departments can remain obtuse in terms of policy delivery. As a response, national jurisdictions often establish a central coordinating authority. For example, in the German context, the Federal Ministry of Transport, Building and Urban Development takes the lead in the German Exclusive Economic Zone (EEZ) establishing targets and principles of spatial planning. It targets sectors such as shipping, fishing, energy, scientific research and environmental protection. Spatial plans for the territorial sea (up to 12 nm) are developed by the German Länder (Federal States) (UNESCO-IOC, 2014). Coordination mechanisms at the vertical scale between Federal and Provincial authorities and at the horizontal scale between departmental interests will influence the delivery and effectiveness of MSP. In the UK, the Marine Management Organisation is the lead authority for delivery of marine plans in England and Wales, while in Scotland the government agency Marine Scotland is the lead coordinator of marine planning. The UK has complex legislative arrangements for devolved management (as evidenced by the challenge from the 2014 referendum on Scottish independence) where most marine powers are granted to the devolved authority scale and coordinated via an overarching Marine Policy Statement across the devolved nations of the UK

(Potts, *et al.*, 2012). While complex, these institutional arrangements are clear and the authority for MSP from UK to devolved scale is well established. Where uncertainty exists is the role for sector management under emerging marine plans for England and Scotland, how sectors interact and resolve conflict, and how any proposed marine plans will have the authority to steer spatial decisions across a contested terrain of maritime development. At the local and regional scale a range of actors including conservation agencies, local government, fishing collectives, aquaculture, ports, energy, tourism and infrastructure will be engaged in spatial negotiation and resolution and in many instances the ability of the sector to engage may depend on historical precedents or policy capability. The role of coordinating 'marine departments' and the power they have to exercise and enforce plans and decisions in the broader context of national government policy is also uncertain and would benefit from further research.

Third order: social–ecological integration

The third tier of integration deals with a more conceptual integration of social–ecological systems into marine planning. Deeper and broader concepts of integration, coordination and cooperation have been developed under the banner of the 'Ecosystem Approach'. The term is frequently used in the research literature relating to environmental governance and is increasingly lauded as a policy goal but with little evidence of systemic delivery. In general, the approach aims to consider the linkages between human processes and ecological systems (Arkema *et al.*, 2006).

The Ecosystem Approach (EA) in its broadest sense has several advantages over traditional approaches to natural resource management. First, it tends to consider ecological, economic and social considerations within a single framework (Grumbine, 1997) and confronts the nexus of conflict, interactions and trade-offs. Second, it recognises that humans, with their cultural diversity, are an integral component of ecosystems (CBD SBSTTA, 2000). Third, it places emphasis on flexible and adaptive methods. All principles have ramifications for MSP and how it is delivered, from initial conception, engagement processes amongst stakeholders, use of local knowledge, examining trade-offs between maritime sectors, incorporating ecosystem services and the ability for MSP to deliver on spatial decisions at relevant scales.

The Convention on Biological Diversity (CBD) is the most well-known exponent of the Ecosystem Approach and is summarized in the 12 'Malawi Principles' (Box 3.1) (CBD SBSTTA, 2000). It includes principles such as the need to decentralize resource management, take into account broader forms of knowledge and involve all relevant actors in decision making. The principles are laudable and relevant, but the problem remains regarding interpretation into the policy context and application into MSP practice. Many principles relate to the distribution of power within the national and regional context and among sectors. Without having a rational understanding of power within the MSP context, any analysis (and practice) will fail to determine the mechanisms and outcomes of trade-offs between sectors that are inherent to MSP delivery. Who wins and who loses, and by what mechanisms of power, is a central, if little explored tenet of MSP and yet critical for its success.

The CBD sets out the EA using 12 principles commonly known as the Malawi Principles (see Box 3.1).

***Box 3.1* The 12 principles of the ecosystem approach.**

1 The objectives of management of land, water and living resources are a matter of societal choice.
2 Management should be decentralized to the lowest appropriate level.
3 Ecosystem managers should consider the effects (actual or potential) of their activities on adjacent and other ecosystems.
4 Recognizing potential gains from management, there is usually a need to understand and manage the ecosystem in an economic context.
5 Conservation of ecosystem structure and functioning, in order to maintain ecosystem services, should be a priority target of the Ecosystem Approach.
6 Ecosystems must be managed within the limits of their functioning.
7 The Ecosystem Approach should be undertaken at the appropriate spatial and temporal scales.
8 Recognizing the varying temporal scales and lag-effects that characterize ecosystem processes, objectives for ecosystem management should be set for the long term.
9 Management must recognize that change is inevitable.
10 The Ecosystem Approach should seek the appropriate balance between, and integration of, conservation and use of biological diversity.
11 The Ecosystem Approach should consider all forms of relevant information, including scientific and indigenous and local knowledge, innovations and practices.
12 The Ecosystem Approach should involve all relevant sectors of society and scientific disciplines.

The relationship of maritime sectors to MSP

The policy environment for the coasts is complex, with instruments differing in spatial extent and jurisdiction. Regulation can focus on individual sectors (e.g. aquaculture or fisheries or waste water) or the cumulative impact on multiple sectors in relation to environmental quality (e.g. biodiversity conservation or marine protection). In general the marine environment is home to a vast number of different activities, many of which have evolved over centuries or conversely have evolved in recent times and embrace technological innovation. This mix of the 'old and new' raises challenges for sector integration in the marine planning context and competition for space and resources may have detrimental impacts on sectors through conflict and on the quality of the marine environment. It is important to note that MSP is not a replacement for sector policy or management. Operational plans and instruments for fisheries, transportation, marine energy, tourism and marine conservation will continue even when MSP is put into practice. The contribution of MSP is strategic, identifying reforms to single-sector management that should reduce conflicts across sectors, balance development and conservation, increase institutional efficiency and address the cumulative impacts of different activities. Focusing on the integrative nature of MSP, the process can raise a number of challenges and opportunities to maritime sectors. We explore the impacts and opportunities for four existing and emerging sectors below. While not comprehensive in terms of covering all activity in the marine environment, they provide a window into the issues and opportunities that face maritime industries in the marine planning process.

Fisheries

Fishing is an ancient activity that occurs across all the oceans of the planet. For decades there has been growing recognition of the need to reduce the impact of industrial fisheries on global marine ecosystems and to reduce levels of catch to both ecologically and economically sustainable levels (Browman *et al.*, 2004). The emergence of the ecosystem approach to fisheries, where broader ecological relationships and social–ecological elements are considered in the management planning process, has changed the nature of fisheries management. In particular, the drive to establish marine-protected areas and the substantial effort to reduce bycatch and discards within the industry has been a feature of the ecosystem approach (Bellido *et al.*, 2011).

As new uses of the ocean emerge, the fishing industry is increasingly under pressure from competition for space and to maintain viability. In fact the industry is under pressure on two fronts: the need to reduce capacity to sustainable levels including the reducion of subsides (Sumaila *et al.*, 2010) and a need to share marine space with new users of the marine environment, such as marine renewable energy (Alexander *et al.*, 2013). At a recent European workshop in 2013 on MSP in Fisheries[2] concerns emerged from industry representatives that highlighted large-scale fishing areas, necessary for maintaining a productive industry, that were reducing and that MSP should not only facilitate cooperation but identify areas that are critical for maintaining activity. In this context MSP could support the identification of important fishing grounds and identify trade-offs and development opportunities that maintain these grounds in the face of cumulative pressures. The loss of space is an issue that has also been reflected in the Nordic region, with the industry concerned that MSP may result in reduced fishing areas and damage to key habitats, particularly with a view to the emergence of large-scale offshore wind energy and the use of marine-protected areas (Blæsbjerg *et al.*, 2009).

The inclusion of improved spatial data on fishing activity and critical habitats is an important area for development. Traditionally, data on spatial activity, like many maritime activities in the marine environment, suffers from poor resolution or is non existent. A reluctance by the industry to map critical habitats and areas of activity (Blæsbjerg *et al.*, 2009), due to mistrust and uncertainty over future spatial use, in particular marine-protected areas, has undermined emerging MSP efforts. Undoubtedly the role of fisheries' expertise, both technical and from the fishermen themselves, is critical for developing successful MSP programmes and building trust. While inevitable tradeoffs will occur over use, placing fishing activity within a broader ecosystem-based framework and integrated sector strategy will benefit the industry. This includes the identification of important use areas, reducing conflicts, and establishing working relationships with other sectors such as marine energy, aquaculture and tourism and shipping that interact at both the national and transboundary scale.

The 2013 EU MSP workshop on Fisheries and Aquaculture held in Vilnius, Lithuania (ibid.) identified a number of key principles and objectives for improving the relationship between MSP and fishing and mechanisms to improve engagement and effectivness. They include:

- Resourcing fishermen to participate in MSP.
- Creating a transparent process, including independent facilitation, to enable participants to plan participation in advance.
- Capturing the spatial extent, resolution and distribution of fishing activities accounting for the behaviour of fishermen.
- Data must be accessible through quality controlled harmonized systems. It is unlikely that data collection alone will provide cost-effective requirements for MSP, so data and monitoring can be supplemented by modelling.
- Essential fish habitats should be taken into account by MSP as they are valuable both for fisheries and nature conservation. The ecosystem services provided by these habitats should also be articulated in MSP.
- The involvement of the fisheries sector in MSP should be prepared and facilitated through good practices such as pilot projects, cross-border fora, discussions and data compilations.
- Fisheries' spatial measures (e.g. seasonal, gear type) could be discussed as part of MSP in order to enhance fish resources.
- Synergies between fisheries and other activities and potential co-uses should be emphasized in the planning process.

Marine energy

Around the world, offshore marine renewable energy has become an important player in delivering carbon-free energy. The sector is particularly important in Europe with investment, construction and expansion in the offshore wind sector aiming to provide a significant component of European energy demands. Several

European countries are embracing wind for renewable energy production and include the Netherlands, Denmark, Sweden, Germany, United Kingdom and Ireland, which are installing large amounts of capacity around the North Sea, the North East Atlantic and the Baltic Sea (Blæsbjerg *et al.*, 2009). In 2013, 418 new offshore wind turbines, in 13 wind farms, worth between €4.6 billion and €6.4 billion were grid connected with a total of 1,567 MW of capacity (EWEA, 2014). To date over 2,080 offshore turbines have been installed and grid connected in eleven European countries with a cumulative total of 6,562 MW in 69 wind farms (EWEA, 2014) concentrated in the North Sea and Baltic Sea regions. Future projections are ambitious with forecasts of 40 GW of offshore wind power by 2020, meeting 4 per cent of the EU's total electricity demand and a further 110 GW of offshore wind capacity forcast to be installed between 2020 and 2030 that would cover 14 per cent of EU electricity demand (EWEA, 2011). The bulk of this capacity (60 per cent) will be located in the North Sea basin and around 20 per cent in the Atlantic basin which comprise key areas for a number of existing activities, including fishing, navigation and coastal development.

The construction and maintenance of offshore wind farms can cause significant changes and impacts on marine systems. This includes construction of foundations that can suspend sediments, remove benthic habitats and cause underwater noise which can elevate stress levels in marine mammals and alter the migration of fish (Bergström *et al.*, 2014). During operation the obvious impact is with collisions with birds, obstruction of migratory paths and changing local circulation and oceanographic conditions. On the positive side, wind farms can generate potential reef effects acting as reservoirs of marine biodiversity and acting as de facto marine-protected areas (Bergström *et al.*, 2014).

The expansion of wind energy has naturally led to increasing conflicts with a range of users as increasing demands for space materialize. Often offshore projects are caught between existing users such as fisheries, large-scale conservation designations, interest groups and legal regimes. Existing planning for wind farms has been sectoral in nature, where areas of potential development are identified with environmental impact and strategic environmental assessments carried out to determine interactions with other users and the marine environment. These assessments however are *ex post* and somewhat reactionary and lack the strategic vision that MSP aims to provide. Marine spatial planning therefore provides an important tool both for this emerging and critically important sector and for addressing the interactions and effects with other sectors. Furthermore, marine spatial planning as an *ex ante* activity allows for the rational exploration of spatial overlaps and interactions identifying not only potential conflicts but opportunities for co-development. This does depend on the quality of data sources used in MSP and for the process to be sufficiently designed for stakeholder input, engagement and decision making (Kerr *et al.*, 2014). In a recent paper on establishing a social research agenda for marine renewables, the authors highlight that the consultation processes surrounding energy development were of variable quality and a lack of trust, transperancy and credibility were issues that led to the diminishment of stakeholder engagement (Kerr *et al.*, 2014). While not specific to this sector, these are clear issues that affect the quality and effectivenss of the marine planning process. MSP, if delivered effectively, can therefore provide a number of benefts to the wind sector. One of the most important is the ability to provide clarity and stability for the sector where clear areas of development potential are identified and the processes established to work with overlaps and conflicts.

The creation of stability through MSP may address a key topic for the industry – that of bringing down costs. While technology development and supply chain integration are major drivers for reducing costs in the industry (EWEA, 2011) strategic MSP can reduce the regulatory burden brought about by overlapping laws, imprecise planning and enduring conflict. MSP will play a major role in reducing risk in offshore projects and potentially increase the speed and efficiency of the planning process. The European Commisson identified in a study in 2011 that MSP would provide benefits in coordination efficiency, lower transaction costs and an enhanced investment climate. These benefits accrue not only from the certainly and stability provided by a MSP process but also from identifying co-development opportunities where uses of the marine environment align. In part a major driver of the emergence of a pan-European approach to marine planning has been the opportunity for stability and efficiency in developing the maritime economy of which marine renewable energy plays a significant part. Europe has been progressing maritime spatial planning as a part of its Integrated Maritime Strategy (European Commission, 2012) and in July 2014 the EU adopted a Directive that establishes a common framework for marine spatial planning throughout the EU (European Parliament and Council of the European Union, 2014).

Conservation

Spatial conservation measures can be considered one of the precursors to marine spatial planning, taking into account multiple use activities and interacting sectors, stakeholder engagement and the Ecosystem Approach (Agardy, 2010; Jentoft and Knol, 2014). While conservation outcomes are a distinct component of MSP and are usually 'hardwired' into the objectives of any plan, marine protected areas (MPAs) focus exclusively on conservation of marine species and habitats and adjust maritime activity to achieve conservation outcomes (Blæsbjerg *et al.*, 2009). The common factor is that both forms have underlying stakeholder and sector interactions that must be accounted for in achieving their respective objectives and integration of both regimes is necessary for success.

While MPA planning has progressed in many parts of the world, fewer examples exist of integrated MSP and MPA programmes. Across the EU, Natura 2000 and the Habitat and Bird Directives are the cornerstones of conservation policy with a range of designations for habitats and species of European importance. Implementation of marine Special Areas of Conservation (SACs) and Special Protection Areas (SPAs) contribute to the overall Natura 2000 network of protected area sites. The development of European MPAs is further strengthened by the implementation of the EU Marine Strategy Framework Directive (European Parliament, 2008) whose aim is to manage human and balance maritime development with environmental protection. It is seen as a milestone in European marine policy and as evidence towards the EU fulfilling its international obligations for the protection of the marine environment. The main goal of the MSFD is to achieve 'Good Environmental Status' across the European marine environment by 2020 by developing and monitoring marine strategies for each marine region (Potts *et al.*, 2012). Member states can achieve good environmental status by a number of management approaches, including MSP, and the Directive identifies and supports MPAs as a specific instrument to achieve its outcomes. Conservation measures under the Habitats Directive should be part of any programme of measures to meet the requirements of MSFD and therefore help deliver more integrated policy and planning.

In addition to European designations and directives, several countries are exploring and experimenting with additional MPA processes that strengthen the national networks. For example, in July 2014, the Scottish Government oversaw the designation of 30 new MPA sites consisting of 17 inshore MPAs designated under the Marine (Scotland) Act 2010 and 13 offshore MPAs designated under the Marine and Coastal Access Act 2009 – in addition to the existing 47 European SAC designations. They represented the culmination of a lengthy stakeholder and science-led process since 2001 to identify and designate additional Scottish MPAs. The process of determining the management processes and interactions that influence the conservation objectives within each MPA is only beginning at the time of writing (October 2014) and represents an opportunity for MSP to link the MPA process in order to engage across maritime sectors.

As multiple and cumulative impacts from maritime and coastal activities increase in the marine environment the need for MPAs to protect and manage important reservoirs of biodiversity becomes increasingly important. Since MPAs themselves can be classified as a particular use of a marine system, albeit one for biodiversity conservation on which most other activities and human well-being depends, user conflicts and interactions are likely to intensify as more MPAs emerge, particularly in crowded coastal systems (Jentoft and Knol, 2014). MPA plans will often call for an alteration, shift or removal of spatial activities that impact upon the conservation status on designated habitats and species. In most situations this refers to fishing but new sectors that can have serious impacts such as offshore energy infrastructure are increasingly interacting with MPA designation and management. This underscores the need to increasingly bring together the MPA and MSP planning communities in order to rationally explore and allocate different uses through participatory, open and accountable processes. While MPAs have an explicit conservation purpose, MSP is also based on the Ecosystem Approach to management and is the most appropriate platform for negotiation over access, space and development. Taking into account the fluid nature of the marine environment, both activities within and external to but still affecting MPAs would be an element of the MSP dialogue. While the process could identify and manage activities that impact conservation objectives within the MPA boundaries, an important aspect of MSP is the identification and promotion of complementary activities that drive the sustainable use of marine regions.

Shipping

Shipping is an international maritime sector that is responsible for approximately 90 per cent of global trade (International Maritime Organization, 2014; Ardron *et al.*, 2008) and is regulated at the international scale through the legal regimes developed within the International Maritime Organization (IMO). The IMO is an agency of the United Nations and the global standard-setting authority for the safety, security and environmental performance of the shipping industry (International Maritime Organization, 2014). Conventions under the IMO include the International Convention for the Safety of Life at Sea (SOLAS), the International Convention for the Prevention of Pollution from Ships (MARPOL) and the International Convention on Maritime Search and Rescue (SAR). These conventions are operationalized via policy processes both at the regional (e.g. EU) and national levels, with the IMO aiming to maintain a consistent global standard to ensure a level playing field both in terms of maritime safety and environmental protection.

Both short sea shipping – where maritime transport occurs over short distances – and deep sea shipping raise important issues for MSP. Shipping interacts with a variety of traditional and new uses of the marine environment, ranging from interactions with inshore fisheries in the coastal zone through to recent challenges associated with the emergence of large offshore infrastructure projects associated with marine wind farms. These interactions can have ramifications for shipping in terms of safety and environmental protection and increasing demands for alteration of existing maritime routes have ramifications for both navigational safety and commercial viability.

Developing a common vision for the use of marine space is an outcome of MSP and the shipping sector has an important role to play despite the sector not having been traditionally engaged in the MSP process, particularly at the subnational scale. This includes contributing data on short sea and deep water routes, providing expertise on navigational protocols and tracking systems, identifying the implications for maritime authorities and ports and harmonizing MSP plan outputs with international authorities such as the IMO and the requirements of conventions such as MARPOL and SOLAS (Patraiko and Holthus, 2013). Furthermore, monitoring of MSP outcomes should occur using standard international shipping approaches and impacts – particularly where changes to shipping routes have been proposed. Changes and incidents should be regularly reported through the IMO and marine plans adapted accordingly (Patraiko and Holthus, 2013).

Conclusion

Marine Spatial Planning is a major evolution in the management of the ocean. It builds upon existing sector approaches and perspectives and subscribes to the Ecosystem Approach to management where deeper links between human processes and ecological systems are explored and assessed. It is critical to note that MSP has not emerged from a blank canvas where negotiations over access and use are a recent endeavour. On the contrary, the marine environment has experienced decades of single sector exploitation and associated management. Where MSP is new and novel is the fact that it moves beyond sector interests to identify common visions and holistic outcomes for marine space, including the rational use of this space. MSP is primarily a negotiation process. Sectors will generally defend their interests and maximise their economic rent from the ocean, and where the current approach favours existing power relationships arrangements, MSP will need to demonstrate its feasibility, relevance and opportunities for reform. The challenge for MSP is to clearly articulate and progress the idea that integrated, collaborative and ecosystem-based approaches offer opportunities for new and existing sectors, not least, the sustainable development of the global marine environment.

Notes

1 http://www.sams.ac.uk/laurence-mee; http://laurence-mee.tumblr.com/
2 The workshop presentations and outputs are available from: http://www.amiando.com/MSPworkshops_Vilnius.html?page=1022769

References

Agardy, T. (2010) *Ocean Zoning: Making Marine Management More Effective*, Earthscan, London.

Alexander, K., Potts, T. and Wilding, T. (2013) 'Marine renewable energy and Scottish west coast fishers: exploring impacts, opportunities and potential mitigation' in *Ocean & Coastal Management*, vol. 75, pp. 1–10.

Ardron, J.A., Gjerde, K.M., Pullen, S., Tilot, V. (2008) 'Marine spatial planning in the high seas', in Douvere, F. *et al.* (Ed.) (2008) 'The role of marine spatial planning in implementing ecosystem-based, sea use management', *Marine Policy*, vol. 32 (Spec. Issue 5), pp. 832–9.

Arkema, Katie K., Abramson, Sarah C. and Dewsbury, Bryan (2006) 'Marine ecosystem-based management: from characterization to implementation', *Frontiers in Ecology and the Environment*, vol. 4, pp. 525–32.

Bainbridge, J.M., Potts, T. and O'Higgins, T.G., (2011) 'Rapid policy network mapping: a new method for understanding governance structures for implementation of marine environmental policy' in *PlOS one*, vol. 6, no. 10.

Bellido, J.M., Santos, M.B., Pennino, M.G., Valeiras, X., Pierce, G. (2011) 'Fishery discards and bycatch: solutions for an ecosystem approach to fisheries management?', *Hydrobiologia*, vol. 670, issue 1, pp. 317–333.

Bergström, L., Kautsky, L., Malm, T., Rosenberg, R., Wahlberg, M., Capetillo, N., Wilhelmsson, D. (2014) 'Effects of offshore wind farms on marine wildlife – a generalized impact assessment', *Environmental Research Letters*, vol. 9, no. 3, pp. 1–12.

Blæsbjerg, M., Pawlak, J., Sorenson, T.K., Vestergaard, O. (2009) *Marine Spatial Planning in the Nordic region – Principles, Perspectives and Opportunities*, Copenhagen: Norden.

Browman, H., Cury, P., Hilborn, R., Jennings, S., Lotze, H.K., Mace, P., Murawski, S., Pauly, D., Sissenwine, M., Stergiou, K. and Zeller, D. (2004) 'Perspectives on ecosystem-based approaches to the management of marine resources' in H. Browman and K. Stergiou (eds) *Marine Ecology Progress Series*, vol. 274, pp. 269–303.

CBD (2000) *Convention on Biological Diversity: Principles of the Ecosystem Approach.* Available at: https://www.cbd.int/ecosystem/principles.shtml

Center for Ocean Solutions (2011) *Decision Guide: Selecting Decision Support Tools for Marine Spatial Planning*, The Center for Ocean Solutions, Monterey, CA, USA, pp. 1–54.

Costanza, R., Andrade, F., Antunes, P., den Belt, M., Boersma, D., Boesch, D.F., Catarino, F., Hanna, S., Limburg, K., Low, B., Molitor, M., Pereira, J.G., Rayner, S., Santos, R., Wilson, J. and Young, M. (1998) 'Principles for Sustainable Governance of the Oceans' in *Science*, vol. 281, no. 5374, pp. 198–9.

Ehler, C.N. and Douvere, F. (2009) 'Marine Spatial Planning: A Step-by-step Approach toward Ecosystem-based Management' in *IOC Manual and Guides* No. 53, ICAM Dossier No. 6, Paris: UNESCO. Available at: http://www.vliz.be/imisdocs/publications/153333.pdf.

European Commission Maritime Affairs and Fisheries (2012) 'Blue Growth: Opportunities for Marine and Maritime Sustainable Growth', COM (2012) 494 final. Luxembourg: Publications Office of the European Union.

European Commission Maritime Affairs and Fisheries (2011a) 'Developing a Maritime Strategy for the Atlantic Ocean Area', COM (2011) 782 final. Luxembourg: Publications Office of the European Union. Available at: http://ec.europa.eu/maritime-affairs/policy/sea_basins/atlantic_ocean/documents/com_2011_782_en.pdf [Accessed October 7, 2014].

European Commission Maritime Affairs and Fisheries (2011b) 'Study on the Economic Effects of Maritime Spatial Planning: Final Report', Luxembourg: Publications Office of the European Union.

European Parliament and Council of the European Union (2008) Directive 2008/56/EC of the European Parliament and of the Council of 17 June 2008, 'Establishing a framework for community action in the field of marine environmental policy' (Marine Strategy Framework Directive).

European Parliament and Council of the European Union (2014) 'Directive of the European Parliament and of the Council 2014/89/EU, 'Establishing a framework for maritime spatial planning'. Available at: http://eur-lex.europa.eu/legal-content/EN/TXT/PDF/?uri=CELEX:32014L0089&from=EN [Accessed October 17, 2014].

EWEA (European Wind Energy Association) (2011) 'Maritime Spatial Planning: supporting offshore wind and grid development', pp. 1–3. Available at: http://www.ewea.org/fileadmin/ewea_documents/documents/members_lounge/1._Make_the_right_connections/Offshore_Wind_Industry_Advisory_Group/110921_EWEA_briefing_on_Maritime_Spatial_Planning.pdf [Accessed October 17, 2014].

EWEA (European Wind Energy Association) (2014) 'The European offshore wind industry – key trends and statistics 2013', pp. 1–22. Available at: http://www.ewea.org/fileadmin/files/library/publications/statistics/European_offshore_statistics_2013.pdf [Accessed October 17, 2014].

Gilliland, P.M. and Laffoley, D. (2008) 'Key elements and steps in the process of developing ecosystem-based marine spatial planning', in *Marine Policy*, vol. 32, no. 5, pp. 787–96.

Grumbine, Edward R. (1997) 'What is Ecosystem Management', *Conservation Biology*, vol. 11, no. 1, pp. 41–47.

Haward, M. and Vince, J. (2008) *Oceans Governance in the Twenty First Century*, Cheltenham, Edward Elgar.

International Maritime Organization (2014) *Introduction to the IMO*. Available at: http://www.imo.org/About/Pages/Default.aspx [Accessed October 17, 2014].

Jentoft, S. and Knol, M. (2014) 'Marine spatial planning : risk or opportunity for fisheries in the North Sea?', *Maritime Studies*, vol. 13, no. 1, pp. 1–16.

Kerr, S., Watts, L., Colton, J., Conway, F., Hull, A., Johnson, K., Jude, S., Kannen, A., MacDougall, S., McLachlan, C., Potts, T. and Vergunst, J. (2014) 'Establishing an agenda for social studies research in marine renewable energy', *Energy Policy*, vol. 67, pp. 694–702.

Patraiko, D. and Holthus, P. (2013) *The Shipping Industry and Marine Spatial Planning*, The Nautical Institute and The World Ocean Council, pp. 1–14. Available at: http://www.nautinst.org/en/forums/msp/ [Accessed October 18, 2014].

Plasman, I.C. (2008) 'Implementing marine spatial planning: A policy perspective', *Marine Policy*, vol. 32, no. 5, pp. 811–15.

Pomeroy, R. and Douvere, F. (2008) 'The engagement of stakeholders in the marine spatial planning process', *Marine Policy*, vol. 32, no. 5, pp. 816–22.

Potts, T., O'Higgins, T. and Hastings, E. (2012) 'Oceans of Opportunity or Rough Seas? What does the future hold for developments in European marine policy?', *Philosophical Transactions of the Royal Society* A, vol. 370, no. 1980, pp. 5682–700.

Potts, T., Burdon, D., Jackson, E., Atkins, J., Saunders, J., Hastings, E. and Langmead, O. (2014) 'Do marine protected areas deliver flows of ecosystem services to support human welfare?', *Marine Policy*, vol. 44, pp. 139–148.

Sumaila, U.R., Khan, A., Dyck, A.J., Watson, R., Munro, G., Tydemers, P. and Pauly, D. (2010) 'A bottom-up re-estimation of global fisheries subsidies', *Journal of Bioeconomics*, vol. 12, no. 3, pp. 201–25.

UNESCO-IOC (2014) *MSP Around the World: Germony*. Updated 6th May 2014. Available at: http://www.unesco-ioc-marinesp.be/msp_around_the_world/germany_lander_or_states

Zacharias, M., (2014) *Marine Policy: An introduction to governance and international law of the oceans*. Oxon: Routledge Earthscan.

Chapter 4

United Nations Convention on the Law of the Sea as a framework for marine spatial planning

Daud Hassan and Niko Soininen

Introduction

Marine spatial planning (MSP) is a planning instrument,[1] resembling land-use planning and consisting of two parts. First, a textual formulation of the important goals, priorities and principles of the plan, reasons for adopting the plan and guidance for the interpretation of the plan. Secondly, it usually includes a map, which indicates the spatial distribution of different activities (zoning).[2] A key aspect of MSP is that it is place-based or area-based, which means that it covers only a certain geographical area and does not concentrate on a certain sector or on a particular environmental problem in isolation (Ehler and Douvere, 2009, p. 78).[3] It has been claimed that place-based measures of marine governance, such as zoning, can aid in targeting economic and ecological goals simultaneously (Arkema, *et al.*, 2006, p. 531).[4] According to Craig (2012, p. 94): '[t]he quest for a more holistic approach to ocean governance leads naturally to an increased use of place-based management. The basic premise of place-based marine management is that regulators can delineate a particular area of the ocean (large or small) and create a governance regime for that area that simultaneously addresses all values to be protected and all activities of concern.'

Until recently, the idea of planning, let alone zoning, was mainly considered as a terrestrial instrument. Jay (2010) argues that this is closely related to the basic purposes of planning in controlling the development and use of (terrestrial) space. This control is based on land ownership and parcelling of land by visible and accurate boundaries. Furthermore, terrestrial planning has usually had the objective of making organized construction and settlement possible. According to Jay (2010), the marine environment, by its very nature, resists all the above basic elements of terrestrial planning (Agardy, 2010, p. 175).[5] This is to a certain extent echoed in the view of the Commission of the European Union (2008, p. 10) as well: 'MSP does not replicate terrestrial planning at sea, given its tri-dimensionality and the fact that the same sea area can host several uses provided they are compatible. However, in the same way that terrestrial planning set up a legally binding framework for the management of land, MSP should be legally binding if it is to be effective.'[6]

With the present prospects of major offshore wind farms, as well as renewable marine energy, spatial planning of marine areas is starting to share more and more elements with terrestrial land-use planning and zoning (Jay, 2010, p. 177).[7] However, there are also major differences. MSP operates in three dimensions by simultaneously addressing activities that take place: (a) on the seabed; (b) in the water column; and (c) on the surface. Land use planning is typically concerned with activities that involve a fair degree of permanence with regard to a specific area of land, such as the construction of a building, road or other structure. In contrast, MSP must take in to account fixed structures, such as oilrigs and wind farms, as well as temporary activities such as navigation (both surface and submarine) and fishing. Land use planning takes place against the background of private land tenure rights. In contrast the sea (including the column and surface) and seabed are not subject to private tenure rights.[8] By nature, the marine environment, in addition to limiting spatial planning, also offers different possibilities for accomplishing reconciliation between interests, even within the same spatial area.[9] This is made possible by the three-dimensional and temporal allocation of activities.

Despite certain similarities and differences between marine and land-use planning, the legal aspect of spatial planning of the sea, due to its transboundary character, is different from that of the land. Since maritime boundary delimitation is an international operation having an international character (Tanaka, 2006, p. 8),[10] a state is only entitled to plan its marine space after having defined maritime boundaries in course of maritime delimitation between its adjacent or opposite coastal state(s). In line with this view, rules governing activities over marine spaces are subject to international law.

The *United Nations Convention on the Law of the Sea* (UNCLOS)[11] has codified various maritime zones for the use and allocation of marine resources and spaces. Furthermore, part XII of UNCLOS has provided a comprehensive framework for the protection and preservation of the marine environment. UNCLOS forms the international legal basis for the allocation of marine space and consequently the legal basis for marine spatial planning and marine zoning. By way of doing this, UNCLOS provides a framework for an orderly and rational conduct of historic and modern maritime activities.[12]

The chapter begins with a brief analysis of the maritime delimitation system of UNCLOS and continues with a discussion of the Convention in the light of protection and preservation of the marine environment. This analysis is followed by a discussion on the role and effectiveness of UNCLOS in implementing marine spatial planning, taking into account characteristics such as integration between sectors and transboundary cooperation discussed earlier in Chapter 1 of the book. The argument is that in order for an MSP to be effective in achieving these aims, the regulatory framework of MSP has to be seen in a broader light. Here, principles of international environmental law, such as sustainability, precautionary principle and polluter pays principle come into the picture in complementing the framework of UNCLOS. Based on this discussion we evaluate whether a complementary legal framework for MSP would be required, *de lege ferenda*, in order to reach these aims.

UNCLOS and the legal framing of MSP

Legally binding maritime zones

UNCLOS has been remarked as one of 'the world's most significant legal instruments' and the 'living monument to international cooperation negotiated by more than 150 States' (United Nations 2012).[13] The scope of UNCLOS is extremely broad. It seeks to reconcile a range of competing interests including the rights of coastal states, land-locked states and flag states. Part of this balance is achieved through dividing the sea into maritime zones. UNCLOS has established seven maritime areas in which coastal states can exercise jurisdiction regarding MSP: internal waters, archipelagic waters, territorial seas, contiguous zones, exclusive economic zones (EEZ), continental shelf, and fishing zones.[14] Under UNCLOS, the rights and jurisdiction of states differ from zone to zone (Maes, 2008, p. 799). Although UNCLOS makes no explicit reference to the establishment of MSP, the ability of a coastal state to engage in marine spatial planning has to start with the constraints set by UNCLOS. The rights of the coastal state are narrowed down when moving from the territorial sea to the EEZ (Directorate General for Marine Affairs and Fisheries, 2009).

Art. 8 of UNCLOS states that waters on the landward side of the baseline[15] of the territorial sea form part of the internal waters of the State. Internal waters include bays, estuaries and ports. Furthermore, under UNCLOS, every coastal state has the right to establish a territorial sea, which extends up to 12 nautical miles (nm)[16] from the baseline (art. 3). An archipelagic state may draw straight archipelagic baselines joining the outermost points of the outermost islands and drying reefs of the archipelago provided that within such baselines are included the main islands and an area in which the ratio of the area of the water to the area of the land, including atolls, is between 1 to 1 and 9 to 1 (UNCLOS, art. 47).

A coastal state has full sovereignty over its internal waters and can, in most circumstances, restrict entry into them. Consequently a coastal state enjoys the widest possible freedom to undertake MSP within its internal waters (UNCLOS, art. 8).[17] In many cases, as in Finland, the land-use planning regime extends to internal waters. The coastal state also has sovereignty over its archipelagic waters and territorial sea (UNCLOS, art. 2 and 49).[18] However, in these zones, the coastal state's sovereignty is subject to the freedom of innocent passage by foreign vessels and particular rules for certain international straits. From a legal perspective this limits marine spatial planning by setting legal requirements for MSP in terms of maritime transportation and navigation (UNCLOS, art. 2 and 17–26).[19]

According to art. 33 of UNCLOS, the Contiguous Zone extends 24 nm from the baselines from which the territorial sea is measured. The coastal state has a right to exercise control over the contiguous zone to (a) prevent infringement of its customs, fiscal, immigration or sanitary laws and regulations within its territory or territorial sea; and (b) punish infringement of the above laws and regulations committed within its territory or territorial sea. However, these rights have not been seen to contribute much to MSP since they do not contribute to solving conflicts between different uses of the marine area (Maes, 2008, p.799). In other words, the rights of the coastal state to regulate the use of the continental shelf are more limited compared to the territorial sea and internal waters.

The EEZ extends to a maximum of 200 nm from the baseline and comprises parts or whole of the continental shelf. The continental shelf comprises the seabed and subsoil of the submarine areas that extend beyond a coastal state's territorial sea throughout the natural prolongation of its land territory to the outer edge of the continental margin, or to a distance of 200 nm from the baselines from which the breadth of the territorial sea is measured where the outer edge of the continental margin does not extend up to that distance. However, the outer limit of the continental shelf shall not in any case exceed 350 nm (UNCLOS, art. 76).

In the EEZ, the sovereignty of the coastal state is limited and according to art. 56 of UNCLOS the coastal state possesses only certain sovereign rights for the purposes of exploring, exploiting, conserving and managing living and non-living natural resources (e.g. fish and hydrocarbons) and other activities for the economic exploitation and exploration of the zone (such as the production of energy from the water, currents and winds). In the EEZ, the coastal state also has jurisdiction with regard to artificial islands, installations and structures, marine scientific research and the protection of the environment (UNCLOS, art. 60). The competence of a coastal state to undertake MSP in its EEZ is therefore restricted to these issues and may not derogate from the rights enjoyed by other states in such waters including the freedom of navigation[20] and the right to lay submarine cables. Similarly, the coastal state has sovereign rights for the purpose of exploring its continental shelf and exploiting its natural resources (such as the harvesting of sedentary fish species, drilling, tunnelling etc.). As with the EEZ, something less than full sovereignty is conferred and it follows that the right of a coastal state to undertake MSP in respect of its continental shelf is restricted to activities that relate to the exercise of its sovereign rights (UNCLOS, art. 77–82 and 85).

Finally, no state may claim sovereignty over the high seas, the international commons beyond the EEZ, and consequently no coastal state has the requisite legal capacity to give unilateral effect to MSP in the high seas: the most that any state acting alone can do is to regulate the activities on the high seas of its nationals and vessels that fly its flag (UNCLOS, art. 87 and 89).

With regard to legally designated maritime zones, although it may be used in many countries, MSP is typically applied to internal and territorial waters

(UNCLOS, art. 8 and 23–26) and may also extend to the EEZ.[21] Within its scope, it recognizes certain rights (e.g. public access rights, riparian rights, development rights and fishing rights) calling for them to be exercised in a sustainable manner. Sectoral and jurisdictional issues are also involved in the management process. For example, Australia is a federal state which addresses marine issues in federal as well as state legislative arrangements. Internal waters up to three nautical miles seaward of the shore are under state control while from the three nautical miles to the extent of the EEZ, the waters are federally governed (Alder and Ward, 2001, p. 274).

The maritime zones discussed set some legal requirements for the coastal states' capacity to adopt marine spatial plans. It is also interesting to note the role UNCLOS can be seen to have played in bringing land use planning and marine spatial planning closer. Traditionally, the lack of property rights has been used as an argument against MSP and any efforts to zone the marine areas. It has also been used as an argument to highlight that terrestrial land use planning principles cannot be used in marine areas. While the terrestrial instrument may not be directly applicable to marine areas, the lack of property rights also creates possibilities for the zoning of marine areas. Eagle *et al.* (2008, pp. 656 and 663) have argued that zoning efforts could create group property rights in which case the holders of certain interests would belong to a certain group and manage the area jointly. Referring to Carr (2008), Agardy (2010, p. 26) has argued that this would 'provide stewardship incentives and lead to rationalization of uses'. From a planning perspective, it is interesting to note that by recognizing certain rights of coastal states and creating legally binding zones, UNCLOS has been responsible for lessening the gap between terrestrial and marine spatial planning by eliminating some of the key-problems of spatial planning in marine areas.[22] In other words, UNCLOS can be seen as contributing and constituting certain essential elements to MSP.

Protection and preservation of the marine environment

In addition to the delimitation of maritime zones, UNCLOS contains more substantive provisions aiming to protect and preserve the marine environment. Part XII of UNCLOS (art. 192–237) provides a wide array of general obligations to coastal states towards the marine environment (Charney, 1994, p. 888). Firstly, it sets out the general provisions for control of all sources of marine pollution (art. 192–206). Furthermore, article 192–206 covers general rights and obligations of states; international and regional cooperation in formulating rules, standards and recommended practices; research and exchange of information; and technical and scientific assistance for the protection and preservation of the marine environment. These provisions establish general obligations, a foundation to develop more specific regional and global rules, standards and practices to control marine pollution.[23]

Substantiating on these general rules and the overall obligation to protect and preserve the marine environment (UNCLOS, art. 192), UNCLOS also makes general reference to 'special areas' in the EEZ (UNCLOS, art. 211(6)) and particular reference to ice-covered areas (UNCLOS, art. 234). This means that any measure taken by a state must be in compliance with the jurisdictional provisions on the protection and preservation of the marine environment (Dux, 2011, p. 179). Also, in taking these measures, states are to refrain from unjustifiable interference with activities carried out by other states in the exercise of their rights in conformity with the Convention (UNCLOS, art. 194(4)). In respect of measures, UNCLOS refers to any kind of measure to prevent, reduce and control pollution of the marine environment, be it from dumping, from vessels, from land-based sources, from seabed activities subject to national jurisdiction, or from the atmosphere (Tullio, 1999, p. 186). Transboundary cooperation is one of the available avenues for preventing and controlling pollution. For example, art. 194 of UNCLOS provides: '1. States shall take, individually, or jointly as appropriate, all measures consistent with this Convention that are necessary to prevent, reduce and control pollution of the marine environment from any source, using for this purpose the best practicable means at their disposal and in accordance with their capabilities, and they shall endeavour to harmonize their policies in this connection.'[24]

One of the procedural instruments designed to implement the requirements for prevention of marine pollution and enhancing transboundary cooperation is environmental impact assessment (EIA). To understand whether a proposed development activity is sustainable, evaluations of potential environmental effects are needed.[25] On a general level, EIA is based on a prediction of the changes in environmental quality, which would result from the proposed action, and it attempts to weigh environmental effects with economic costs and benefits. EIA includes studying the effects of a proposed action on the environment and comparing various alternatives by which a desired objective may be realized (Yusuf and George, 1985, p. 2). It aims to ensure that environmental impacts are recognized and taken into account early in project designs so that the proposed action will not adversely affect the environment (Le Prestre, 1995, p. 89).

Art. 206 of UNCLOS explicitly requires, in relation to matters under coastal states' jurisdiction or control that 'states shall as far as practicable assess the potential effects of those activities that may cause substantial pollution of, or, significant and harmful changes to, the marine environment'. In order to protect and preserve the marine environment, EIA requirements have been developed as a 'preventive tool' at an international level through international law, either impliedly or explicitly.[26] In this regard, art. 12 of the 1985 Montreal Guidelines for the Protection of the Marine Environment from Land Based Marine Pollution requires states to 'assess the potential effects, or, impacts of, proposed projects under their jurisdiction and control, particularly, in coastal areas.' The United Nations Joint Group of Experts of Scientific Aspects of Marine Pollution (GESAMP, 1984) has recommended EIA for effective control of marine pollution.

With regard to transboundary cooperation in MSP, the limitation of EIA under UNCLOS is that it is conducted within a state's jurisdiction and controls (Alheritiere, 1982, p. 54), which gives a state the option of acting as the sole judge of the environmental effects of activities within its territory. In this sense EIA can be seen as a procedural safeguard with little effect on enhancing transboundary cooperation or integration of sectoral decision making. However, some regional agreements have been conducted in relation to transboundary EIA[27] which significantly increase its potential for creating positive obligations for coastal states in conducting an EIA within or outside the context of marine spatial planning.[28]

In addition to establishing maritime zones and setting certain requirements for the protection of the marine environment, UNCLOS also provides an international framework for the conservation and management of marine living resources. The coastal states are empowered to establish and determine fishery zones in their territorial sea. In the EEZ, they are empowered to determine the allowable catch of the living resources and have the duty to maintain and restore the living resources through proper conservation and management measures, taking into account a multi-species approach and ensuring that the living resources are not endangered by over-exploitation (UNCLOS, art. 61).

The jurisdiction of the coastal state is only limited by the obligation to agree with states' fishing stocks straddling in the EEZ, to ensure conservation of these stocks in the high seas and to coordinate measures to ensure conservation of these stocks within the EEZs of two or more coastal states (UNCLOS, art. 63). Under article 64 and 65 of UNCLOS there are also several duties for states to cooperate in conserving certain species (highly migratory species and marine mammals) (UNCLOS, art. 64 and 65). Besides the duty to conserve marine living resources in the territorial seas and EEZ, the same duty applies on the high seas. Rather than imposing additional requirements to cooperate or consult, these provisions do not represent any important progress with respect to the effective management of fisheries resources. Questions remain as to the positive obligation to cooperate and to the nature and extent of duty to cooperate.

Fisheries in the EEZ by third parties are very much dependent on agreements and arrangements that give those states access to the surplus of the allowable catch. Nationals of the third party states fishing in the EEZ of the coastal state have to comply with the laws and regulations of the coastal state.[29] Despite the coastal states' right to take enforcement measures (like boarding, inspection, arrest and judicial proceedings) (UNCLOS, art. 73), in practice enforcement is difficult. In order to enhance cooperation and enforcement in the conservation and management of straddling and highly migratory fish stocks, an Agreement for the Implementation of the Provisions of the United Nations Convention on the Law of the Sea Relating to the Conservation and Management of Straddling Fish Stocks and Highly Migratory Fish Stocks (Fish Stock Agreement)[30] was adopted. The Preamble of the Fish Stock Agreement indicates that the management of high seas fisheries is inadequate in many areas by pointing out that: '. . . some resources are over utilized, there are problems of unregulated fishing, problems of over capitalization, excessive fleet sizes, vessel re-flagging in order to escape regulatory controls, insufficiently selective fishing gear, unreliable databases and a lack of sufficient cooperation between States.' (Freestone, 1999, p. 313)

On the basis of principles 4 and 15 of the Rio Declaration and paragraph 17.21 of the Agenda 21 of the United Nations Conference on Environment and Development (UNCED) 1992,[31] article 2 of the Fish Stocks Agreement intends to ensure the long term conservation and sustainable use of straddling fish stocks and highly migratory fish stocks through effective implementation of fisheries-related provisions of the UNCLOS (Fish Stock Agreement, art. 2). The Agreement contains general principles of stock management and obliges coastal states to utilize the principles by adopting measures to ensure the long-term sustainability of straddling fish stocks and highly migratory fish stocks and promoting the objective of their optimum utilization (Fish Stocks Agreement, art. 5(a)). It incorporates the precautionary approach and the ecosystem approach to the conservation, management and exploitation of fish stocks in waters under national jurisdiction and in the high seas.[32]

The Fish Stocks Agreement is the first international convention regarding fisheries that makes a reference to the precautionary approach. It requires that states should be more cautious when using information that is potentially uncertain, unreliable or inadequate, as well as in the absence of adequate scientific information it shall not be used as a reason for postponing or failing to take conservation and management measures (Fish Stock Agreement, art. 6(2)). When new or exploratory fisheries are being undertaken, the Agreement also obliges states to take special precautions providing that states shall adopt as soon as possible cautious conservation and management measures, including catch limits and effort limits (Hayashi, 1999, p. 60). Importantly, article 6(3) of the Fish Stock Agreement also lays down ways of implementing the precautionary approach by providing the following:

> . . . improve decision-making for fishery conservation and management by obtaining and sharing the best scientific information available and implementing improved techniques for dealing with risk of uncertainty; apply the guidelines set out in Annex II and determine, on the basis of the best scientific information available, stock-specific reference points and the action to be taken if they are exceeded; take into account, *inter alia*, uncertainties relating to the size and productivity of the stocks, reference points, stock condition in relation to such reference points, level of distribution of fishing mortality and the impact of fishing activities on non-target and associated or dependent species, as well as existing and predicted oceanic, environmental and socio-economic conditions; and develop data collection and research programmes to assess the impact of fishing on non-target and associated or dependent species and their environment, and adopt plans which are necessary to ensure the conservation of such species and to protect habitats of special concern.

The Fish Stocks Agreement emphasizes the compatibility of conservation and management measures and obliges states to take into account various matters in accordance with UNCLOS which include biological unity and other biological characteristics of the stocks and the relationship between the distribution of the stocks, the fisheries and the geographical particularities of the region concerned as well as to ensure that such measures do not result in harmful impact on the living marine resources as a whole (Fish Stock Agreement, art. 7). It also provides more stringent obligations on the flag state for fishing on the high seas.[33]

To implement these aims and principles, the Fish Stock Agreement promotes the establishment of sub-regional and regional fisheries management organizations and arrangements (Fish Stock Agreement, art. 6). The Agreement has outlined several functions for regional and sub-regional fisheries management organizations and strengthened the arrangements of conservation and management of fish stocks.[34]

The Fish Stock Agreement also places more stringent enforcement procedures compared to UNCLOS. Article 20 provides that: '(1) States shall cooperate, either directly or through sub-regional or regional fisheries management organisations or arrangements, to ensure compliance with and enforcement of sub-regional and regional conservation management measures for straddling fish stocks and highly migratory fish stocks. (4) States shall assist each other in identifying vessels reported to have engaged in activities undermining the effectiveness of sub-regional regional or global conservation management measures. (6) Where there are reasonable grounds for believing that a vessel on the high seas has been engaged in unauthorized fishing within an area under the jurisdiction of a coastal State, the flag State of that vessel, at the request of the coastal State concerned, shall immediately and fully investigate the matter. The flag State shall cooperate with coastal State in taking appropriate enforcement act on cases and may authorize the relevant authorities of the coastal State to board and inspect the vessel on the high seas.'

The Agreement also provides that apart from coastal states, states that are members of a sub-regional or regional fisheries organization or participants in a sub-regional or regional fisheries management arrangement may take action in accordance with international law. These actions can include for instance a recourse to sub-regional or regional procedures established for this purpose but member states also have a right to deter vessels which have engaged in activities which undermine the effectiveness of or otherwise violate the conservation and management measures established by that organization or arrangement from fishing on the high seas in the sub-region or region until such time as appropriate action is taken by the flag State (Fish Stock Agreement, art. 20(7)). It has emphasized sub-regional and regional cooperation in enforcement (ibid., art. 21) and outlined the procedures for boarding and inspection (ibid., art. 22).

Overall, it has been asserted that from an MSP perspective the Agreement lacks immediate contribution since it is dominantly focusing on fish species (Maes, 2008, p. 804). It provides sectoral remedies without an integrated approach. While this may be the case within the Fish Stocks Agreement, evaluating the overall framework of UNCLOS suggests that there are some elements that point toward sectoral integration. The instruments and legal obligations stated in the part XII of UNCLOS provide certain minimum requirements for bringing different sectors under the same framework also in the context of MSP. By way of doing this, UNCLOS places certain minimum requirements for sectoral integration as well.

In terms of scope and transboundary cooperation, there is an interesting dynamic between the Fish Stocks Agreement and UNCLOS. While UNCLOS includes the necessary breadth of scope for the integrated management of the marine environment, it lacks to a certain extent strict legal obligations to implement this aim. In contrast, the Fisheries Agreement has a more limited scope and stricter obligations on managing of one sectoral resource (fisheries) and its transboundary cooperation. They both include some building blocks for an effective MSP.

Despite this background, UNCLOS has been considered as a bare framework for the marine and coastal resources management.[35] A question remains as to the effective management of the ocean environment in a sustainable and integrated manner. In line with this, it has been asserted that UNCLOS cannot be seen in isolation from other developments of international environmental law when giving normative content to marine spatial planning and interpreting its normative requirements. While it is clear that UNCLOS and agreements made under this framework form the legal basis for marine spatial planning, they do not portray a full picture of legal obligations relating to MSP. UNCLOS may be complemented from a legal perspective to ensure effective implementation of MSP.

Complementing UNCLOS with substantive principles

Sustainable development

The principle of sustainable development is founded on the concept of harmony between environmental protection and economic development.[36] Recently, the global climate system as a common natural resource[37] has attracted much attention and rightly so. In this context, the principle is under consideration as a means of allowing states to anticipate, prevent and minimize the causes of climate change,[38] and to mitigate its adverse effects for the benefit of present and future generations in accordance with Article 3(4)[39] of the UNFCCC. The Convention calls for integration of social, economic and environmental issues with climate change responses and places emphasis on the priority needs of developing states for the achievement of sustainable economic growth and eradication of poverty.[40]

Again, considering the global climate as a common natural resource, the International Law Association Committee has drawn attention on the legal principles to the notion of 'common concern of humankind' with contrast to the established principle of permanent sovereignty of states over natural resources.[41] The committee admitted the increasing emergence of international legal regimes for the cooperative management of natural resources pursuant to sustainable development.[42] Furthermore, it emphasized that the development of international environmental law and prominence of sustainable development means that the 'permanent sovereignty must be exercised pursuant to environmental and development policies and should not cause damage to other states' (ibid.).

In terms of MSP, the applicability of this principle is indispensable in order to protect the marine environment and resources from conflicting offshore activities as well as from transboundary environmental damage.[43] With regard to oceans, sustainable development requires maintaining a clean ocean environment suitable for rational management and optimum utilization of marine resources (Dzidzornu, 1998, p. 97) and thus the sustainable manner of oceans usage requires the minimization of marine pollution. In practice, sustainable development, in terms of MSP, requires organizational and managerial procedures and equipment, human resource development, the availability and accessibility of scientific information and financial and technological assistance. Again many countries of the world whose sources of income are very much dependent on ocean activities, like fishing and tourism, may face sustainability challenges due to pollution and the reality is that many of those countries have no legal and institutional arrangements in regard to sustainable use of resources and the protection of the marine and coastal environment from pollution. The shortcomings of sustainable development are well known and documented: 'Heads of nations must commit themselves to improving overseas development practices to ensure that the projects are sustainable. One of the best ways of doing this is to increase the transparency of lending practices so that local communities and non-governmental groups have the opportunity to commit on proposals.' (Gore, 1992)

Legal and institutional arrangements are poor in many countries with regard to the sustainable use of resources and the protection of the marine and coastal environment from pollution. Improvement in this situation requires international and regional cooperation (Hassan, 2006, p. 52). Active participation and cooperation of the NGOs and local communities are also significantly important in this context.

Precautionary principle

The precautionary principle is usually taken to mean that, when making policy decisions, one should err on the side of the environment, or caution, or both (Bodansky, 1991). This approach maintains that it is not permitted to carry out an activity unless it can be shown that the activity in question will not cause unacceptable harm to the environment (Birnie and Boyle, 2002, p. 118). This principle is aptly formulated in the Bergen Ministerial Declaration on Sustainable Development: 'Environmental measures must anticipate, prevent and attack the causes of environmental degradation. Where there are threats of serious or irreversible damage, lack of full scientific certainty should not be a reason for postponing measures to prevent environmental degradation.'[44]

Furthermore, principle 15 of the Rio Declaration on Environment and Development calls for a wide application of this principle: 'In order to protect the environment, the precautionary approach shall be widely applied by States according to their capabilities.'[45]

Despite some debate among scholars,[46] the precautionary principle is considered as one of the most important normative requirements for an effective MSP. It was developed in the practices of the European States, and subsequently accepted in the international forums as well.[47] In fact, this principle refers to a preventive approach for the policy makers to act in an anticipatory manner to ensure that potential environmental harms do not occur in the first place, irrespective of scientific uncertainty (Van Dyke *et al.*, 1993, p. 477).

The precautionary principle operates in two ways. First, it shifts the burden of proof and, secondly, it encompasses a dynamic element that requires all users of the ocean commons to develop alternative non-burdensome technologies.[48] However, application of this principle in an equitable manner poses a number of challenges such that it is not well received in domestic laws and in the governmental decision-making process.[49] In fact, what should exactly trigger precautionary actions remains controversial within the Rio Declaration, which only suggests a threshold of 'serious or irreversible' harm,[50] but leaves open the question as to which persons or institutions within states should make precautionary determinations and judgments.[51] Furthermore, whether the precautionary principle should be determined by sound science and risk assessment, or social values and public perceptions, remains contentious.[52]

Despite this, and being well aware of the problems with the precautionary principle, some scholars have advocated that this principle favours the coastal states and the potential opportunity to extend their jurisdiction under international law. This extension would include powers of intervention towards international shipping, when a vessel is considered to pose an unacceptable risk to the coastal and marine environment of the coast prior to the occurrence of any incident or accident. This precaution would be taken in order to prevent or minimize the risk of occurrence of the accident or incident leading to damage.[53] By way of doing this, the principle can be seen as substantiating some of the requirements set under UNCLOS.

In recent times this principle has also gained traction in terms of response to the impacts of climate change. The ILA Committee on the Legal Principles Relating to Climate Change has adopted this principle to a large degree. According to the Committee, states can take anticipatory, preventive or adaptive measures without waiting for conclusive scientific proof, not only in a situation where there is a reasonably foreseeable threat of serious or irreversible damage within national jurisdiction, but also in a situation where a proposed activity may cause serious damage to the environment of other states or areas beyond national jurisdiction.[54]

In terms of a new understanding of traditional resource management, the precautionary principle has assumed a significant status in terms of MSP. Chapter 17B of Agenda 21, entitled 'Marine environment protection', stresses a precautionary and anticipatory approach to prevent marine environment degradation. In this way, the principle has become one of the normative cores of sustainable marine development. Paragraph 9a of the GPA states that: '. . . to protect the marine environment . . . in the context of sustainable development it is necessary to apply preventive, precautionary, and anticipatory approaches so as to avoid degradation of the marine environment, as well as to reduce the risk of long term or irreversible adverse effects upon it.'

In terms of MSP, both the traditional and the upcoming implications of the precautionary principle have a big role to play. This is the case in MSP on a general level but includes fisheries, for example, as well.[55] The importance of the precautionary principle will certainly require the attention of the international actors for evaluating the necessity of an international legal framework for MSP, which would complement the minimum requirements presently set by UNCLOS. At present, it is one of the normative requirements to be taken into consideration when fleshing out the normative content of sustainability in marine spatial planning.

The polluter pays principle

The 'polluter pays' principle encourages polluters, or potential polluters, to undertake waste control measures. This is done by government incentives to polluters in the form of tax incentives or a pollution tax.[56] Alternatively, a waste discharge permit system may allow the purchase of pollution rights (Stewart, 1985, p. 2) so as to keep discharges at a permissible level.[57]

The polluter pays principle has originated as an economic tool applied in domestic contexts to allocate the costs of pollution prevention and control measures to the polluter (Smets, 1994, p. 131) encouraging the rational use (as opposed to wasteful exploitation and utilization) of scarce environmental resources. According to the Organisation for Economic Co-operation and Development (OECD), this principle means that the 'polluter should bear the expense of carrying out the pollution prevention and control measures decided by public authorities to ensure that the environment is in an acceptable state.' (OECD, 1972) It is applicable both at national and international level. The British Petroleum oil spill in 2010 in the Gulf of Mexico established an example of paying such compensation.[58] This principle has been incorporated in many international and regional marine environmental instruments including Agenda 21, Global Program of Action GPA (1995), the Helsinki Convention,[59] and the Paris Convention.[60]

The importance of this principle in the context of marine environmental issues has been underlined and reflected in Agenda 21 and the GPA, where states have agreed to: '. . . develop economic incentives, where appropriate, apply clean technologies and other means consistent with the internalisation of environmental costs, such as the Polluter Pays Principle, so as to avoid degradation of the marine environment.' (Agenda 21, para. 17 22(d); GPA, para. 9(d).)

In terms of MSP, it assumes the role of marine pollution control by way of encouraging polluters, or potential polluters, to undertake waste control measures to protect the marine and coastal environment. It is a means of preventing unnecessary harm to other uses of the marine area or to the marine environment itself. By way of doing this, the principle functions as a mechanism to implement sustainable development and to achieve reconciliation between the different uses (or non-uses) of the marine environment.

Conclusions

UNCLOS has indirectly provided a firm legal basis for MSP and also some basis for sustainable development of the marine and coastal environment and resources (Dux, 2011, p. 179). However, due to the increased pressure on the marine environment, increased protection and conservation measures are required for functional and sustainable marine governance.[61] While it can be said that the framework of UNCLOS does set certain minimum criteria for sectoral integration and transboundary cooperation also in terms of MSP, they can be said to be lacking in the present time when facing wicked problems[62] such as that of climate change. The present authors suggest that in evaluating the legal requirements for MSP, several principles of international environmental law have to be taken into consideration in complementing the overall framework of UNCLOS. As such, sustainability, the precautionary principle and the polluter pays principle were considered as examples. Taking into account the fragmentation of the legal framework for MSP, it may also be asked whether effective implementation of MSP would require, for instance, a specific agreement under the framework of UNCLOS.[63]

The reasons for the broadening of legal framework of MSP are manifold. First and most importantly, there are limitations and a lack of comprehensiveness of UNCLOS in terms of MSP. UNCLOS successfully shapes a decisive legal framework for maritime zones and its delimitation process as well as providing measures to control the fishing activities of the states to ensure the long-term conservation and sustainable use of straddling and highly migratory fish stocks. However, it makes no express reference to the establishment of MSP. Since maritime boundary delimitation is an international operation (Tanaka, 2006, p. 8), activities taking place on marine areas are also of international character. It is estimated that in less than 10 years, globally, roughly 20 countries have prepared or are preparing over 40 marine spatial plans, and over the next 10 years at least 80 MSP will be completed globally (Ehler, 2012). The obligations set in UNCLOS may have to be recalibrated to address environmental issues, such as climate change, through an effective framework on marine spatial planning and to facilitate for these new developments with regard to MSP.

Secondly, although UNCLOS has provided a legal basis to implement the management principles of sustainable development (Tsamenyi, 1995, p. 22), UNCLOS does not itself provide a framework for substantive management.[64] Many of the principles discussed in this chapter are not explicitly mentioned in UNCLOS, nor does it encourage the ecosystem approach, which attains clear support from international law as a whole (Maes, 2008, pp. 806–9). Some of these principles are explicitly mentioned in the Fisheries Agreement but they are limited to fisheries only. However, neither UNCLOS nor the Fisheries Agreement pay considerable attention to integrated governance of marine areas, or how to deal with the effects between different uses of the sea, or how to bring ocean and coastal management together (Cicin-Sain and Knechtm, 1998, p. 72). The guidance provided by the UNCLOS-regime is limited in this regard and, from the MSP viewpoint, inadequate.

These shortcomings are becoming increasingly visible as problems with the marine environment increase. It is succinctly articulated that 'water does not respect boundaries' (Backer and Frias, 2012, p. 14). Furthermore, it is indisputably affirmed that healthy oceans are one of the most important sources for human prosperity (The Secretary General of the United Nations, 2012, p. 2). In light of this, and in order to promote state activities in terms of ocean governance, the Secretary General of the United Nations has taken a remarkable initiative to set out a strategic vision for the UN system to deliver on its ocean-related mandates, consistent with the Rio+20 outcome document 'The Future We Want', in a more coherent and effective manner (ibid.). He seems to hold a quite clear view that if the oceans do not remain in good health, the well-being and prosperity of all humankind may have to face the challenge of sustaining the planet (ibid.). Therefore, any dangerous activities in any part of the oceans could endanger the whole of the oceans. MSP tries to tackle these types of issues and any shortcomings in the present legal framework, by emphasizing the importance of integrated and transboundary MSP. It remains to be seen whether this can be achieved within the context of the present legal arrangements, or whether they have to be complemented by other tools to facilitate and encourage MSP on a wider scale.

Notes

1 See further, Chapter 1 of this book.

2 For a good overview of planning and spatial planning in general and their relationship to MSP, see Backer (2011, p. 280–281). MSP is often confused with ocean zoning or other already existing governance instruments, or is mistakenly thought to replace some or all of the existing instruments of governance, see Agardy (2010, p. 13): 'Though zoning is one of the central components of MSP, contrary to the public perception, the two are not one and the same.' However, Agardy has argued that any MSP-system *not using* zoning as an implementation mechanism '– is not taking advantage of the power of ocean zoning as a problem-solving tool.' To Agardy, zoning represents the concrete implementation of the aims set in MSP. See ibid., p. 14. See on the misconceptions related to marine zoning, ibid., p. 34.

3 See Agardy (2010, p. 13): 'Marine Spatial Planning (MSP) is a generic term describing the process leading to place-based marine management.'

4 According to the synthesis report of a project known as 'Baltic Sea Management – Nature Conservation and Sustainable Management of the Ecosystem through Spatial Planning' there are generally four types of zones in MSP: (1) General Use Zones: areas in which all activities are allowed as long as they are permitted by law and fulfil some requirements such as permits and environmental impact assessment; (2) Targeted Management Zones: areas in which some restricted activities and uses are allowed, so that overlapping activities and uses may occur; (3) Exclusive-Use Zones: areas to be used for a specific type use only, although certain activities such as agriculture facilities, gas pipelines and renewable energy could take place in the zone if they are compatible with the main purpose of the zone; and (4) Restrictive-Access Zones: areas to which access is highly restricted for adequate protection of certain areas or issues (unique ecological habitat, military use). The project is also known as the Balance project and was partly funded by the EU through its regional development fund. Running from 2005–2007, and coordinated through the Balance secretariat located in Copenhagen, Denmark, its main aim was to develop adequate management tools based on spatial planning and transnational and cross-sectoral cooperation for Baltic Sea governance. For additional details, see <www.balance-eu.org>. See also Merrie (2010, p. 10).

5 In addition, Peel and Lloyd (2004, p. 374) have argued that one must be careful when contemplating the transfer of terrestrial planning instruments to marine environments, stating that '[t]here is little evidence that land-based policy solutions will readily transfer offshore.'

6 A land use plan may have direct or indirect impacts on activities beneath the ground (in terms of mineral extraction for example) or above the ground (a land area that is zoned as a city may preclude the use of the airspace above that city as a flight corridor). But these restrictions are peripheral or incidental to the land use plan. They are not directly addressed in the plan itself except to the extent that they impact on surface land use. See European Commission (2008, p. 3).

7 The building of wind farms has been one major driver behind the development of MSP in many of the European Countries, see UNESCO, 'Marine Spatial Planning Initiative, Marine Spatial Planning (MSP)', available at <http://www.unesco-ioc-marinesp.be/marine_spatial_planning_msp>, accessed on 5 February 2013. On specific wind farm projects, see for instance Schoukens, H., Cliquet, A. and Maes, F. (2012) 'Wind Farm Development in the Belgian Part of the North Sea: A Policy Odyssey Without Precedent', *Zeitschrift für europäisches Umwelt- und Planungsrecht*, vol. 6, pp. 304–312.

8 Although some rights in the form of concessions, leases and licences, that are somewhat analogous to land tenure rights, or which may even be a type of land tenure right, may be typically granted in respect of the use of the sea bed. See European Commission (2008, p. 5)

9 Despite this advantage, the present writers agree with (2008) *et al.* in their assessment that any zoning system within MSP should first prioritize a certain use or uses in a particular area of the zone. However, the zoning should also 'permit non-priority uses where that use can be conducted in a manner consistent with the overall purpose of that zone'. See Eagle, Sanchirico and Thompson (2008, p. 654).

10 This term 'international character' actually relates to the dicta made in *Anglo-Norwegian Fisheries Case* where the International Court of Justice stated that

'The delimitation of sea areas has always an international aspect; it cannot be dependent merely upon the will of the coastal State as expressed in its municipal law. Although it is true that the act of delimitation is necessarily a unilateral act, because only the coastal State is competent to undertake it, the validity of the delimitation with regard to other States depends upon international law.' See, ICJ Report/1951/132.

11 United Nations Convention on the Law of the Sea (UNCLOS), Montego Bay, 10.12.1982, in force 16.11.1994, 21 International Legal Materials (1982) 1261. It took nine years to finalise the text of the convention and it entered into force on 16.11.1994, consistent with art. 308 of UNCLOS, one year after the date of deposit of the sixtieth instrument of ratification or acceptance.

12 For the significance of UNCLOS, see Birnie (1993).

13 The sources of the Law of the Sea include customary international law as well as a range of treaties and agreements. The elements of UNCLOS that are most relevant to this study are generally held to be declaratory of customary international law, see Directorate General for Marine Affairs and Fisheries (European Commission) (2009) *Legal Aspects of Maritime Spatial Planning: Summary Report*, p. 2.

14 See also Maes (2008, p. 799). However, territorial disputes still prevent the establishment of EEZs in some parts of the world, see ibid. (2008, p. 800).

15 There are numerous methods and exceptions to the definition of the baseline but the general rule is provided in the art. 5 of UNCLOS: the normal baseline for measuring the breadth of the territorial sea is the low-water line along the coast as marked on large-scale charts officially recognized by the coastal State.

16 1 nautical mile = 1.852 kilometre. See Carleton and Schofield (2001, p. 23).

17 This sovereignty is complete in internal waters, in which even the right to innocent passage does not apply.

18 Similarly to internal waters, the coastal state can exercise full sovereignty in archipelagic waters with the exception that freedom of innocent passage, as defined in art. 19 of UNCLOS.

19 In this respect UNCLOS is complemented, *inter alia*, by International Convention for the Safety of Life at Sea (SOLAS, London, 1.11.1974, in force 25.5.1980, 1184 *International Legal Materials* (1980) 278) and Traffic Separation Schemes approved by the International Maritime Organization (IMO), see IMO Resolution A.572(14) 'General Provisions on Ships' Routeing'.

20 It is notable that, freedom of navigation in the EEZ is not absolute, but a balancing exercise between the coastal State and the flag State, inasmuch as by UNCLOS art. 58(3) its exercise is subjected to due regard to the coastal State's rights and duties and compliance with its laws in so far as they are not incompatible with Part V of the Convention.

21 On the areal aspects of MSP, see Backer (2011, p. 280). In Europe, the situation is somewhat different, as the Framework Directive on Maritime Spatial Planning does not apply to coastal waters (Directive 2014/89/EU of the European Parliament and of the Council of 23 July 2014 establishing a framework for maritime spatial planning, OJ L 25, 28.8.2014, p. 135). See further Chapter 9 of this book.

22 See also Maes (2008, pp. 799–806).

23 UNCLOS emphasises cooperation on a global and regional basis. Art. 197 of states: 'States shall cooperate on a global basis and, as appropriate, on a regional basis, directly or through competent international organizations, in formulating and elaborating international rules, standards and recommended practices and procedures consistent

with this Convention, for the protection and preservation of the marine environment, taking into account characteristic regional features.'

24 Specific provisions for particular types of marine pollution have been laid down in art. 207–222 of UNCLOS. These provisions have addressed all sources of marine pollution, along with the specific duties of states with respect to these sources of pollution, and established a framework for the conservation and development of marine resources, see Charney (1994, pp. 734–35). Furthermore, art. 122 and 123 emphasise cooperation in relation to the protection of enclosed and semi-enclosed seas.

25 EIA, UNEP *Regional Seas Reports and Studies*, No.130, UNEP, 1990, p. 1.

26 Both the Stockholm Declaration and the Rio Declaration also include a reference to EIA. Principle 21 of the Stockholm Declaration implies an EIA requirement by giving states the responsibility to ensure activities carried out on their territory do not harm the environment of other states. Likewise, Principle 17 of the Rio Declaration and paragraph 22(c) of the Global Program of Action (GPA) for the Protection of the Marine Environment from Land Based Activities emphasises the identification and assessment of problems in the same manner. According to para. 22 of the GPA, priority basis for action is the relative importance of impacts upon food, security, public health, coastal and marine resources, ecosystem health, and socio-economic benefits.

27 See for instance the UNECE Convention on Environmental Impact Assessment in a Transboundary Context (Espoo, 25.2.1991, in force 10.9.1997).

28 See further on the relationship between EIA and MSP, Chapter 1 of this book.

29 The laws and regulations of the coastal state may relate to licensing of fishermen, fishing vessel and equipment, determination of species that may be caught through quotas or catch per vessel over a period of time, seasonal and area limitations or prohibitions, number of vessels and gear specifications etc. See art. 62 of UNCLOS.

30 Agreement for the implementation of the provisions of the United Nations Convention on the Law of the Sea of 10 December 1982 relating to the conservation and management of straddling fish stocks and highly migratory fish stocks (Fish Stock Agreement, New York, 4.8.1995, in force 11.12.2001, A/CONF.164/37).

31 Principle 4 of the Rio Declaration provides: 'In order to achieve sustainable development, environmental protection shall constitute an integral part of the development process and cannot be considered in isolation from it.' Principle 15 provides: 'Where there are threats of serious irreversible damage, lack of full scientific certainty shall not be used as a reason for postponing cost effective measures to prevent environmental degradation.'

32 An ecosystem is a functional unit of physical and biological organization with characteristic trophic structure and material cycles, some degree of internal homogeneity, and recognizable boundaries. Odum (1977, p. 1289). Ecosystem management was advocated in the 1984 FAO Strategy for Fisheries Management and Development and also reflected in the Code of Conduct (particularly art. 6). For details see Kaye (2001, pp. 269–81).

33 The Fish Stocks Agreement has elaborated the duties of the flag state (art. 18(2), 18(3) and art. 20(6)) impose an additional obligation on the flag state to cooperate with coastal states in taking appropriate enforcement measures where there are reasonable grounds for believing that flag states vessel has been engaged in unauthorized fishing within areas under the jurisdiction of a coastal state (Hayashi, 1999, p. 65).

34 These functions include the ability to: '[a]gree on and comply with conservation and management measures to ensure the long term sustainability of fish stock; adopt and

apply generally recommended international minimum standards for the responsible conduct of fishing operations; agree on standards of collection, reporting, verification and exchange of data on fisheries for the stocks; promote and conduct scientific assessments of the stocks and relevant research and disseminate the result thereof; establish appropriate cooperative mechanisms for effective monitoring, control, surveillance and enforcement; ensure the full cooperation of their relevant national agencies and industries in implementing the recommendations and decisions of the sub-regional or regional fisheries management organization or arrangement; and give due publicity to the conservation and management measures established by the organization or arrangement.' Art. 10 of the Fish Stock Agreement.

35 UNCLOS does not make an explicit reference to MSP but this does not mean that would prevent coastal states in engaging in marine spatial planning, see Maes (2008, p. 799).

36 Sustainable development is '[d]evelopment that meets the needs of the present without compromising the ability of future generations to meet their own needs' (World Commission on Environment and Development (1987) *Our Common Future*, Oxford University Press, p. 8). This term appears to have been first introduced in a 1980 report by the International Union for the Conservation of Nature and Natural Resources (IUCN), and has been brought to the top of the agenda, with institutions such as the United Nations and the World Bank, through the *Brundtland Report* (ibid.). It goes with principle 4 of the Rio Declaration which stated that '[i]n order to achieve sustainable development, environmental protection shall constitute an integral part of the development process and cannot be considered in isolation from it.'

37 The climate system as a common natural resource is an emerging concept of international law. It got its foundation in the preamble of the United Nations Framework Convention on Climate Change ((UNFCCC), New York, 9.5.1992, in force 21.3.1994, 31 International Legal Materials (1992) 849) where it is stated that 'change in the Earth's climate and its adverse effects are a common concern of humankind' which is universally accepted. See UNFCCC preamble; UN General Assembly (6 December 1988). For details discussion see generally Brunnee, (2007, pp. 550 and 564–67); Birnie, Boyle, and Redgwell, (2009, pp. 338–339); Murase (2011).

38 Climate Change as defined by UNFCCC is 'a change of climate which is attributed directly or indirectly to human activity that alerts the composition of the global atmosphere –'. See UNFCCC, art. 1. See Bodansky (1993, p. 451).

39 UNFCCC, art. 3(4) which states as follows: 'The Parties have a right to, and should, promote sustainable development. Policies and measures to protect the climate system against human-induced change should be appropriate for the specific conditions of each Party and should be integrated with national development programmes, taking into account that economic development is essential for adopting measures to address climate change.'

40 See *Draft Report on the Legal Principles relating to Climate Change* (submitted by the ILA Committee on the Legal Principles relating to Climate Change in the 76th Conference of the International Law Association, held in Washington D.C., the United States of America, 7–11 April 2014), pp. 3–8, <http://www.ila-hq.org/en/committees/index.cfm/cid/1029>, accessed on 17 April 2014; *Declaration of Legal Principles Relating to Climate Change* (Resolution 2/2014, adopted by the ILA Committee on the Legal Principles relating to Climate Change in the 76th Conference of the International Law Association, held in Washington, D.C., the United States of America, 7–11 April 2014), pp. 2–3.

41 The permanent sovereignty principle is enshrined in the UN General Assembly Resolution. See UN General Assembly, *Permanent Sovereignty over Natural Resources*, UNGA Res. 1803(XVII), (14 December 1962). The preamble of the UNFCCC preamble affirms the principle of permanent sovereignty as it recalls that states have the sovereign right to exploit their own resources. The present scholars are motivated to counter the permanent sovereignty principle, as being practised in contemporary international law, in terms of management of natural resources through an intensive global action based on nations such as the common concern of humankind. See generally Trindade (2010), Scholtz (2008), Schrijver (2008), Chimni (1998), Schachter (1977).

42 See *Draft Report on the Legal Principles relating to Climate Change* (submitted by the ILA Committee on the Legal Principles relating to Climate Change in the 76th Conference of the International Law Association, held in Washington, D.C., the United States of America, 7–11 April 2014) p. 6, <http://www.ila-hq.org/en/committees/index.cfm/cid/1029>, accessed on 17 April 2014.

43 For background of this concept, see *Draft Report on the Legal Principles relating to Climate Change* (submitted by the ILA Committee on the Legal Principles relating to Climate Change in the 76th Conference of the International Law Association, held in Washington, D.C., the United States of America, 7–11 April 2014), pp. 1–3.

44 ECE/RMP 6, Draft Report of the Meeting on the Mediterranean (1990). See also principle 15 of the *Rio Declaration on Environment and Development.*

45 See also Agenda 21, Chapter 17.22, A/CONF, 151/26 (Vol. II), 1992.

46 This matter of debate is reflected in the writings of Benedicte Sage-Fuller. See Sage-Fuller (2013, p. XIII).

47 For example, it seemed to originate in the national law of Germany and be accepted by the states bordering the Wadden Sea. Later on, its essence seemed to be accepted then in Principle 15 of the *Rio Declaration on Environment and Development:* 'In order to protect the environment, the precautionary approach shall be widely applied by States according to their capabilities. Where there are threats of serious or irreversible damage, lack of scientific certainty shall not be used as a reason for postponing cost-effective measures to prevent environmental degradation'. See generally, Hohmann (1994) *Precautionary Legal Duties and Principles of Modern International Environmental Law*, Graham & Trotman, p. 333; Freestone (1991).

48 See Hassan (2006, p. 60). See also Hey (1992, p. 308).

49 The possible challenges are: t has no consistent interpretation, nor any consensus, as to how this principle should be applied; it begs the questions of where a threshold for possible adverse effects should be set; and it does not prescribe the specific measures by means of which it might be operationalized. See Hassan (2006, pp. 61–62). See also Grinlinton (1995); Freestone and Hey (1996).

50 *United Nations Conference on Environment and Development: Rio Declaration on Environment and Development*, 14 June 1992, *International Legal Materials*, vol. 31, p. 879 (hereinafter Rio Declaration). Principle 15 of the Rio Declaration states: 'In order to protect the environment, the precautionary approach shall be widely applied by States according to their capabilities. Where there are threats of serious or irreversible damage, lack of full scientific certainty shall not be used as a reason for postponing cost-effective measures to prevent environmental degradation.'

51 See generally Leiss and Tyshenko (2002).

52 For discussions, see Lin-Easton (2001) and Douma (2000).

53 For a clear view, see Sage-Fuller (2013) and VanderZwaag *et al.* (2006).

54 See generally *Draft Report on the Legal Principles relating to Climate Change* (submitted by the ILA Committee on the Legal Principles relating to Climate Change in the 76th Conference of the International Law Association, held in Washington, D.C., the United States of America, 7–11 April 2014) pp. 20–26, <http://www.ila-hq.org/en/committees/index.cfm/cid/1029>, accessed on 17 April 2014; *Declaration of Legal Principles Relating to Climate Change* (Resolution 2/2014, adopted by the ILA Committee on the Legal Principles relating to Climate Change in the 76th Conference of the International Law Association, held in Washington, D.C., the United States of America, 7–11 April 2014) pp. 5–6.

55 For details, see VanderZwaag *et al* (2006).

56 A tax incentive authorizes a deduction from regularly imposed tax, and the pollution tax is charged and calculated as the same rate as the marginal pollution control cost at the point where it equals the marginal damage cost to society (see Sandbach (1979). As a fiscal instrument, pollution tax internalizes pollution cost and provides an incentive to reduce pollution adopting the least expensive pollution abatement technologies.

57 To use this system the permissible level of pollution is assessed and 'rights to pollute' are then sold in the market (Sandbach, 1992).

58 More than 750 million litres of oil spewed into the Gulf of Mexico after the undersea well blew out 100 miles (160 km) off the Louisiana coast on 20 April 2010 and was not capped until July. *The Guardian* 'Gulf of Mexico oil spill: BP loses bid to make others pay compensation', Friday 27 January 2012 13.18 AEST, <http://www.theguardian.com/environment/2012/jan/27/gulf-mexico-oil-bp-compensation>, accessed on 2 April, 2014.

59 UNECE Convention on the Protection and Use of Transboundary Watercourses and International Lakes, Helsinki, 19.3.1992, in force 17.1.2000, Art. 2(5).

60 The Convention for the Protection of the Marine Environment of the North-East Atlantic, Paris, 22.9.1992, in force 25.3.1998, art. 2(2)(b).

61 These problems of marine governance have been highlighted in Chapter 1 of this book.

62 Climate change has been considered as a 'wicked problem' in that there is not even a conclusive defition of the problem or its causes. See further on framing the problem and a good overview of the literature Van Asselt (2013, p. 330).

63 We are not arguing that UNCLOS should be re-opened but only that one should consider complementing UNCLOS with international regulations relating to MSP.

64 The adoption of management principles in marine environmental resource planning and implementation in Chapter 17 of Agenda 21 is recognition that current sectoral approaches are inadequate for resource management (Tsamenyi (1995) 'Mechanisms for Integrated Resource Management', paper presented in *29th Annual Conference of the Law of the Sea Institute*, Denpasar, Bali, 19–22 June).

References

Agardy, Tundi (2010) *Ocean Zoning: Making Marine Management More Effective*, Earthscan.

Alder, J. and Ward, T. (2001) 'Australia's Ocean Policy: Sink or Swim?', *Journal of Environment and Development*, vol. 10, no. 3, pp. 266–89.

Alheritiere, D. (1982) *Environmental Impact Assessment and Agricultural Development: A Comparative Study*, FAO, Rome.

Arkema, Katie K., Abramson, Sarah C. and Dewsbury, Bryan (2006) 'Marine Ecosystem-Based Management: From Characterization to Implementation', *Frontiers in Ecology and the Environment*, vol. 4, pp. 525–32.

Backer, Hermanni and Frias, Manuel (eds) (2012) *Planning the Bothnian Sea: Key Findings of the Plan Bothnia Project*, Finepress.

Backer, Hermanni (2011) 'Trans-boundary Maritime Spatial Planning: a Baltic Sea Perspective', *Journal of Coastal Conservation*, vol. 15, pp. 278–89.

Birnie, P. (1993) 'The Law of the Sea and the United Nations Conference on Environment and Development' 10, *Ocean Yearbook*.

Birnie, P.W. and Boyle, A.E. (2002) *International Law and the Environment*, Oxford University Press.

Birnie, P., Boyle, A. and Redgwell, C. (2009) *International Law and the Environment*, Oxford University Press.

Bodansky, D. (1991) Remarks of 'Panel Discussion: New Developments in International Environmental Law,' *American Society of International Law Proceedings*, vol. 85.

Bodansky, D. (1993) 'The United Nations Framework Convention on Climate Change: A Commentary', *Yale Journal of International Law*, vol. 19, no. 2.

Brunnee, J. (2007) 'Common Areas, Common Heritage and Common Concern' in Bodansky, D., Brunnee, J. and Hey, E. (eds), *Oxford Handbook of International Environmental Law*, Oxford University Press, 2007.

Carleton, Chris and Schofield, Clive (2001) 'Development in the Technical Determination of Maritime Space: Charts, Datums, Baselines and Maritime Zones' *Maritime Briefing*, vol. 3, no. 3.

Carr, S. (2008) 'Comprehensive Ocean Zoning: Answering Questions about this Powerful Tool for EBM' *Marine Ecosystems and Management*, vol. 2, no. 1, p. 2. Available at: < http://depts.washington.edu/meam/MEAM5.pdf>, accessed on 19.2.2013.

Charney, J.I. (1994) 'The Marine Environment and 1982 United Nations Convention on the Law of the Sea', *International Lawyer*, vol. 28, no. 4.

Chimni, B.S. (1998) 'The Principle of Permanent Sovereignty over Natural Resources: Toward a Radical Interpretation', *Indian Journal of International Law*, vol. 38, p. 208.

Cicin-Sain, B. and Knechtm, R.W. (1998) *Integrated Coastal Zone Management: Concept and Practice*, Island Press.

Craig, Robin Kundis (2012) *Comparative Ocean Governance: Place-Based Protections in an Era of Climate Change*, Edward Elgar Publishing.

Directorate General for Marine Affairs and Fisheries (2009) *Legal Aspects of Maritime Spatial Planning: Summary Report*, European Commission.

Douma, Wybe (2000) 'The Precautionary Principle in the European Union', *Review of European Community and International Environmental Law*, vol. 9, p. 142.

Dux, Thomas (2011) *Specially Protected Marine Areas in the Exclusive Economic Zone*, LIT Verlag.

Dzidzornu, D.M. (1998) 'Four Principles in Marine Environmental Protection: A Comparative Analysis' *Ocean Development and International Law*, vol. 29, no. 2.

Eagle, Josh, Sanchirico, James N. and Thomson, Barton J. Jr. (2008) 'Ocean Zoning and Spatial Access Privileges: Rewriting the Tragedy of the Regulated Ocean' *New York University Environmental Law Journal*, vol. 17, pp. 646–68.

ECE/RMP 6, Draft Report of the Meeting on the Mediterranean (1990).

Ehler, Charles N. (2012) 'Maritime Spatial Planning: International Experience with MSP' (Conference Paper presented at SHAPE Conference, Venice, Italy, 5–6 June 2012),

<http://shape.ervet.it/download/listbox/Venice%20Slides/Ehler_IOC_Unesco.PDF>, accessed on 28 December 2013.

Ehler, Charles and Douvere, Fanny (2009) 'New Perspectives on Sea Use Management: Initial Findings from European Experience with Marine Spatial Planning', *Journal of Environmental Management*, vol. 90.

European Commission (2008) *Legal Aspects of Maritime Spatial Planning*, Final Report to DG Maritime Affairs and Fisheries, Framework Service Contract No. FISH/2006/09-LOTS2 (October, 2008).

Freestone, David (1991) 'The Precautionary Principle' in Churchill, R. and Freestone, D., *International Law and Global Climate Change*, Graham & Trotman, p. 32; Agenda 21, ch. 17.22, A/CONF, 151/26 (Vol. II), 1992.

Freestone, D. (1999) 'Implementing Precaution Cautiously: The Precautionary Approach in the Straddling and Highly Migratory Fish Stocks Agreement', in Hey, E. (ed.) *Developments in International Fisheries Law*, Kluwer Law International.

GESAMP (1984) *Reports for the Second Session of the GESAMP Working Group on the Methodologies and Guidelines for the Assessment of the Impact of Pollutants on the Marine Environment*, GESAMP, XV/6.

Gore, A., 'Life Beyond the Earth Summit', *Financial Times*, 20 June 1992.

Grinlinton, D. (1995) 'Natural Resources Law Reform in New Zealand – Integrating Law, Policy, and Sustainability', *Australian Journal of Natural Resources and Policy*, vol. 2, no. 1, p. 14.

Hassan, Daud (2006) *Protecting the Marine Environment from the Land Based-Based Sources of Pollution*, Ashgate Publishing.

Hayashi, M. (1999) 'The Straddling and Highly Migratory Fish Stocks Agreements' in Hey, E. (ed.) *Developments in International Fisheries Law*, Kluwer Law International.

Hey, E. (1992) 'The Precautionary Concept in Environmental Policy and Law: Institutionalising Caution', *Georgetown International Environmental Law Review*, vol. 4.

Jay, Stephen (2010) 'Built at Sea: Marine Management and the Construction of Marine Spatial Planning', *Town Planning Review*, vol. 81, pp. 173–91.

Kaye, S.M. (2001) *International Fisheries Management*, Kluwer Law International, pp. 269–81.

Leiss, William and Tyshenko, Michael (2002) 'Some Aspects of the 'New biotechnology' and its Regulation in Canada', in Van Nijnatten, Debora and Boardman, Robert (eds), *Canadian Environmental Policy: Context and Cases*, 2nd ed., Oxford University Press, ch.17.

Le Prestre, P.G. (1995) 'Environmental Learning at the World Bank' in Bartlett, B.V. *et al.* (eds) *International Organizations and Environmental Policy*, Greenwood Press, p. 89.

Lin-Easton, Paul (2001) 'It's Time for Environmentalists to Think Small – Real Small: A Call for the Involvement of Environmental Lawyers in Developing Precautionary Policies for Molecular nanotechnology', *Georgetown International Environmental Law Review*, vol. 14, pp. 128–29.

Maes, Frank (2008) 'The International Legal Framework for Marine Spatial Planning' *Marine Policy*, vol. 32.

Merrie, A. (2010) *Managing the Marine Mosaic: A Briefing on Marine Spatial Planning with an Ecosystem Approach*, Spatial Planning Stockholm Resilience Centre.

Murase, S. (2011) 'Protection of the Atmosphere and International Lawmaking' in Pogacnik, Miha (ed.) (2011) *Challenges of Contemporary International Law and*

International Relations: Liber Amicorum in Honour of Ernest Petric, Evropska Pravna Fakulteta Nova Gorica, Slovenia.
Odum, E. (1977) 'The Emergence of Ecology as a New Integrative Discipline', *Science*, vol. 195.
OECD Environment Committee, *Guiding Principles Concerning the International Economic Aspects of Environmental Policies*, OECK Doc C (72).
Peel, Deborah and Lloyd, Greg M. (2004) 'The Social Reconstruction of the Marine Environment: Towards Marine Spatial Planning?', *Town Planning Review*, vol. 75.
Sage-Fuller, Benedicte (2013) *The Precautionary Principle in Marine Environmental Law: With Special Reference to High Risk Vessels*, Routledge.
Sandbach, F.R. (1979) 'Economics of Pollution Control', in Lahan, J. and Fletcher, W.W. (eds), *Economics of the Environment*, New York, 1979, p. 7.
Sandbach, F.R. (1992) 'Economics of Pollution Control', in Leihan, J. and Fletcher, W.W. (eds), *Economics of the Environment*, New York, p. 12.
Scholtz, W. (2008) Custodial Sovereignty Reconciling Sovereignty and Global Environmental Challenges Amongst the Vestiges of Colonialism', *Netherland International Law Review*, vol. 53, no. 3, p. 333.
Schrijver, N. (2008) 'Unravelling State Sovereignty: The Controversy on the Right of Indigenous Peoples to Permanent Sovereignty over Natural Wealth and Resources', in Boerefijn, I. and Goldschmidt, J. (eds), *Changing Perceptions of Sovereignty and Human Rights: Essays in Honour of Cees Flinterman*, Intersentia, pp. 85–98.
Schachter, O. (1977) *Sharing the World's Resources*, Columbia University Press.
Secretary General of the United Nations (2012) *The Oceans Compact: Healthy Oceans for Prosperity – An Initiative of the United Nations Secretary-General* (United Nations, July 2012) p. 2. <https://www.un.org/Depts/los/ocean_compact/oceans_compact.htm>, accessed on 29 March 2014.
Smets, H. (1994) 'The Polluter Pays Principle in the Early 1990s' in Campiglio, L. *et al.* *The Environment after Rio: International Law and Economics*, Graham & Trotman.
Stewart, R.B. (1985) 'Economics, Environment, and the Limits of Legal Control', *Harvard Environmental Law Review*, pp. 1–22.
Tanaka, Yoshifumi (2006) *Predictability and Flexibility in the Law of Maritime Delimitation*, Hart Publishing.
Trindade, A.A.C. (2010) *International Law for Humankind*, Martinus Nijhoff, pp. 327–52.
Tsamenyi, B. M. (1995) 'Mechanisms for Integrated Resource Management', paper presented in *29th Annual Conference of the Law of the Sea Institute*, Denpasar, Bali, 19–22 June.
Tullio, Sovazzi (ed.) (1999) *Marine Specially Protected Areas: The General Aspects and the Mediterranean Regional System*, Kluwer Law International.
UN General Assembly, *Protection of Global Climate for Present and Future Generations of Mankind*, UN Doc A/RES/43/53 (6 December 1988), <http://www.un.org/documents / ga/res/43/a43r053.htm>, accessed on 17 April 2014.
United Nations (2012), *Secretary-General's remarks at Law of Sea conference and launch of UN Oceans Compact* (Yeosu International Conference, Yeosu, Republic of Korea, 12 August 2012), <http://www.un.org/sg/statements/index.asp?nid=6239>, accessed on 27 December 2013.
Van Asselt, Harro (2013) 'Managing the Fragmentation of International Climate Law' in Erkki J. Hollo, Kati Kulovesi and Michael Mehling (eds) *Climate Change and the Law*. Springer (2013).

Van Dyke, J.M. *et al.* (1993) *Freedom for the Seas in the 21st Century*, Island Press.

VanderZwaag, David, D., Fuller, Susanna and Myers, Ransom (2006) 'Canada and the Precautionary Principle/approach in Ocean and Coastal Management: Wading and Wandering in Tricky Currents' in Rothwell, Donald and VanderZwaag, David (2006) *Towards Principled Oceans Governance*, Routledge, p. 154.

Yusuf, J.A. and George, K.S. (1985) *Guidelines to Environmental Impact Assessment in Developing Countries*, UNEP, Hodder and Stoughton Ltd.

Chapter 5

Marine spatial planning

Global and regional conventions and organizations

Frank Maes and An Cliquet

Introduction

Marine spatial planning (MSP) can be broadly seen as a planning process to designate or identify preferential zones for various activities at sea with the aim to reduce user conflicts. As a tool, MSP can also be used to designate marine protected areas (MPAs) and to support area-based nature conservation as well as introduce a long-term vision to regulate new activities at sea. MSP is considered to be an appropriate tool and process to achieve an ecosystem-based sustainable management of activities at sea.

In the last decade an increasing number of coastal states, particularly in Europe, started to develop marine spatial plans for maritime areas under their jurisdiction (Collie *et al.*, 2013; UNESCO, 2014). Recently, much more attention has been paid to MSP initiatives in the European Union (EU), partly due to its well known MSP policy documents, its support for MSP projects and finally its MSP Directive adopted in 2014 (see Chapter 9). On the other hand, less attention has been paid to transboundary MSP and the role it plays in international and regional organizations outside the EU. So far, the implementation of MSP has taken place at the national level, confined within national jurisdictional boundaries.

Nevertheless, states have accepted, in most conventions and within various organizations, the need to cooperate on a large number of issues. In terms of transboundary MSP, it seems that regional seas are the most appropriate scale to start transboundary MSP, while large sea areas outside regional seas are subdivided into regional ecosystem areas (e.g. the Great Barrier Reef). Regional MSP is about the willingness of coastal states to take into account each other's national policy priorities in exercising their sovereignty and sovereign rights, and to adjust them towards common goals for the benefit of the whole region. Precisely this transboundary element of MSP is a great challenge for regional MSP developments.

As it stands now, there is a growing exchange of information relevant to MSP among scientists and public authorities at a national level and in some cases reaching the appropriate policy decision-makers. So far, no regional organization has been mandated to design binding spatial plans for its Member States (MS). The European Commission's Green Paper, 'Towards a future Maritime Policy for the Union: A European vision for the oceans and seas' (2006) recognized that under the current legal circumstances individual decisions on activities should be taken at a national or local level but that 'a degree of commonality between the systems will be needed to ensure that decisions affecting the same ecosystem or cross-border activities . . . are dealt with in a coherent manner.' (European Commission, 2006, p. 34.) The EU MSP Directive adopted in 2014 (Directive 2014/89/EU) for example does not interfere with MS competences to conduct MSP, but aims to stimulate cooperation among neighbouring states and to assure their plans will be implemented (see Chapter 9). So far, only in the Baltic Sea have scientists, government representatives and stakeholders been closely co-operating in a more structural manner to agree upon common MSP objectives in the framework of a regional approach (see Chapter 7).

The focus of this chapter is on global and regional conventions and institutions whose decision-making can contribute to the development of transboundary MSP from a legal perspective. Ocean governance has been approached at two international governance levels: universal and regional. At the universal level the basic rules of ocean governance are laid down in the Law of the Sea Convention (LOSC), supplemented by sectoral rules and standards, such as for shipping (International Maritime Organization (IMO) and its conventions); fisheries (implementing agreements and efforts by the Food and Agriculture Organisation); and biodiversity protection (Convention on Biological Diversity (CBD)).

This chapter does not provide an overview of the various MSP issues to which international and regional organizations can contribute (e.g. data exchange about effects of maritime activities on the marine environment), but aims to describe some developments that might stimulate or contribute to transboundary cooperation in MSP. Although decisions taken by most governmental organizations are considered to be soft law or not legally binding within the context of MSP (with the exclusion of the EU and decisions taken by the Oslo and Paris Commission (OSPARCOM)), they could still have a legal relevance. Soft laws often pave the way or can set in motion policies for the development of legally binding commitments. For that reason, a selection of soft law approaches for transboundary MSP will be discussed below.

MSP at universal level

MSP: the Law of the Sea Convention and the International Court of Justice

The 1982 Law of the Sea Convention (LOSC) does not refer to MSP directly but, in art. 123 of the LOSC, it promotes cooperation and coordination among states bordering enclosed or semi-enclosed seas to manage, conserve, explore and exploit the living resources of the sea as well as to protect and preserve the marine environment. Art. 123 confirms a regional seas approach that already started before the adoption of the LOSC (Maes, 2008). Furthermore, art. 192 of the LOSC obliges all states, not only parties to the LOSC, 'to protect and preserve the marine environment'. Despite states having the right to exploit their natural resources based on national environmental policies, they still have the duty to protect and preserve the marine environment (art. 193, LOSC) and to cooperate in this respect at a global and regional level (art. 197, LOSC). Important for MSP is the additional duty for states to take measures to protect and preserve rare and fragile ecosystems, as well as the habitat of depleted, threatened or endangered species and other forms of marine life (art. 194 (5), LOSC).

In its advisory opinion on the 'Legality of the Threat or Use of Nuclear Weapons', the International Court of Justice (ICJ) reaffirmed the customary law status of the obligation for states to ensure that activities within their jurisdiction and control respect the environment of other states or of areas beyond their national jurisdiction or control (ICJ, 1996, pp. 241–42 para. 29). In the Pulp Mills Case (ICJ, 2010), the ICJ repeated the customary law status of the principle of prevention: 'A State is thus obliged to use all the means at its disposal in order to avoid activities which take place in its territory, or in any area under its jurisdiction, causing significant damage to the environment of another State' (ICJ, 2010, pp. 55–56 para. 101). Co-operation between states is a necessary requirement to fulfil their obligation of prevention (ICJ, 2010, pp. 55–56 para. 102).

In order to assess significant and harmful changes to the marine environment, states 'shall, as far as practicable', make use of environmental impact assessments (EIA) for activities under their jurisdiction or control (art. 206, LOSC). The ICJ in the Pulp Mills Case was of the opinion that ' . . . the obligation to protect and preserve . . . has to be interpreted in accordance with a practice, which in recent years has gained so much acceptance among States that it may now be considered a requirement under general international law to undertake an environmental impact assessment where there is a risk that the proposed industrial activity may have a significant adverse impact in a transboundary context, in particular, on a shared resource' (ICJ, 2010, p. 83 para. 204). Although this case was about the Uruguay River that was considered a shared resource between Argentina and Uruguay, this dictum can equally be applied to oceans and seas, which are also shared resources.

EIAs are required before the adoption of a particular project, while strategic environmental assessments (SEAs) have to be taken into account before the adoption of plans or programmes, such as marine spatial plans. EIAs and SEAs are dealt with at a regional treaty level within the United Nations Economic Commission for Europe (UNECE) (see Chapter 8.1). International law also requires that a decision in respect of an activity which might cause significant harm should be based on an EIA of the possible harmful transboundary effects on people, property and the environment in other states (International Law Commission, 2001, art. 2(b) and 7). It is the view of the ICJ that each state determines, in its domestic legislation or in the authorization process, the specific content of the EIA, 'having regard to the nature and magnitude of the proposed development and its likely adverse impact on the environment as well as to the need to exercise due diligence in conducting such an assessment' (ICJ, 2010, p. 83 para. 205). The ICJ is further of the opinion that 'Once operations have started and, where necessary, throughout the life of the project, continuous monitoring of its effects on the environment shall be undertaken' (ICJ, 2010, p. 83, para. 205).

MSP and the United Nations Conferences on sustainable development

Chapter 17 of 'Agenda 21', adopted at the United Nations Conference on Environment and Development (UNCED) in Rio in 1992, sets forth some governance suggestions for states to pursue the protection and sustainable development of the marine and coastal environment and its resources. Chapter 17 does not explicitly refer to MSP, but suggests that: 'Each coastal State should consider establishing, or where necessary strengthening, appropriate coordinating mechanisms (such as a high-level policy planning body) for integrated management and sustainable development of coastal and marine areas and their resources, at both the local and national levels. . . . Such national coordinating mechanisms could provide, inter alia, for: . . . (b) Implementation of integrated coastal and marine management and sustainable development plans and programmes at appropriate levels; . . . '(17.6). The 1992 Rio Declaration adopted at UNCED introduced the ecosystem approach to conserve, protect and restore the health and integrity of the Earth (Principle 7), globalizes the use of public participation in handling environmental issues (Principle 10) and calls upon states to apply the precautionary approach (Principle 15).

Ten years later, ministers at the 2002 World Summit on Sustainable Development (WSSD) in Johannesburg adopted the 'Plan of Implementation' (UN Report 2002). In the Plan, the ministers are encouraging states, *inter alia*, to apply the ecosystem approach (para. 30d), to urgently restore depleted fish stocks (para. 31a), to establish MPAs in a context of representative MPA networks and to adopt time/area closures for the protection of nursery grounds (para. 32c). The Plan of Implementation, as well as 'Agenda 21', are not legal documents and do not intend to create direct legal obligations for states. Follow-up and implementation of those environmental targets need to be done by states, as well as within the framework of international conventions and international organisations to which the Plan of Implementation refers. The universal conventions in this respect are mainly the 1982 LOSC and the 1992 CBD.

The outcome of the 2012 Rio+20 UN Conference on Sustainable Development was the adoption of a document called 'The future we want', approved by the United Nations General Assembly (UNGA) in 2012 (UNGA 2012) to increase its political profile and in particular to mandate various UN organizations, institutions, commissions and programmes to implement the policy directions as well as the targets it puts forward. In the section on 'Oceans and Seas', state representatives committed themselves again to protect and restore oceans and marine ecosystems by effectively applying an ecosystem and the precautionary approach in the management of activities having an impact on the marine environment (para. 158). Para. 177 of UNGA 2012 comes close to one of the objectives of zoning under MSP, including area-based measures as a tool for the conservation of biological diversity through effectively and equitably managed, ecologically representative and well-connected systems of protected areas.

MSP and UNICPOLOS

In 2006, the seventh meeting of the United Nations Open-ended Informal Consultative Process on Ocean and the Law of the Sea (UNICPOLOS-7) was dedicated to ecosystem approaches and oceans (UN Report, 2006). According to UNICPOLOS-7, the implementation of an ecosystem approach can be achieved, by inter alia, the use of a broad range of management tools for the conservation and sustainable use of marine biodiversity. It also included an integrated area-based management to make use of best available scientific advice and the precautionary approach, cross-boundary integrated management and planning as well as integrating management across sectors. In 2006, at its sixty-first session, the UNGA welcomed the Report and adopted Resolution 61/222 on 'Oceans and the law of the sea'.[1] The Assembly inter alia noted: (1) 'that . . . . increasing competing demands require an urgent response and the setting of priorities for management interventions aimed at conserving ecosystem integrity'; and (2) 'that ecosystem approaches to ocean management should be focused on managing human activities in order to maintain and, where needed, restore ecosystem health . . . .' (UNGA Resolution 2006, para. 119). This is the closest the UN got to MSP in the Law of the Sea reform processes until now. In fact, MSP as a spatial planning tool or a spatial management approach has not yet been explicitly mentioned in any official UN Law of the Sea document, nor in the various UNGA Resolutions on 'oceans and the law of the sea' that are adopted every year (status 2014).

MSP and the CBD

The main objectives of the 1992 CBD are the conservation and sustainable use of biodiversity (art. 1).[2] An ecosystem approach is the key to conservation, by establishing a system of protected areas, promoting the protection of ecosystems and to rehabilitate and restore degraded ecosystems (art. 8). Marine and coastal biological diversity is considered as a priority by the Conference of the Parties (COP). The COP meets every two years to review the implementation of the Convention as well as to consider and undertake additional actions, if required, for the achievement of the objectives of the Convention. Decisions of the COP are taken by consensus and are considered soft law, but have an important political and moral value for future initiatives. The 1995 COP 2 Decision II/10 in Jakarta encouraged Parties to use integrated marine and coastal area management as the most suitable framework for addressing the human impact on marine and coastal biological diversity (para. 2). Institutional, administrative and legal arrangements should be established for this integrated management, as well as plans and strategies for marine and coastal areas (para. 3). Since then marine and coastal diversity is regularly addressed by the COP and by the Subsidiary Body on Scientific, Technical and Technological Advice (SBSTTA).[3] In 1998, COP 4 in Bratislava adopted Decision IV/5 including a programme of work on conservation and sustainable use of marine and coastal biological diversity (COP, 1998). The programme has five thematic elements, of which one is on integrated marine and coastal area management (IMCAM) and seeks to promote the development and implementation of it at all levels (e.g. local, national and regional). The 2000 COP 5 in Nairobi adopted Decision V/18 that promotes EIA as a means of addressing loss of marine and coastal biological diversity and the interrelated socio-economic, cultural and human-health aspects of marine and coastal biological diversity. Interested and affected stakeholders should be involved in a participatory process at all stages of this assessment process, including local communities. Furthermore, governments are encouraged to assess not only the impact of individual projects, but also their global and cumulative effects, incorporating biological diversity considerations at the decision and/or environmental planning level (para. 2(a)) (COP, 2000). Decision VI/7 contains guidelines for incorporating biodiversity related issues into all stages of EIA and SEA legislation and/or processes, as well as taking into account the ecosystem approach (COP, 2002). Furthermore, MSP can enhance the implementation of IMCAM to achieve an ecosystem approach (COP, 2006, Decision VIII/22). MSP, taking into account the precautionary approach,[4] as embedded in the preamble of the CBD, can significantly contribute to this goal by inter alia the designation of MPAs. MPAs are one of the essential tools and approaches in the conservation and sustainable use of marine and coastal biodiversity (*Ad Hoc* Technical Group, 2003, p. 78; COP, 2004, Decision VII/5, p. 147). The designation and management of MPAs is an important objective for the Parties to the CBD (art. 8). This includes a global network of comprehensive, representative and effectively managed national and regional protected areas, ecological corridors, buffer zones and other related approaches, as well as the integration of protected areas and their systems into the wider land and seascape (COP, 2004, Decision VII/28, p. 345 and p. 352). The Programme of Work adopted in Decision VII/28 further calls upon the following: (1) to establish by 2012 trans-boundary protected areas (TBPAs) and to collaborate between Parties regarding neighbouring protected areas across national boundaries; (2) to improve site-based area planning and management, including effective management by 2012, making use of participatory and science-based site planning processes; and (3) a long-term management plan with active stakeholder involvement (COP, 2004, Decision VII/5). The 2008 COP 9 did not take any relevant decisions, both indirectly or directly, related to MSP. In 2010, MSP was more prominently mentioned in the COP Decisions. In the Decision X/29, Parties and other governments are invited 'to increase efforts to apply marine spatial planning tools, as appropriate, in accordance with Parties' national planning and strategies, for better integration of conservation objectives in marine and other sectoral development programmes, and in overall plans for economic development' (para. 78) (COP, 2010). In the Decision X/29, MSP is seen as a tool for long-term conservation, management and sustainable use of marine resources and coastal habitats, and to effectively manage MPAs (para. 15). The Executive Secretary was requested to compile and synthesize available information on experiences and uses of MSP (para. 75) as well as to organize a workshop to review tools 'such as marine spatial planning that might assist Parties in their efforts to establish and manage marine protected areas (MPAs) and integrate these areas with other human uses allocations' (para. 76). Following the mandate given to the Executive Secretary, a study on 'Marine Spatial Planning in the context of the Convention on Biological Diversity' was finalized in 2012 (Secretariat CBD, 2012) and submitted to the SBSTTA in April 2012 (SBSTTA, 2012a). As a whole, the study supports MSP in the framework of the CBD and at the level of the Global Environment Facility (GEF), and perhaps beyond. To mention only a few conclusions briefly, which are relevant for this chapter, the study concludes that although MSP initiatives are relatively new, a legal framework to support MSP can contribute to the application of its essential elements, such as multi-objectives, long-term planning, participatory process and good governance with support of stakeholders. MSP as an approach in support of ecosystem-based management can improve existing management frameworks, reduce loss of ecosystem services, avoid user conflicts and promote economies of scale, but requires at international level sufficient capacity-building and public awareness activities (SBSTTA, 2012a, pp. 32–3). The key messages of the study were summarized in a note by the Executive Secretary of the CBD, supported by a draft recommendation on MSP (SBSTTA, 2012b). In 2012, the COP 11 adopted for the first time, a decision on MSP (COP, 2012, Decision XI/18, section c). This Decision was a start to bring MSP under the universal attention of the CBD Parties, other governments and competent organizations by disseminating MSP awareness-raising material and by initiating the development of a web-based information sharing system on MSP.[5] The aim was to compile and share information on MSP experiences, to organize training workshops, to convene a workshop with focus on guidance and toolkits on MSP, to identify gaps and proposals to fill them and, if considered necessary, to prepare practical guidance and a toolkit on MSP. A technical meeting on MSP in practice took place in Cambridge (United Kingdom) from 6 to 8 May 2014,[6] followed by a CDB Expert Workshop in Montreal from 9 till 11 September 2014 to provide consolidated and practical guidance and a toolkit for MSP.[7] In the draft decisions[8] for COP 12 of the CBD (2014),[9] prepared by SBSTTA 17 and SBSTTA 18, MSP gained an increasing role and support by the Parties to the CBD as a tool and method to implement the 'Strategic Plan for Biodiversity' 2011–2020.[10] In particular, Parties were encouraged to make use of scientific information describing areas meeting the criteria for ecologically or biologically significant marine areas (EBSA) and the development of representative networks of MPAs[11] when carrying out MSP. Different processes related to

MSP and area-based management should be linked to relevant information on the adverse impacts of underwater noise on sound-sensitive species.[12] MSP is recognized as a useful tool for applying the ecosystem approach to marine and coastal management and relevant organizations are invited to advance their work on enhancing methods and tools, including monitoring measures, for MSP.[13] The Executive Secretary is requested to enhance methods and tools for MSP and to facilitate, through technical training and information-sharing mechanisms on EBSA, efforts at national or regional level on the use of MSP by Parties and competent intergovernmental organizations.[14] Also coral reef ecosystems in coastal development and land-use and sea-use management should be protected and prioritized through the application of area-based management measures, such as marine and coastal protected areas and/or MSP.[15] Cross-sectoral, inter-agency area-based management tools, including MSP approaches should be applied, to effectively reduce local stressors from multiple sources and mitigate their impacts to coral reefs and closely associated ecosystems.[16]

MSP at regional sea level in Europe

MSP on the basis of regional co-operation is still under development. The EU, in its Marine Strategy Framework Directive, relies inter alia on marine regions delimitated on the basis of European regional seas, such as the Baltic Sea, the North Sea, the Mediterranean Sea and the Black Sea (Directive 2008/26/EC, art. 4). This confirms regional seas as management units for ecosystem-based MSP in Europe. For European regional seas, there are regional conventions that have established regional commissions.[17] In particular, the Helsinki Commission (HELCOM) in the Baltic Sea (see Chapter 7) and the OSPAR Commission (OSPARCOM) in the North-East Atlantic region have set up Working Groups (WG) on MSP.

OSPAR and transboundary cooperation on MSP

At the regional sea level, attention for MSP was triggered by the Ministers of Environment of the countries bordering the North Sea at their 5th International Conference on the Protection of the North Sea (Bergen, 2002). The Bergen Declaration, adopted at the end of this Conference, raised awareness for potential conflicts between the conservation of the marine environment and the cumulative effects of human activities. The Ministers agreed that co-operation among states in the spatial planning processes of the North Sea was required (Ministerial Declaration, 2002, Section XI, para. 76). To that end, OSPAR was asked to improve arrangements for the exchange and experiences of national spatial planning processes, to investigate the possibilities for further international cooperation in spatial planning and to consider the improvement of environmental assessment of human activities. The OSPAR Biodiversity Committee (BDC) was invited 'to investigate the possibilities for further international cooperation in planning and managing marine activities through spatial planning of the North Sea States taking into account cumulative and transboundary effects' (Ministerial Declaration, 2002, Section XI, para. 77(ii)).

The first Joint Ministerial Meeting (JMM) of HELCOM and OSPARCOM (Bremen, June 2003) issued a 'Statement on the Ecosystem Approach to the Management of Human Activities: Towards an Ecosystem Approach to the Management of Human Activities' to promote the cooperation in spatial planning between competent authorities with a focus on the development of spatial tools for the maritime areas (para. 24c.).[18] The OSPAR Secretariat presented to the first Workshop on Spatial Planning in the North Sea (SPINS 1) in January 2004 a first attempt to survey the existing spatial control mechanisms of the North Sea states as a basis for discussions on how to take forward the work on MSP. The survey 'showed that there was a wide range of spatial controls in all North Sea States covering most, if not all, relevant human activities. However, no North Sea State (except possibly Belgium) had clear arrangements to demonstrate that consistent approaches were being applied in the many different fields, though no doubt in practice there was much informal cooperation to ensure consistency' (OSPARCOM 2004, 04/5/1, Annex 1, para. 2.3). The document was to be completed before the second SPINS Workshop in February 2005, but regrettably the document was not developed further. On the MSP process, SPINS 1 concluded that: 'Within the framework of international laws and obligations (including the UN Convention on the Law of the Sea), it is for each State to define its priorities for the use of the marine resources available to it. The main focus of spatial planning of the North Sea should therefore be at the national level' (OSPARCOM 2004, 04/5/1-E, para. 6). The SPINS 2 Workshop further concluded that: ' . . . it was premature to develop guidance on good practice. More time was needed to accumulate and assess experience with the new techniques and procedures that were being developed' (OSPARCOM 2005, 05/5/1, para. 3.1). On the issue of information exchange, the Workshop did not consider it necessary to gather all material on MSP in a single information source. A portal was suggested to guide the reader to specific sites of interest, even through an intermediary stage of other portals (OSPARCOM 2005, 05/5/1, para. 3.3.c). Up till now OSPAR does not have a MSP portal, in sharp contrast to HELCOM.[19] The first MSP portal was developed after the First International Workshop on MSP organized by Fanny Douvere and Charles Ehler at UNESCO in November 2006 (Ehler and Douvere, 2007). Since then the EU has gradually taken over the MSP initiative.

After the two SPINS workshops with focus on the North Sea, three workshops on Marine Spatial Management (MASMA) followed in 2005, 2006 and 2007, extending their scope outside the North Sea. At MASMA 2006, the chairman concluded that the task of information collection and exchange should continue to be on the agenda for OSPAR work on marine spatial management and endorsed the need for an overview of national spatial planning systems, recognizing the diversity of national systems. MASMA 2006 concluded that the focus for OSPAR should continue to be on transboundary and cumulative impacts (MASMA 06/8/1-E.).[20]

The OPSAR Biodiversity Committee (BDC) adopted in 2007 the 'Terms of Reference for an Intersessional Correspondence Group on Marine Spatial Planning' (ICG-MSP) with the aim of making a compilation of national spatial planning and control systems. To achieve this, summaries or updates of national spatial planning systems should be collected from Contracting Parties (CPs). An overview of national spatial planning and control systems in the OSPAR area was presented by Ireland at MASMA 2007 on behalf of the IGG MSP (MASMA 07/4/1-E.). Information was still missing and it was the intention to ask CPs to respond to the questions in the document before the end of December 2007. Due to work commitments in other areas, no request for this information was sent to CPs, indicating that MSP was then not a priority for OSPAR.

To raise the profile of Marine Spatial Management (MSM) within OSPAR, MASMA 2007 proposed to the BDC that MSM should become a mainstream activity to be considered by the WG on Environmental Impacts of Human Activities (EIHA) and ensure that experts in MSP were given an opportunity to meet and exchange views in EIHA. The EIHA 2007 agreed to discontinue the MASMA workshop series and proposed that MSM activities should again become products in the BDC work programme (OSPAR Commission, 2007, para. 4.17). At the EIHA 2008, Ireland presented a draft overview report on national MSP and control systems relevant to the OSPAR area. IEHA invited CPs for comments on the draft report and recommended that BDC 2009 adopt the final report for publication on the OSPAR website (OSPAR Commission, 2008, para. 6.3). ICG-MSP was invited to develop conclusions for submission to BDC 2009 on how to progress work in MSP, while taking into account, inter alia: (1) the need for a better linkage of existing national plans and continued exchange of information; (2) the development of a joint regional MSP perspective; and (3) options for MSP in Region V (i.e. North East Atlantic, excluding the Gulf of Biscay and the Irish Sea areas) and Areas Beyond National Jurisdiction (ABNJ) (EIHA 08/8/1-E, para. 6.10). The 2008–2009 meetings of ICG-MSP were held back to back with other workshops and conferences on MSP. One of the conclusions of these meetings was that OSPAR has the benefit of solving MSP issues collectively. Furthermore the relevance of MSP for an ecosystem approach should be reflected in the OSPAR strategies. EIHA 2009 recommended to OSPAR to invest further in global information system (GIS) expertise within the Secretariat (OSPAR Commission, 2009, para. 6.6).

The Ministerial meeting of the OSPARCOM in Bergen adopted the Bergen Statement (2010), which mainly focused on the contribution by OSPAR to the implementation of the EU Marine Strategy Framework Directive (MSFD) to protect species and habitats, including MPAs, within and beyond national jurisdiction, and to focus on various sources of pollution and adverse impacts of human activities. An overview of human activities with an impact in the region is given in the 2010 OSPAR 'Quality Status Report'.[21] The ecosystem approach has been reaffirmed in the Bergen Statement and MSP is considered as a tool to support this approach (OSPAR 10/23/1-E, Annex 49, para. 8). No other references can be found in the Bergen Statement.

In contrast, the 2010 HELCOM Ministerial Declaration on the implementation of the HELCOM Baltic Sea Action Plan pays a lot of attention to MSP. MSP should be developed for the different Baltic Sea areas in close transboundary cooperation with the aim of having long-term sustainable management and planning for the whole Baltic Sea. The Ministers agreed to establish a joint, co-chaired HELCOM-VASAB (Visions and Strategies around the Baltic Sea)[22] WG on Maritime Spatial Planning enabling coordination and integration of MSP related actions and projects within the framework of the EU Strategy for the Baltic Sea Region and its Action Plan. This joint WG HELCOM-VASAB was asked to finalize a set of joint HELCOM-VASAB broad-scale transboundary MSP principles by 2010. HELCOM agreed to test, apply and evaluate the use of these joint principles when developing national MSP initiatives, as well as regional ones (HELCOM Ministerial Declaration, p. 4).

The OSPAR working group on EIHA took up MSP again in 2011 and agreed to re-establish an ICG-MSP and to propose the adoption of its Term of Reference (ToR) (OSPAR Commission, 2011a, Annex 11), which was afterwards agreed by the Commission (OSPAR Commission, 2011b, Annex 17). This came after being reminded by Ireland of the origin of the OSPAR MSP work within the North East Atlantic Environmental Strategy, in particular in its Biodiversity Strategy (OSPAR Commission 2011c, para. 5.9 and 5.15). 'The North East Atlantic Environmental Strategy 2010–2020' requires the further development of appropriate measures, in line with the ecosystem approach, to facilitate MSP in the OSPAR maritime area. This includes: '1. cooperation on transboundary issues arising from MSP; 2. where necessary, additional mechanisms for transnational consultations on marine spatial plans and issues arising from them; 3. region-specific, tailor-made approaches to applying MSP to support the Ecosystem Approach; 4. exchange of best practices and experiences with regard to MSP' (OSPAR 10/23/1-E, Annex 25, p. 11, para. 4.2.m; Agreement 2010-03, p. 11). The issue of transboundary consultation was taken forward in the IEHA ToR for the ICG-MSP tasks 2011–2013 based on a draft OSPAR Recommendation for a MSP 'Consultation Procedure' that would serve to further develop mechanisms for transnational consultations (OSPAR Commission 2011a, Annex 11, para. 2(ii); OSPAR Commission 2012, Annex 11, para. 3.b). The EIHA 2011 forwarded the draft recommendation to the EIHA 2012 (OSPAR Commission 2011b, Annex 17), however, the United Kingdom and France retained their previous reservations (OSPAR Commission, 2011c, para. 5.10 and 5.11). The draft recommendation remained a draft and transnational MSP consultations ceased to be an action for EIHA or OSPAR ICG-MSP 2013 and 2014 ToRs. From 2012 onwards, any direct or indirect link to potential OSPAR recommendations for a transboundary MSP consultation procedure through the work of EIHA or ICG-MSP disappeared from the agenda of the OSPAR COP meetings.

Previously, in 2011, a joint NGO position paper on EU MSP emphasized that there was no need to develop a legally binding MSP instrument as suggested by the European Commission. In case a legal MSP instrument should be considered essential, these NGOs believed that it should rather be enshrined in the MSFD (OSPAR Commission 2011b, para. 5.9). These NGOs misjudged the potential of a forthcoming EU Directive to stimulate transboundary consultations and cooperation on MSP, in particular to achieve an ecosystem-based management.

The EIHA 2013 agreed on a new ICG-MSP ToR for 2013–2014 (OSPAR Commission, 2013, Annex 13), slightly expanded by EIHA 2014 for the ICG-MSP period 2014–2015. The latter introduces the 'evaluation of possible cooperation' with the HELCOM/VASAB MSP WG and to discuss knowledge on bird migration routes and offshore wind power (OSPAR Commission, 2014, Annex 17). The scope of the work of ICG-MSP 2014–2015 is to provide a platform for the exchange of best practices and experiences related to MSP. For ICG-MSP, MSP is the responsibility of governments and the focus of ICG-MSP should be on issues and working methods that are relevant in a transboundary context. The major role of IGG-MSP will be facilitating the MSP learning process, as well as exchanging spatial data and information on cross-border MSP approaches (e.g. mapping and data standards, working methods). Information exchange will, in particular, focus on user-ecosystem relations (e.g. effects of wind farms, relation between MSFD and MSP, eco-system approach in MSP), user–user relations (e.g. co-use of wind farms, cumulative effects of wind farms on shipping), future spatial developments such as aquaculture and the implementation of SEAs. Furthermore, possible networking and cooperation with other international organizations relevant for MSP (e.g. IMO, the International Council for the Exploration of the Sea – ICES, HELCOM VASAB) is foreseen (OSPAR Commission, 2014, Annex 17).

From this MSP overview within OSPAR it becomes clear that OPSAR has no strong ambition to play an active role in stimulating cross-border cooperation on MSP between its members, as is the case with HELCOM VASAB (see Chapter 7). It seems that cross-border cooperation in the North East Atlantic Region has been taken over by the EU.

Conclusion

The LOSC provides coastal states with new rights and duties, especially in the exclusive economic zone. Most of those rights and duties are implicitly supportive of MSP, while transboundary cooperation is mainly seen in a regional seas context. There is a general obligation to cooperate to prevent significant damage to the marine environment, as expressed in the LOSC and by the ICJ. However, this obligation does not mean that there is a clear duty to cooperate in transboundary MSP. The obligation to cooperate is often linked to activities that can potentially cause significant damage to the environment or hazardous activities with potential transboundary effects. The best tool to assess this in the planning stage is a transboundary SEA that takes into account environmental impact assessments of most activities taking place at regional sea level. In addition to EIAs and SEAs, the ICJ in the Pulp Mills case goes a step further in supporting the necessity of continuous monitoring of the environmental effects of certain activities already taking place.

The CBD is the most important global convention in support of MSP in order to protect marine biological diversity. To improve conservation and sustainable use of the marine and coastal biological diversity, the Parties to the CBD advocate the main principles underlying MSP, such as the integration of the marine environment under jurisdiction of coastal states within their IMCAM approach; the application of EIAs for separate activities affecting marine biological diversity and a SEA for the planning of all those activities together; the underlying active stakeholder participation in a science-based planning process; and the necessity to establish MPAs and to incorporate them in transboundary networks of protected areas. The CBD mainly considers MSP as a tool to implement an ecosystem approach, with focus on the designation and management of MPAs and recently, the protection of coral reefs.

From a regional policy and legal perspective the EU became the major player in stimulating transboundary MSP at the expense of OSPAR. OSPAR seems to have no strong ambition to play an active role in supporting cross-border cooperation on MSP between its members. Its contribution to MSP is mainly focused on collecting scientific data and the assessment of the impacts of human activities on the marine environment, as a contribution to the implementation of the EU MSFD by its Parties. In contrast to OSPAR, HELCOM has set up a Joint HELCOM-VASAB Maritime Spatial Planning Working Group which is very active and whose lessons learned and the projects that have been supported can contribute to the identification of processes necessary to facilitate transboundary MSP in the Baltic Sea.

Notes

1 The UNGA Resolution 61/222 was adopted by 157 votes to 1 (Turkey), with 3 abstentions (Colombia, Libyan Arab Jamahiriya and Venezuela) on 20 December 2006, A/61/49 (Vol. I), 2007, pp. 97–110.

2 See for the Convention text: Secretariat of the Convention on Biological Diversity. *Handbook of the Convention on Biological Diversity* (CBD Handbook), London, Earthscan, 2001, p. 690.

3 Established according to article 25 of the CBD, SBSTTA inter alia prepares decisions to be taken by the COP.

4 The precautionary approach is considered to play a role to halt losses in biodiversity and encourage recovery, notwithstanding our imperfect knowledge of the marine environment see Decision VII/5: *Marine and coastal biological diversity, Appendix 3 Elements of a marine and coastal management framework* UNEP/CBD/COP7/21, 166 at www.cbd.int/doc/decisions/COP-07-dec-en.pdf, para. 2

5 Reference is made to the website of the UNESCO Intergovernmental Oceanographic Commission, in particular the programme 'marine spatial planning initiative' initiated and updated by Charles Ehler and Fanny Douvere, and sponsored by Belgium and other partners at www.unesco-ioc-marinesp.be/

6 Marine Spatial Planning in Practice – Transitioning from Planning to Implementation: UNEP/CBD/SBTTA/18/INF/23 of 18 June 2014 at http://www.cbd.int/doc/meetings/sbstta/sbstta-18/information/sbstta-18-inf-23-en.pdf
7 http://www.cbd.int/doc/?meeting=MCBEM-2014-04
8 UNEP/CBD/COP/12/1/Add.2 of 1 August 2014 at http://www.cbd.int/doc/?meeting=cop-12.
9 COP 12 took place in Pyeongchang in the Republic of Korea from 6 to 17 October 2014.
10 UNEP/CBD/COP/12/1/Add.2 , Annex II Key Scientific and Technical Needs related to the Implementation of the Strategic Plan for Biodiversity 2011–2020, para. (d), p. 8.
11 UNEP/CBD/COP/12/1/Add.2, Marine and coastal biodiversity, para. 8, p. 45.
12 UNEP/CBD/COP/12/1/Add.2, Marine and coastal biodiversity: Impacts on marine and coastal biodiversity of anthropogenic underwater noise and ocean acidification, priority actions to achieve Aichi Biodiversity Target 10 for coral reefs and closely associated ecosystem, and marine spatial planning and training initiatives, para. 3 (n), p. 111.
13 Ibid., para. 16, p. 113.
14 Ibid., para. 17, p. 113.
15 UNEP/CBD/COP/12/1/Add.2, Priority actions to achieve Aichi biodiversity target 10 for coral reefs and closely associated ecosystems, para. 8.4.a, p. 116.
16 Ibid., para. 10.b, p. 116.
17 The Black Sea Commission (www.blacksea-commission.org), the Helsinki Commission (www.helcom.fi), the OSPAR Commission (www.ospar.org), the North Sea Commission (www.northsea.org), UNEP Mediterranean Action Plan (www.unepmap.org).
18 Joint Meeting of the Helsinki & OPSAR Commissions, Record of the Meeting – Annex 5.
19 See http://helcom.fi/action-areas/maritime-spatial-planning.
20 The Secretariat informed the workshop that the organization of a marine spatial management internet forum on the OSPAR website had been investigated, but that a detailed evaluation was needed to assess the costs for upgrading the OSPAR website, OSPAR Workshop, MASMA 2006 Report, para. 4.2.
21 OSPAR Quality Status Report (2010) at http://qsr2010.ospar.org/
22 VASAB is the intergovernmental multilateral co-operation of 11 countries of the Baltic Sea Region in spatial planning and development, guided by the Conference of Ministers responsible for spatial planning and development: see www.vasab.org/

References

Ad Hoc Technical Group on Protected Areas (2003) *Protected areas and the conservation and sustainable use of biological diversity*, UNEP/CBD/AHTEG-PA/1/2, 30 May.

Collie, J. S., Adamowicz, W.L., Beck, M.W., Craig, B., Essington, T.E., Fluharty, D., Rice, J. and Sanchinico, J.N. (2013) 'Marine spatial planning in practice', *Estuarine, Coastal and Shelf Science*, vol. 117, pp. 1–11.

Convention on Biodiversity (CBD) COP (1998), Decision IV/5: *Conservation and sustainable use of marine and coastal biological diversity, including a programme of work*, www.cbd.int/doc/decisions/cop-04/full/cop-04-dec-en.pdf, pp. 32–43.

Convention on Biodiversity (CBD) COP (2000), Decision V/18: *Impact assessment, liability and redress*, UNEP/CBD/COP/5/23, www.cbd.int/doc/decisions/cop-05/full/cop-05-dec-en.pdf, pp.148–150.

Convention on Biodiversity (CBD) COP (2002), Decision VI/7: *Identification, monitoring, indicators and assessments*, UNEP/CBD/COP6/20, www.cbd.int/doc/decisions/COP-06-dec-en.pdf, pp. 93–109.

Convention on Biodiversity (CBD) COP (2004), Decision VII/28: *Protected areas and the Annex concerning a programme of work on protected areas*, UNEP/CBD/COP/7/21, www.cbd.int/doc/decisions/COP-07-dec-en.pdf, pp. 344–364.

Convention on Biodiversity (CBD) COP (2004), Decision VII/5: *Marine and coastal biological diversity*, UNEP/CBD/COP7/21, www.cbd.int/doc/decisions/COP-07-dec-en.pdf, pp. 134–77.

Convention on Biodiversity (CBD) COP (2006), Decision VIII/22: *Marine and coastal biological diversity: enhancing the implementation of integrated marine and coastal area management*, www.cbd.int/doc/decisions/cop-08/full/cop-08-dec-en.pdf, pp. 202–203.

Convention on Biodiversity (CBD) COP (2010), Decision X/29: *Marine and coastal biological diversity*, UNEP/CBD/COP/10/27, www.cbd.int/doc/decisions/cop-10/full/cop-10-dec-en.pdf, pp. 229–44.

Convention on Biodiversity (CBD) COP (2010), *Draft Decisions for the Twelfth Meeting of the Conference of the Parties to the Convention on Biological Diversity. Annex II Key Scientific and Technical Needs related to the Implementation of the Strategic Plan for Biodiversity 2011–2020*, UNEP/CBD/COP/12/1/Add.2/Rev.1, http://www.cbd.int/doc/meetings/cop/cop-12/official/cop-12-01-add2-rev1-en.pdf

Convention on Biodiversity (CBD) COP (2012), Decision XI/18: *Marine and coastal biological diversity: sustainable fisheries and addressing adverse impacts of human activities, voluntary guidelines for environmental impact assessment, and marine spatial planning*, UNEP/CBD/COP/11/35, www.cbd.int/doc/decisions/cop-11/full/cop-11-dec-en.pdf, pp. 204–211.

Directive 2008/26/EC of the European Parliament and of the Council of 17 June 2008 establishing a framework for community action in the field of marine environmental policy (Marine Strategy Framework Directive), *Pb L*. 164, 26 June 2008, 164/19, p. 19.

Directive 2014/89/EU of the European Parliament and of the Council of 23 July 2014 establishing a framework for maritime spatial planning (MSP Directive), *Pb L*. 257, 28 August 2014, 257/135.

Ehler, C. and Douvere, F. (2007) *Visions for a Sea Change, Report of the First International Workshop on Marine Spatial Planning: Intergovernmental Oceanographic Commission and Man and the Biosphere Programme*. IOC Manual and Guides No.48, IOCAM Dossier No.4. Paris, UNESCO, www.unesco-ioc-marinesp.be/

European Commission (2006), *Green Paper: Towards a future Maritime Policy for the Union: A European vision for the oceans and seas*, COM (2006) 275 final, 7 June

General Assembly (2006), Resolution 61/222, *Oceans and the law of the sea*, A/RES/61/222, undocs.org/A/RES/61/222

General Assembly (2012), Resolution 66/288, *The future we want*, A/RES/288, undocs.org/A/RES/66/288

HELCOM (2010), *HELCOM Ministerial Declaration on the implementation of the HELCOM Baltic Sea Action Plan*, Moscow, http://helcom.fi/Documents/Baltic%20sea%20action%20plan/HELCOM%20Moscow%20Ministerial%20Declaration%20FINAL.pdf

International Law Commission (2001), 'The 2001 Draft Articles on Prevention of Transboundary Harm from Hazardous Activities', *Yearbook of the International Law Commission*, vol. 2, no. 2, pp. 146–70.

ICJ, 'Legality of the Threat or Use of Nuclear Weapons, Advisory Opinion' *I.C.J. Reports* 1996, 8 July 1996 , p. 226.

ICJ, 'Pulp Mills on the River Uruguay (Argentina v. Uruguay) Judgement', *I.C.J. Reports* 2010, 20 April 2010, p. 14.

Maes, F. (2008) 'The international legal framework for marine spatial planning', *Marine Policy*, vol. 32, no. 5, p. 799.

MASMA (2006) *Report on the OSPAR Workshop on Marine Spatial Planning* MASMA 06/8/1-E, pp. 1–8. *Ministerial Statement on the Ecosystem Approach to the Management of Human Activities: 'Towards an Ecosystem Approach to the Management of Human Activities'*, First Joint Ministerial Meeting of HELCOM and OSPARCOM, 26–26 June 2003, Bremen, at Germany, http://www.ospar.org/content/content.asp?menu=00430109150000_000000_000000

Ministerial Declaration of the Fifth International Conference on the Protection of the North Sea, 20–21 March 2002, Bergen, Norway, at http://www.ospar.org/html_documents/ospar/html/bergen_declaration_final.pdf

OSPAR Commission (2007) Summary Record, EIHA 2007, EIHA 07/8/1-E.

OSPAR Commission (2008) Summary Record, EIHA 2008, EIHA 08/8/1-E.

OSPAR Commission (2009) Summary Record, EIHA 2009, EIHA 09/11/1-E.

OSPAR Commission (2010) Summary Record, OSPAR/MMC 2010, OSPAR 10/23/1-E.

OSPAR Commission (2011a) Draft Summary Record, EIHA 2011, EIHA 11/10/1-E.

OSPAR Commission (2011b) Summary Record, OSPAR 11/20/1-E.

OSPAR Commission (2011c) Summary Record, EIHA 2011, EIHA 11/10/1-E.

OSPAR Commission (2012) Summary Record, EIHA 2012, EIHA 12/10/1-E.

OSPAR Commission (2013) Summary Record, EIHA 2013, EIHA 13/10/1-E.

OSPAR Commission (2014) Summary Record, EIHA 2014, EIHA 14/10/1-E.

OSPAR Workshop (2006) MASMA 2006 Report, MASMA 06/8/1-E.

OSPAR Workshop (2007) MASMA 07/4/1-E.

OSPARCOM (2004) Workshop Report, SPINS 2004, 04/5/1-E.

OSPARCOM (2005) Workshop Report, SPINS 2005, 05/5/1.

SBSTTA (2012a), *Synthesis document on the experience and use of marine spatial planning*, UNEP/CBD/SBSTTA/16/INF/18, www.cbd.int/sbstta16/documents/

SBSTTA (2012b), *Marine Biodiversity: Marine Spatial Planning and Voluntary Guidelines for the Consideration of Biodiversity in Environmental Impact Assessments and Strategic Environmental Assessments in Marine and Coastal Areas*, UNEP/CBD/SBSTTA/16/7, www.cbd.int/sbstta16/documents/

Secretariat of the Convention on Biological Diversity and the Scientific and Technical Advisory Panel – GEF (2012), *Marine Spatial Planning in the Context of the Convention on Biological Diversity. A study carried out in response to CBS COP 10 decision X/29*, Montreal, Technical Series N. 68.

UN Report 2002: United Nations, *Report of the World Summit on Sustainable Development*, A/Conf.199/20, 26 August–4 September 2002, undocs.org/A/Conf.199/20.

UN Report 2006: United Nations, *Report on the work of the United Nations Open-ended Informal Consultative Process on Oceans and the Law of the Sea at its seventh meeting*, A/61/156.

UNESCO (2014) www.unesco-ioc-marinesp.be/msp_around_the_world

UNGA (2012): *UNGA Resolution A/RES/288.*

Part III

Marine spatial planning in transboundary contexts

Chapter 6

Marine spatial planning

One of the fundamental tools to help achieve effective marine conservation in the Great Barrier Reef[1]

Jon C. Day

Introduction

This chapter discusses marine spatial planning (MSP) in the context of a very large marine protected area (MPA). The Great Barrier Reef (GBR) is one of the best known MPAs in the world; as spatial planning has been used there for over 35 years, the GBR provides an excellent case study to examine some of the lessons learned about MSP.

For this chapter, MSP is defined as 'a process of analysing and allocating parts of three-dimensional marine spaces to specific uses, to achieve ecological, economic, and social objectives that are usually specified through the political process' (Ehler and Douvere, 2007).

A range of spatial and temporal management tools, including a multiple-use zoning network, are today used to ensure the conservation and management of the GBR. The statutory Zoning Plan is the primary planning instrument and a cornerstone of GBR management, but is only one of many management tools used in the GBR.

While zoning is a well-recognized form of MSP, it is not necessarily the most effective way to manage all ocean activities or impacts, and it is important to recognize that many issues facing MPAs cannot be effectively addressed by zoning alone; for example:

- Water quality – ocean zoning usually does not apply outside the marine area up onto the land where most WQ issues arise.
- Fishing impacts – zoning may address some but not all unsustainable fishing impacts.
- Climate change – zoning can help build resilience, but does not address such factors as acidification or rising sea temperatures.
- Coastal developments, especially ports – zoning will not apply in ports if they are located outside the jurisdictional control of a marine park.
- Shipping and pollution incidents – a zoning plan may help by delineating shipping lanes but will not address ship groundings/marine pollution.
- Increasing population growth and recreation – marine zoning will not address key issues unless it can help to curtail use or reduce some of the consequential impacts.

Most of these impacts are better managed using other management 'tools' or management approaches rather than zoning, and various examples have been developed by other sectoral agencies using their own specific legislation (e.g. for fisheries management or shipping). However, when management tools from other agencies or sectors are applied in the GBR Marine Park, they are still subject to the overall zoning framework and therefore must be consistent with the underlying zone objectives. The GBR Marine Park Act provides precedence over inconsistent provisions of nearly all other federal laws and, under the Australian Constitution, federal laws have precedence over inconsistent Queensland State laws within the GBR Region (Kenchington and Day, 2011).

Within the GBR Marine Park, other spatial and temporal management tools developed to address particular activities include:

- Plans of Management – statutory plans for high use or high value areas such as popular tourist destinations.
- Special Management Areas – the statutory Zoning Plan has provisions for additional restrictions on access to, or use of, specified areas of the Marine Park for well-defined conservation or management purposes.
- Site Plans – localized plans that prescribe management arrangements for use of a particular site concentrating on specific use issues and cumulative impacts at that site.
- Other spatial arrangements (e.g. Defence Training Areas, designated shipping areas, formal agreements with Traditional Owners).
- Permits – often tied to specific zones or smaller areas within zones, and providing a detailed level of management arrangement not possible by zoning alone.

All these spatial management tools have their own specific objectives and, when superimposed on the underlying zoning in the GBR Marine Park, they must be consistent with the relevant zone objectives.

Collectively these spatial and temporal tools, including the statutory Zoning Plan, make up the comprehensive MSP approach. Together they comprise a key part of the integrated management approach for the GBR which aims to protect and conserve the biodiversity of the GBR ecosystem, while providing opportunities for the ecologically sustainable use of, and access to, the GBR by current and future generations.

Effective marine conservation, however, requires more than just a comprehensive MSP framework within the marine realm, especially given the range of pressures facing MPAs today (e.g. climate change, declining water quality, loss of coastal habitats, increasing coastal development). Many of these pressures originate outside the marine realm and are not directly ameliorated by ocean zoning or MSP.

Figure 6.1 depicts the interrelationship between zoning, MSP and ecosystem-based management as it occurs within, or adjoining, the GBR:

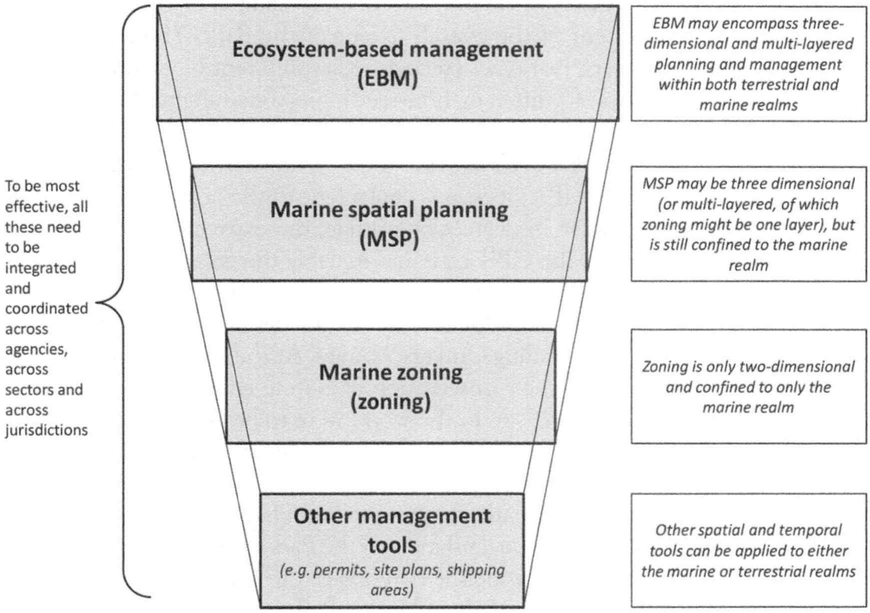

Figure 6.1 Interrelationship of zoning, MSP and ecosystem-based management as they relate to the GBR Marine Park.

- Zoning is normally only a two-dimensional layer (although it can be deemed to act in a three-dimensional space) and is usually confined only to the marine parts of an MPA.
- Marine spatial planning may be multi-dimensional (i.e. multiple layers comprising different plans of which zoning may be one layer) but MSP is still confined only to the marine parts of an MPA.
- A comprehensive ecosystem-based management (EBM) approach encourages 'thinking outside the box' and can encompass three dimensional or multi-layered management and planning within both the terrestrial and the marine realms, which are all relevant for effective marine conservation.

Whenever any of the management tools discussed above are utilized either within or adjacent to an MPA, it is also essential that they are integrated and coordinated across agencies, across sectors and across jurisdictions in order to achieve effective marine conservation.

The Great Barrier Reef Marine Park and World Heritage Area

The GBR is the largest coral reef ecosystem on the planet, stretching over 2,300 km along Australia's north-east coast. While coral reefs initially provided the focus for the GBR Marine Park when it was first proclaimed in 1975, reefs comprise less than 10 per cent of the overall extent of the Park. The Marine Park includes some 30 different reef types (recognized as different bioregions) but the majority is comprised of 40 different non-reef bioregions ranging from shallow inshore waters out to deep oceanic waters.

Today the Marine Park covers an area of 344,400 km^2 and, while it is no longer the world's largest MPA, its size is equivalent to the area of Italy or Japan or Malaysia. Extending over 14 degrees of latitude, the expansive latitudinal and cross-shelf diversity means the GBR contains arguably the greatest biodiversity of any World Heritage Area (WHA) on the planet. An area of 348,000 km^2 (slightly larger than the Marine Park) was added to the World Heritage List in 1981 in recognition of the GBR's Outstanding Universal Value. At the time of its inscription, the International Union for the Conservation of Nature (IUCN) wrote 'It seems clear that if only one coral reef site in the world were to be chosen for the World Heritage List, the Great Barrier Reef is the site to be chosen' (IUCN, 1981, p. 2).

The GBR Marine Park extends from the tip of Cape York in the north to just past Lady Elliot Island in the south. Its western boundary is generally mean low water on the mainland coast of Queensland and the Park extends seaward between 80 and 250 km offshore, well outside the outer reefs into deep oceanic waters (the term 'generally' is used here as the federal Marine Park does not include 13 coastal exclusion areas around ports nor any internal waters of Queensland).

The federal Marine Park also does not include the majority of islands within its outer boundary (only 70 islands or parts of islands that are under federal jurisdiction are part of the GBR Marine Park); however the federal Marine Park does extend to a depth of 1000 metres beneath the seabed and up to a height of 915 metres above sea level in the airspace above.

The federal Marine Park is complemented by the GBR Coast Marine Park established in adjacent state waters under Queensland government legislation, and together both marine parks form the majority of the WHA; the remaining components of the WHA comprise:

- all islands within the outer boundary (about 1050 islands in total, including the 70 Commonwealth islands, with the remaining 980 islands being part of Queensland);
- all waters seaward of low water mark (including internal waters of Queensland such as Hinchinbrook Channel, and port waters); and
- the 13 coastal exclusions (predominantly around ports) that do not form part of the federal Marine Park.

About 70 Aboriginal and Torres Strait Islander clan groups are today recognized as being the 'Traditional Owners' of their 'sea country' occurring within the waters now regarded as the GBR. As Traditional Owners, they have a unique and continuing cultural and historical connections with those waters, as well as the islands and the adjoining coastal areas.

The GBR is an integral part of Australia's national identity and is valued by local, national and international communities. Consequently it is the subject of strong national pride, reflected by an enduring public interest in its future health and management. It is critical to the cultural, economic and social well-being of more than one million people who live mostly in the adjacent coastal zone, but also within the GBR (i.e. on some of the islands). The GBR helps bring billions of dollars annually to Australia's regional and national economies, and supports some 69,000 jobs (Deloitte Access Economics, 2013).

Because of the iconic status of the GBR, some people think the entire area is a marine sanctuary or a marine national park, and therefore equally protected throughout. Many do not understand that while the GBR Marine Park has an overriding main conservation objective of 'long-term protection and conservation of the biodiversity, environment and heritage values of the GBR Region', it also has other objectives, including 'allow ecologically sustainable use of the Great Barrier Reef Region'; however, the legislation is very clear that these other objectives can only occur 'so far as is consistent with the main object' (*Great Barrier Reef Marine Park Act 1975*, s.2A).

Consequently a wide range of activities and uses are allowed in the GBR, including many extractive industries, while still doing much to protect one of the world's most diverse marine ecosystems. The comprehensive, multiple-use zoning system governs all human activities, providing high levels of protection for specific areas, while allowing a variety of other uses, including shipping, boating, diving, many types of tourism, most forms of commercial fishing and recreational fishing, aquaculture, developmental works including dredging and spoil disposal, and military training to occur in certain zones, often with a permit containing specific conditions. Indigenous hunting by Traditional Owners also occurs throughout much of the coastal waters, but increasingly with self-imposed restrictions in some areas.

Institutional and legal framework

A complex, but effective, legal and institutional framework has developed over the past 40 years for the protection and management of the GBR.

The principal legislation that provides for the protection and management of the GBR, the *Great Barrier Reef Marine Park Act 1975*, and its supporting Regulations, was specifically developed as the primary federal legislation for the GBR. It resulted from a Royal Commission which in 1974 recommended ' . . . a special statutory authority should be established responsible to the appropriate Parliament for ecological protection and the control of research and development within the Great Barrier Reef province.'(Queensland State Archives, 1974.)

At that time, the Great *Barrier Reef Marine Park Act 1975* was pioneering legislation enabling 'conservation and reasonable use' of natural resources provided such uses did not compromise the conservation of the GBR, thereby introducing the concept of a multiple-use marine park. The Act established an independent statutory authority (the Great Barrier Reef Marine Park Authority or GBRMPA, the federal agency responsible for the Marine Park), and defined the GBR Region within which the Marine Park could be progressively declared.

The legislation also initiated the emergence of MSP in the GBR through an objectives-based regulatory framework and a comprehensive and systematic process to develop spatially explicit zoning plans. This planning process also included mandatory requirements for certain aspects of public participation during specific phases of planning.

The GBR Marine Park Act is complemented by the following pieces of federal legislation specifically developed for the GBR:

- GBR Marine Park Regulations 1983 – the primary regulations under the Act.
- *GBR Marine Park (Environmental Management Charge–Excise) Act 1993* and *GBR Marine Park (Environmental Management Charge–General) Act 1993* govern the operation of the environmental management charge, a charge associated with many commercial activities undertaken within the GBR Marine Park, including tourism operations.
- GBR Marine Park Zoning Plan 2003 (the Zoning Plan) – subordinate legislation, providing the primary spatial planning instrument for the conservation and management of the Marine Park.
- Cairns Area Plan of Management (1998), Whitsundays Plan of Management (1998), Hinchinbrook Plan of Management (2004) and Shoalwater Bay (Dugong) Plan of Management (1997) establish more detailed management arrangements for specific areas of the Marine Park.

Given the GBR is listed both as a World Heritage Area and a national heritage place, the national environmental legislation, the Environment Protection and Biodiversity Conservation Act 1999, also applies.

A comprehensive list of the federal and Queensland legislation that assists in the protection and management of the GBR, along with Australia's obligations under relevant international conventions, is provided in the recent GBR Strategic Assessment (GBRMPA, 2013, Part 3.5). Some of the most important of these are listed in Table 6.1:

Table 6.1 Some of the key legislative instruments and international conventions relevant to the GBR.

Key Australian (federal) legislation
Great Barrier Reef Marine Park Act 1975
Environment Protection and Biodiversity Conservation Act 1999
Native Title Act 1993
Environment Protection (Sea Dumping) Act 1981
Sea Installations Act 1987
Historic Shipwrecks Act 1976

Key Queensland (State) legislation
Marine Parks Act 2004
Fisheries Act 1994
Nature Conservation Act 1992
Environmental Protection Act 1994
Coastal Protection and Management Act 1995
State Development and Public Works Organisation Act 1971
Key International Conventions
World Heritage Convention 1972
Convention on Biological Diversity 1992
UN Convention on the Law of the Sea 1982 (UNCLOS)
International Convention for the Prevention of Pollution from Ships (MARPOL)
Convention on the Conservation of Migratory Species of Wild Animals 1979

As mentioned previously, the GBR legislation provides precedence over inconsistent provisions of most other federal laws and any inconsistent Queensland laws within the GBR Region (Kenchington and Day, 2011).

Emergence of MSP in the GBR

The 1975 legislation specified that a plan depicting spatially derived zones (i.e. zoning) was to be the key management tool for the Marine Park, and zoning plans were required by the legislation to define the purposes for which certain areas of the Marine Park may be used or entered; however the objects of zoning have 'evolved' from the initial version of the Act (1975) to the latest amendment (2008) as shown in Table 6.2:

Table 6.2 'Evolution' of the statutory objects for zoning in Great Barrier Reef Marine Park Act.

Objects of GBR zoning in 1975 s. 32(7) of the Act	*Objects of GBR zoning in 2008 s. 32(1) of the Act*
The conservation of the Great Barrier Reef; The regulation of the use of the Marine Park so as to protect the GBR while allowing reasonable human use of the GBR Region	To protect areas in the Marine Park that are of high conservation value To regulate the use of the Marine Park so as to: i protect the ecosystem within the GBR Region; and ii ensure the use is ecologically sustainable use; and iii manage competing usage demands

(continued)

Table 6.2 (continued)

Objects of GBR zoning in 1975 s. 32(7) of the Act	*Objects of GBR zoning in 2008 s. 32(1) of the Act*
[no equivalent object in 1975]	To protect and conserve the biodiversity of the Marine Park, including ecosystems, habitats, populations and genes
The regulation of activities that exploit the resources of the GBR Region so as to minimise the effect of those activities on the GBR	To regulate activities that exploit the resources of the GBR Region so as to: i minimize the adverse effect of those activities on the GBR; and ii ensure the ecologically sustainable use of the resources
[no equivalent object in 1975]	To protect the world heritage values of the GBR World Heritage Area
[no equivalent object in 1975]	To provide for the ecologically sustainable use of marine resources by Traditional Owners consistent with their traditional practices
The reservation of some areas of the GBR for their appreciation and enjoyment by the public;	To reserve some areas of the GBR Region for public enjoyment and appreciation
The preservation of some areas of the GBR in its natural state undisturbed by man except for the purposes of scientific research.	To preserve some areas of the GBR Region in a natural state, undisturbed except for the purposes of scientific research that cannot be undertaken elsewhere in the Marine Park.

This evolution of the objectives of zoning illustrates an increased recognition of the significance of such matters as world heritage and the use of marine resources by indigenous Traditional Owners, as well as the need to protect the full range of the biodiversity of the area rather than just keystone species or habitats.

The first zoning plan for the GBR Marine Park covered only an extremely small part of the GBR Region (the Capricorn-Bunker group in the southern GBR), and was finalized in 1981. It introduced a spectrum of zone types, ranging from a General Use Zone (the least restrictive zone, allowing most reasonable uses), through to a Preservation Zone (very small 'no-go' areas, set aside as scientific reference areas, refer to Table 6.3). This spectrum of zones (and most zone names) reflected the wording of the objectives as outlined above in the 1975 legislation.

For each zone, the GBR Zoning Plan sets out in detail two specific lists of 'use or entry' provisions; these then help to determine what activities are appropriate in that particular zone:

1 The first list indicates activities that are allowed to occur in that zone ('as of right') and which do not require a permit; and
2 The second list stipulates which activities may occur in that particular zone but only after a permit has been assessed and, if the application meets all the necessary requirements, a permit has been granted. The Regulations specify the assessment process and criteria for a permit – these vary depending on the proposed activity.

If an activity is not listed in either (1) or (2) above, then it is prohibited in that zone, and the provisions of the Zoning Plan applies to all users. For communicating with the wider public, the allowable activities in the Zoning Plan have been summarized into a simple activity/zoning matrix that is shown on all zoning maps. However, the legal instrument a delegate must consider when making a decision is the statutory Zoning Plan (which is subordinate legislation to the Act).

Over the years zoning has been progressively applied to different sections of the GBR Marine Park and many aspects of zoning have been modified (Day, 2002a, pp. 142–43). It was not until 1988 that the majority of the Marine Park had been sequentially declared and then zoned (i.e. 13 years after the GBR legislation was initially proclaimed). Considerable experience has now been gained as to what has worked well with zoning, and what has needed to be amended, both within the GBR and in other Australian MPAs. Consequently various aspects of zoning have been refined (Day, 2002b, p. 1264; Day, 2011) along with other management approaches.

By the late 1990s, an area approximately 15,500 km^2 of the GBR Marine Park (~4.5 per cent) was zoned as 'no take' areas (locally known as 'green zones'), with a further 470 km^2 (~ 0.13 per cent of the GBRMP) as 'no-access' areas or Preservation Zones. The locations of both these zones reflected a historical focus primarily on coral reefs, with a skewed emphasis in the more remote and 'pristine' areas (72 per cent of the total extent of no-take in the Marine Park was in a single large cross-shelf transect of National Park Zone in the remote Far Northern Section). A further 15 per cent of the total GBR Marine Park was also afforded seabed protection by the Habitat Protection Zone. However by the late 1990s there were concerns that the existing levels of protection did not adequately protect the range of biodiversity known to exist within the GBR, and these levels of protection were inadequate to ensure that the reefs as well as the surrounding non-reef areas remained healthy, productive and resilient into the future.

Consequently, between 1999 and 2003, the GBRMPA undertook a complex planning and consultative programme to develop a new Zoning Plan for the entire Marine Park (Day *et al.*, 2004; Fernandes *et al.*, 2005; Fernandes *et al.*, 2009). The primary aim of the programme was to better protect the range of biodiversity in the GBR, by increasing the extent of 'no-take' areas, ensuring they included 'representative' examples of all the different habitat types (hence the name, the Representative Areas Program or RAP). A further aim was to minimise impacts on the existing users, including fishers, of the GBR Marine Park.

It was a comprehensive but controversial programme comprising considerable scientific input, community involvement and innovation and, to the surprise of many, it achieved its aims.

During the rezoning programme, all components of the existing Zoning Plans were open for comment and amendment. Given that the previous Zoning Plans had been progressively developed for different sections of the Marine Park over some 18 years, various terms, management provisions and zone names differed across different parts of the Marine Park. The rezoning programme saw the development of a single Zoning Plan for the entire Marine Park that removed these inconsistencies and enabled GBRMPA to address several other important planning tasks; for example:

- zoning, for the first time, 28 new coastal sections added to the federal Marine Park in 2000 and 2001; and
- implementing coordinate-based descriptions for all zone boundaries.

The current GBR Zoning Plan was finalized in 2003 and came into effect in July 2004, providing far greater protection of this internationally acclaimed area. The multiple-use zoning network which was the outcome of the rezoning provides high levels of protection (in 'no-take' zones, and very small 'no-go' zones) for one third (33.3 per cent or 117,000 km^2) of the Marine Park. Today this comprises the world's largest representative network of marine no-take zones protecting typical examples of each of the 70 broad habitat types (or bioregions) identified across the entire GBR (Fernandes *et al.*, 2005).

The current Zoning Plan divides the Marine Park into eight zones – seven marine zones and one zone for Commonwealth Islands as shown in Table 6.3 (see page 116). The General Use Zone allows the widest range of activities and most reasonable uses in some 33 per cent of the Marine Park, while a further 33 per cent is Habitat Protection Zone, and zoned such that the benthic habitat is fully protected including a prohibition on bottom-trawling or any activities that might impact the benthos.

The Preservation Zone is the most restrictive zone, delineating small areas as 'scientific baselines' or reference areas, not impacted by human use. The Commonwealth Islands Zone provides for the use or entry of areas of the Marine Park above low water mark on the 70 Commonwealth islands.

There are also complementary zoning arrangements in adjacent areas under Queensland jurisdiction within the GBR Coast Marine Park, so effectively similar laws apply in all waters of the GBR seaward of high water mark.

The Zoning Plan is only one of many types of MSP applying in the GBR

As a consequence of the most recent amendments to the Act, the Authority is today required to manage the GBR in a way that is consistent with the objects of the Act, including the principles of ecologically sustainable use and the protection of the World Heritage values of the GBR World Heritage Area.

This means that virtually all reasonable activities are allowed to occur in some part of the GBR Marine Park, but all areas are zoned and regulated to minimise impacts and conflicts between activities. The comprehensive zoning network, along with the wide range of other management tools and approaches, provides for effective and integrated protection of this huge and complex area. The obligations under the World Heritage Convention are an important reinforcement of the objectives of the Act.

Effective management of the GBR therefore relies upon the cooperation of a number of management agencies (both federal and State), using a number of management tools, including many that are regarded as components of MSP (e.g. zoning plans, plans of management, other spatial plans) along with various management approaches (e.g. education, planning, partnerships, enforcement) to control and/or mitigate impacts of various activities (e.g. tourism, fishing, shipping) and to address various pressures/threats such as climate change, water quality, and population growth.

Other layers of MSP used in key parts of the GBR were listed in the introduction of this chapter; two of the more comprehensive MSP layers are:

- Plans of Management – Plans of Management have been prepared for intensively used areas, particularly 'at risk' groups of islands and reefs, or for the protection of species of conservation concern or ecological communities. They provide greater detail than the broader GBR-wide Zoning Plan by way of specific management provisions, and impose controls on the granting of permissions. Four plans of management currently exist, covering about 8 per cent of the Marine Park. The plans for the Cairns Area, the Whitsundays and Hinchinbrook set out detailed management arrangements applying to all users of these areas, with a focus on protecting key natural values while allowing a range of uses. The Shoalwater Bay (Dugong) Plan of Management manages activities in the bay that threaten the dugong population or impact on the seagrass meadows.
- Traditional Owner agreements – formal Traditional Use of Marine Resources Agreements (TUMRAs) describe how indigenous Traditional Owner groups work with the Australian and Queensland governments to manage traditional use activities in their sea country. TUMRAs support cultural practices while protecting species and ecosystems critical to the health of people, culture and country. Indigenous Land Use Agreements are agreements between one or more native title groups and other people or parties about the use and management of land and waters.

The above agreements address issues including the sustainable take of culturally significant species, like turtle and dugong, and incorporate traditional and contemporary scientific knowledge and environmental management for the ongoing conservation and management of the GBR.

Zoning remains the key management tool for conservation and management over the entire GBR, with each type of zone contributing to varying degrees to ensuring the overriding conservation objective. However, as outlined above, there are various misconceptions about the role that zoning actually plays; some of the misconceptions are discussed in the section below on 'Key lessons learnt'.

In accordance with the GBR Marine Park Act, the Authority may amend a Zoning Plan if it (or its most recent amendment) has been in operation for at least seven years; however the current legislation requires the entire plan to be amended, so amendments to only small areas cannot currently be considered.

The planning approach in the GBR is effectively transboundary MSP

While MSP in the GBR has been applied in only one country (Australia), the sheer size of its application and its use across differing jurisdictional arrangements all help to clarify the magnitude of this achievement. As previously outlined, the GBR Marine Park is, on a global scale, equal in size to many countries (or equivalent to the area of the UK, Switzerland and the Netherlands combined). If the GBR were to be overlaid on the west coast of North America, it would stretch from Vancouver to the Mexican border (i.e. the entire west coast of the USA).

The MSP methodology in the GBR has elements of a transboundary approach in that the State of Queensland 'mirrored' the federal zoning in nearly all the adjoining State waters. The result is that today there is complementary zoning for virtually all the State and Federal waters across the entire GBR from high water mark out to a maximum distance of 250 km offshore. This in itself is fairly unique on a global scale, and provides for more effective marine conservation and public understanding of the entire area as the regulatory provisions are the same irrespective of which jurisdiction applies.

Other complementary management approaches, both spatial and temporal, operate across the jurisdictional boundaries (e.g. TUMRAs as outlined above). These have been developed with differing levels of government, and with various industries, stakeholders or community groups, and are designed to provide more effective and integrated protection of the GBR and thereby increase the resilience of the GBR to cope with escalating pressures.

In most other Australian marine waters, MSP has only been conducted within jurisdictional limits either by one of the States or by the Commonwealth with little consideration of the artificiality of such jurisdictional boundaries or the problems likely to arise for effective marine conservation. There are some examples of effective marine spatial planning undertaken within jurisdictional limits in Australia (e.g. South Australia), but regrettably very few transboundary examples.

Key lessons learnt about zoning and MSP in the GBR

Kenchington and Day (2011) identified six misunderstandings about the management of the GBR, particularly around zoning. This part of the chapter addresses some further lessons learnt about zoning, marine spatial planning and ecosystem-based management, along with some challenges for other MPAs and MPA networks bearing in mind the adaptive management and planning approaches developed in the GBR.

Lesson #1 – the GBR zoning is based around the zone objectives rather than on specific activities

Zoning in the ocean can provide a spatial basis for determining where many marine activities are able to occur and therefore separate conflicting uses, and may provide gear restrictions (for example, on some types of fishing gear) while providing differing levels of protection for different areas.

In some parts of the world, zoning is based solely around allowing, or prohibiting, specific activities in specific areas. In the GBR the emphasis is on providing a spectrum of zones with differing objectives; the objectives for each zone are shown in Table 6.3 (along with the most appropriate IUCN category).

The difference between zoning by objective rather than zoning by activity is best explained by an example; a 'no-trawling' zone may indicate clearly an activity is prohibited (i.e. all trawling is banned in that zone), but it may not be clear as to what other activities may be allowed or not allowed.

The objective of the Habitat Protection Zone indicates that a range of activities which have (relatively) minimal impacts on the habitat(s) are allowed within that zone; for example, boating, diving, and limited impact research, as well as allowing some extractive activities like line fishing, netting, trolling and spear-fishing (i.e. some, but not all, fishing activities). However the zone objective and related zoning provisions clearly prohibit bottom trawling, dredging or any other activity that is damaging to the sensitive habitats in the zone.

In most oceans there are many existing or potential marine activities that need to be managed but many of these activities are complementary and can occur within the same zone; if zoning is used to address all existing activities (and ocean zoning is certainly one important tool to do so), then it is preferable that zoning is by objective rather than by each individual activity.

It is also important to note that in each of the zones that have multiple parts in their objective (for example, providing for both conservation and reasonable use as shown for most zones in Table 6.3), there is a clear hierarchy within the objective, with the second part always being subject to the first (i.e. reasonable use can only occur subject to ensuring conservation).

Table 6.3 Current GBR zones and zone objectives (as of 2014).

Zone name	*Zone colour*	*Objective(s) of the zone*	*Equivalent IUCN category*
General Use Zone	Light blue	To provide for the conservation of areas of the Marine Park, while providing opportunities for reasonable use.	VI
Habitat Protection Zone	Dark blue	a To provide for the conservation of areas of the Marine Park through the protection and management of sensitive habitats, generally free from potentially damaging activities; and b Subject to (a), to provide opportunities for reasonable use.	VI
Conservation Park Zone	Yellow	a To provide for the conservation of areas of the Marine Park; b Subject to (a), to provide opportunities for reasonable use and enjoyment, including limited extractive use	IV
Buffer Zone	Olive Green	a To provide for the protection of the natural integrity and values of areas of the Marine Park, generally free from extractive activities; b Subject to (a), to provide opportunities for: i Certain activities, including the presentation of the values of the Marine Park, to be undertaken in relatively undisturbed areas; and ii Trolling for pelagic species.	IV
Scientific Research Zone	Orange	a To provide for the protection of the natural integrity and values of areas of the Marine Park, generally free from extractive activities; and b Subject to (a), to provide opportunities for scientific research to be undertaken in relatively undisturbed areas.	Ia
Marine National Park Zone	Green	a To provide for the protection of the natural integrity and values of areas of the Marine Park, generally free from extractive activities; and b Subject to (a), to provide opportunities for certain activities, including the presentation of the values of the Marine Park, to be undertaken in relatively undisturbed areas.	II
Preservation Zone	Pink	a To provide for the preservation of the natural integrity and values of areas of the Marine Park, generally undisturbed by human activities.	Ia
Commonwealth Islands Zone	Cream	a To provide for the conservation of the natural integrity and values of areas of the Marine Park above low water mark; and b To provide for use of the zone by the Commonwealth; and c Subject to (a), to provide for facilities and uses consistent with the values of the area.	II

There is not an exact correlation between the GBR zone objectives and the definitions for each of the IUCN categories. However, using the guidelines for applying the IUCN categories to marine-protected areas (Day *et al.*, 2012), the closest equivalent IUCN category for each zone is shown in Table 6.3.

Lesson #2 – the zoning in the GBR has evolved over many years

It can take years to effectively undertake an effective zoning programme.The first zoning plans were progressively developed for parts of the Marine Park in the early 1980s, but it was not until 13 years after the outer boundary of the Marine Park was first declared that the entire GBR was zoned (i.e.1988). From 1988 until mid-2004, less than five per cent of the entire GBR was zoned in highly protected 'no-take' zones.

The Representative Areas Program rezoned the entire Marine Park during a single comprehensive planning process, but it took almost five years to complete. An important lesson is not so much the overall percentage of the Marine Park that was protected; rather the fact it was a representative approach ensuring an adequate example of every bio-region was protected, and more than one example per bio-region was protected in the network (to spread the load and provide some 'insurance' against possible future losses).

Lesson #3 – fishing can occur in more than one zone in the GBR Marine Park

All seven marine zone types, including the General Use Zone, have various restrictions that affect differing aspects of fishing (for example, long-lining and the use of more than six hooks on a single line, are prohibited throughout all zones in the Marine Park). Various types of fishing are normally allowed to occur in four zone types which make up 66 per cent of the Marine Park. Half of this area excludes trawling and related activities that damage seabed habitats/communities but various other types of fishing (line, net, pot, etc.) are allowed. While all these fisheries in the GBR are still subject to the zoning provisions, they are managed primarily by the Queensland fisheries agency.

One misconception is that the Conservation Park Zone (or yellow zone) was intended to be a recreational fishing-only zone. This is incorrect and the provision for essentially only 'one-line, one hook' throughout that zone was intended to ensure limited fishing, but was not intended to distinguish whether such fishing was undertaken by commercial or recreational fishermen.

While various zones prohibit all types of extraction or collection (e.g. the Marine National Park Zone and the Preservation Zone), a special permit may be issued to allow some types of fishing for research purposes in these zones, but only under very strict permit conditions.

Lesson #4 – just because an activity is listed in the Zoning Plan as able to occur with a permit, then it does not automatically mean a permit will be granted for that activity

This misconception may be best illustrated by another example, again using the Habitat Protection Zone. Activities such as aquaculture or harvest fishing that may or may not have an impact may be permitted to occur in that zone but only after undergoing a detailed permit assessment process. The assessment determines whether the specific proposal (such as the actual aquaculture method or proposed location of the harvest fishing) is compatible with the zone objective and meets all the necessary permit criteria.

Once the necessary requirements in the assessment process have been satisfactorily addressed, a permit may be issued with conditions that specify where and how the activity can occur (not necessarily throughout the zone) and to ensure any impacts remain at acceptable levels. Such permits are generally granted for a limited time period (new permits are usually for one year, but existing permittees may be granted permits for up to 15 years in some instances). The permits can include a range of permit conditions, such as the payment of an Environmental Management Charge, and may require a formal deed of agreement covering aspects such as insurance or a bank guarantee for safe removal of structures if directed.

There is also a special 'catch-all' permit provision in the GBR Zoning Plan, 'any other purpose consistent with the objective of the zone . . . '. This provision provides for new technology or activities that were not known when the Zoning Plan was approved and which therefore are not in either of the lists of provisions explained previously. In all zones an activity that is not specifically listed but is assessed to be consistent with the zone objective (see Table 6.3) may be granted a permit. This essential requirement (i.e. to be consistent with the zone objective) is an important first consideration whenever a permit application is considered for a particular zone. The 'any other purpose' provision is an important 'safety net' that has enabled new activities to be considered for a permit while maintaining the integrity of the overall zoning scheme.

Lesson #5 – effective marine conservation requires cooperation across jurisdictions

In 1979, the Queensland and Australian Governments agreed to complementary management of the waters and islands within the GBR Region. Known as the Emerald Agreement, this was fundamental given the complexities of what were deemed to be 'State waters' (extending from high water mark to three nautical miles offshore) versus 'Commonwealth waters'. The Offshore Constitutional Settlement Act 1975, which still applies, determined that zoning by the federal government overrides any conflicting State legislation, even in what had previously been considered the three nautical mile limit of coastal waters.

The Emerald Agreement addressed these jurisdictional complexities as well as a range of other legal and administrative matters including:

- the Commonwealth would take the lead in park planning and overall management;
- Queensland would lead in day-to-day (or field) management; and
- both governments would closely collaborate in joint permitting and enforcement, assisted by 'mirroring' legislation on matters such as complementary zoning and permits.

The Agreement introduced the Field Management Program, which is jointly funded by the State and federal governments, and also created the GBR Ministerial Council (now known as the Ministerial Forum), which facilitates ongoing discussions between relevant federal and State ministers.

Queensland remains responsible for State Marine Parks in intertidal waters (with legislation that 'mirrors' the adjoining federal legislation), as well as for the majority of islands (including national park islands), and for other Queensland waters (such as ports), all of which adjoin the federal Marine Park.

In June 2009, an updated Great Barrier Reef Intergovernmental Agreement replaced the 1979 agreement, providing a contemporary framework for cooperation between both governments, and recognizing challenges such as climate change and catchment water quality that were unforeseen in 1979.

Lesson #6 – the zoning scheme is only one of many spatial management tools applied to regulate activities in the Marine Park

Zoning is only one of many spatial management tools used in the GBR. Other spatial layers that overlay the underlying zoning are depicted in the following diagrams, illustrated by using the same area of the Marine Park but showing differing management layers. If all these management layers were to exist in a single two-dimensional zoning plan, it would be extremely complex and confusing.

In the GBR a range of multi-dimensional management arrangements (spatial, non-spatial and temporal) are applied, some of which are in the Zoning Plan, but others are in additional statutory or non-statutory documents. Non-spatial management arrangements include bag limits, size limits and various permit conditions, and temporal management arrangements include seasonal closures at key fish spawning times or temporary closures for short-term activities like military training.

This multi-layered spatial and temporal management approach does mean the total management 'package' appears complex, but it does not require every aspect to be shown to the public in a two-dimensional zoning plan.

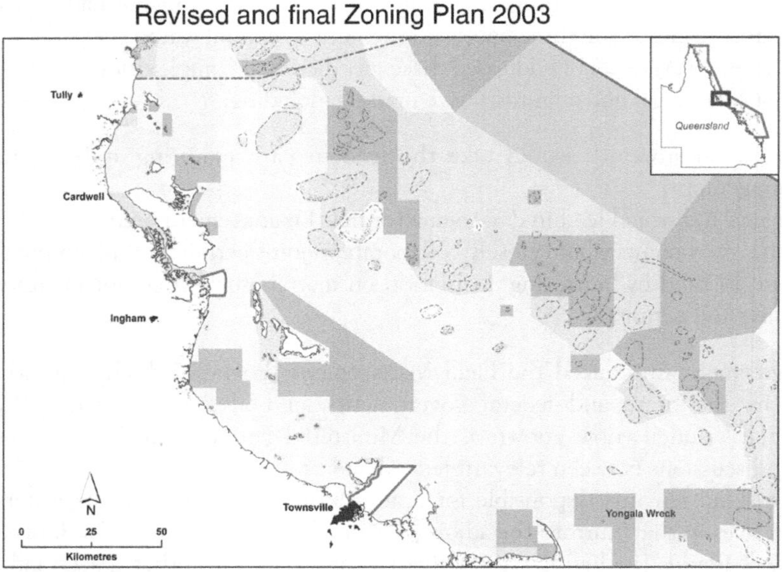

Figure 6.2 Part of the 2003 Zoning Plan showing the range of zones in a small area off Townsville in the central part of the GBR. This same area is then shown below with other spatial management arrangements on top of the underlying zoning.

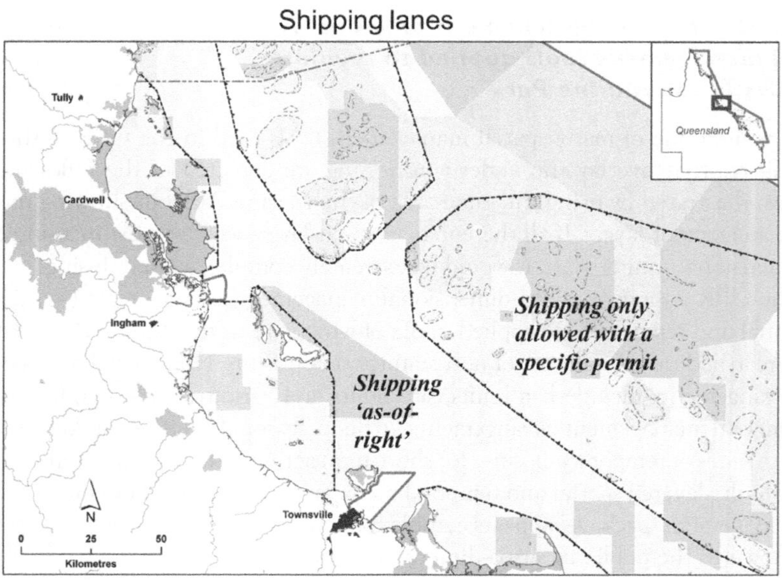

Figure 6.3 Shipping is one of many examples of marine activities that are not limited to a single zone within a multi-use zoning scheme.

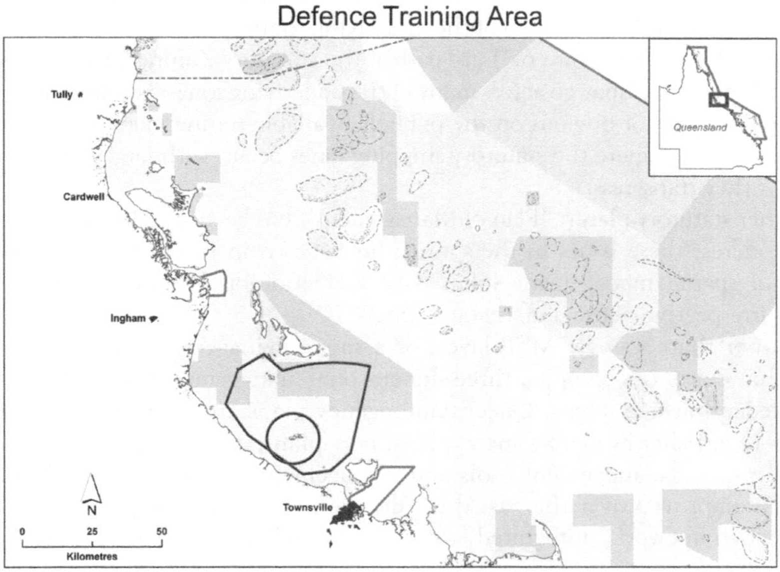

Figure 6.4 While some Defence Training areas in the GBR provide permanent closures to the public, others like this one are not permanent. When this area is being used for defence training purposes, it is closed to all users by Public Notice, but for the majority of the year the area is open with very few restrictions other than the underlying zoning (i.e. both a spatial and a temporal arrangement).

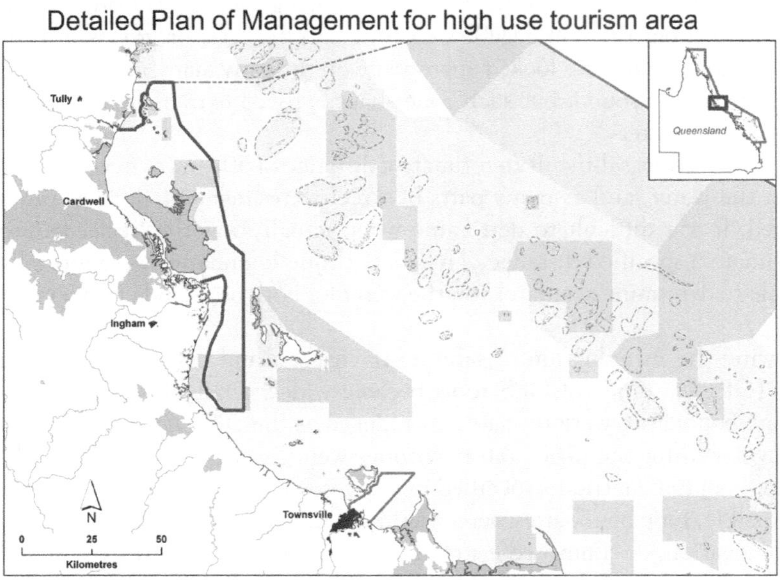

Figure 6.5 A small subset of the mapped area is highly used with potential conflicts between tourism, recreation and conservation aspects.

Figures 6.2 to 6.5 are a small subset of the GBR Marine Park showing various spatial management layers on top of the underlying zoning.

Shipping lanes (see Figure 6.3) are part of the statutory Zoning Plan but, as shown, shipping lanes may go across many of the underlying zones. For most users, shipping lanes are not obvious on the publicly available zoning maps. However all ships are aware where the statutory shipping lanes occur, with large penalties possible if they transgress.

Another statutory plan (a 'Plan of Management') has been specifically developed to address these issues in the specific area shown in Figure 6.5, using an overlay of spatial management (akin to a recreation-opportunity spectrum) which is irrespective of the underlying zoning.

So rather than a single MSP layer, or a single management plan for the GBR, what exists is a complex three-dimensional management 'system' comprising federal agency plans, Queensland agency plans and plans from other agencies (e.g. fisheries management plans, port plans, a shipping plan, etc.). This full suite of management tools and management approaches have been adaptively improved over the past three decades, and today comprise a comprehensive framework, integrated and coordinated across agencies, across sectors and across jurisdictions.

Lesson #7 – Co-ordinate based zone boundaries are far more effective offshore than geographically based boundaries

Early zoning plans within the GBR Marine Park emphasized the protection of coral reefs as they were considered the most important areas. Zone boundaries were initially described as a specified distance from a geographical feature (such as '500 metres from the reef edge'). Depicting specific reefs or groups of reefs within such zones may have looked appropriate on the early maps, and may have seemed ecologically sound, but such zone shapes proved extremely difficult to interpret 'on the water'.

For example, it was difficult to estimate a distance of 500 m (or even 100 m) while on the water, and as many parts of a reef were fragmented, or at times submerged, it was difficult to determine what actually was the 'reef edge' to then estimate a specified distance. This meant zone boundaries were virtually impossible to determine accurately on the water for both users and enforcement officers.

Following the introduction of satellite navigation and Global Positioning Systems (GPS), a range of GPS tools became widely available. Coordinate-based zone boundaries were therefore introduced as the 2003 Zoning Plan was being developed for the GBR. All new zones were described by their coordinates (i.e. longitude/ latitude, specified in degrees and decimal minutes). As far as was possible, zone boundaries were orientated north, south, east and west for ease of navigation, or comprised a straight line between two easily determined points. In addition, wherever possible, the new zone boundaries also included considerable non-reef areas surrounding any coral reefs of interest, in recognition of the connectivity and importance of these surrounding non-reef areas.

Every zone was described in full detail in a schedule to the statutory Zoning Plan, but not every zone coordinate was shown on the freely-available zoning maps. However the coordinates for all no-fishing (green) zones and all no-access (pink) zones were shown on the zoning maps. All zoning coordinates were also made available in an electronic form to commercial suppliers of electronic navigation aids or downloadable from the web (GBRMPA, nd) to enable any user to locate zones using their own electronic device such as a handheld GPS, or to plot the coordinates on a chart.

As far as possible, inshore zoning boundaries are aligned with identified landmarks or other recognizable coastal features (such as 'the no-fishing (green) zone extends north from the eastern extent of the headland at xxx') recognizing that not all users had access to GPS technology.

Lesson #8 – Effective management of the Marine Park also needs to occur outside the 'wet bits'

The federal Marine Park is more or less confined to the waters seaward of low water (Commonwealth Islands are part of the Marine Park) but it does not include various exclusions along the coast within ports or other internal waters of Queensland. In November 2004, the State of Queensland 'mirrored' the Commonwealth zoning in most of the adjoining State waters, so there is now complementary zoning for virtually all the State and Commonwealth waters within the entire GBR World Heritage Area.

The GBR legislation also has provisions to take a broad ecosystem-approach, allowing regulatory controls on specific activities well outside the jurisdictional area (e.g. GBRMPA was able to bring in specific Regulations controlling aquaculture up to 5 km landward of the GBR Marine Park when concerns were raised about the potential adverse impact of discharges associated with aquaculture activities).

The integrated management approach also extends well outside the marine area to include all the islands, all the tidal lands/tidal waters and many activities in the catchments; furthermore most of the management approaches today (e.g. addressing water quality issues) are done in partnerships with local government and industries throughout the catchment.

Lesson #9 – MSP is important, but there is a need to consider the adjacent lands for fully effective marine conservation

MSP has been referred to as having the '. . . potential as a new and integrated solutions tool with capacity to balance conservation with sustainable use and economic development' and '. . . an approach that explicitly offers an integrated way of managing the ocean at relatively large scales' (Merrie and Olsson, 2014).

However, as outlined above, management of the marine realm alone, without working in close partnership with the adjoining coastal waters and catchments, is unlikely to result in effective marine conservation.

The challenge of integrating the land-sea connections was highlighted by Alvarez-Romero *et al.* (2011) stating '. . . land-sea planning should involve explicit conservation objectives for processes that connect the land and the sea as well as explicit ways of accounting for threats that originate in one realm and affect the other'.

Many of the current initiatives undertaken within GBRMPA and other agencies, such as the mapping of coastal ecosystems, the identification of key areas within catchment basins, and working with farmers to minimise their impacts on water quality, are specifically aimed at addressing this land–sea interface and the adjoining coastal waters and catchments (GBRMPA, 2012).

Merrie and Olsson (2014) conclude 'MSP is only one tool for ocean governance, a tool that has been framed as a way forward in being able to implement ecosystem-based management in an even more complex and crowded ocean'. In 2013 the European Commission launched a joint initiative to establish a framework for MSP and Integrated Coastal Management in European Union member States, stressing that planning the marine area cannot be considered independently from what is happening in the coastal zone.

Lesson #10 – Some results of zoning may become apparent quickly while others may take decades

While many are aware of the rezoning in the GBR that led to the 2003 Zoning Plan, few are aware of the significant outcomes that have since resulted, or the speed at which that occurred. For example, research showed coral trout (*Plectropomus leopardus*) numbers rebounded by 31 to 75 per cent on a majority of reefs that were closed to fishing after as little as one and a half to two years (Russ *et al.*, 2008)

Equally exciting is the more recent research results using isotope marking, which demonstrates the connectivity of larvae from areas that have been closed to fishing into adjacent fished areas. Research by James Cook University has provided definitive evidence of the benefits of no-take zones (i.e. green zones) for reef fish conservation and for sustainable harvesting, and the connectivity of local fish populations (Harrison *et al.*, 2012).

The 2003 Zoning Plan and the integrated management framework have brought conservation benefits for the entire GBR ecosystem but equally flow-on social and economic benefits for adjacent communities and industries – including the commercial fishing, recreational fishing and tourism industries that rely on the GBR for their livelihoods.

Adaptive management is a key aspect of managing any marine area (Day, 2008, p. 824); it is also important to recognize that some management actions need to be in place for a reasonable period of time to be effective or to enable a reasonable assessment of their effectiveness. Adopting an adaptive management approach also enables managers to be flexible and to expect, and deal with, the unexpected (e.g. climate change was not even considered an important marine issue a decade ago).

Lesson #11 – Decision support tools are not essential to achieve effective MSP

Merrie and Olsson (2014) outline the views of some planners about the use of Geographic Information Systems (GIS) as a key 'hardware' component of MSP, given they can provide the ability to synthesize large amounts of data in a cost–effective way. They conclude that GIS is 'therefore a key prior-condition . . . but MSP is more than simply a GIS tool'.

It is important to recognize that while a GIS can be extremely useful for planning, it is not essential; furthermore, decision-support systems (DSS) or analytical tools (e.g. Marxan, C-Plan) will never produce the final pragmatic solution for any planning task (Day *et al.*, 2004, p. 262). Lewis *et al.* (2007, pp. 524–25) list some of the key pitfalls when trying to utilize DSS for marine planning:

- Use of a DSS will not compensate for missing and incomplete data, and poor data will lead to poor results.
- Outcomes will be of little practical value if social and economic values are not also included in the DSS. Accurate social, cultural and economic data, at the best possible spatial resolution, significantly improved the conservation outcomes in the GBR and was vital for credibility – but such data are often not readily available in a form amendable to a DSS.
- Some layers of information cannot be effectively incorporated into any DSS nor can a DSS undertake the fine-scale tuning that accompanies the final stages of any plan as political trade-offs inevitably occur.
- It is natural for DSS users to hope that the DSS will generate 'the answer', providing a quick, cheap and reliable solution to a planning problem. However all DSS tools have limitations, and cannot match the complexity of real-world planning problems. More often than not they produce simplistic results and unintended side-effects. Most contemporary DSS tools are unlikely to meet all the needs of any user and even simple 'rules' such as 'all reserves should be no smaller than (xx) square kilometres . . .' were not able to be directly implemented using the DSS in the GBR planning program.

The DSS capabilities were matched to certain parts of the problem during the major rezoning of the GBR between 1999 and 2003. For example, DSS generated an initial 'footprint' as an option for various 'no-take' zones, but could not cater for the required eight zone types, each with its own objective. Once this initial 'footprint' was developed, other planning methods needed to be applied. This is demonstrated in Pressey *et al.* (2013) with a diagram showing the best results that Marxan could produce in the GBR and how much that differed from both the draft and the final Zoning Plans.

Lesson #12 – the adaptive-management approach applied in the GBR is an essential part of effective ecosystem-based management

The GBR is considered by many as one of the world's better-working examples of marine zoning and EBM. For example, Ruckelshaus *et al.* (2008) concluded 'The Great Barrier Reef ecosystem boasts a system-wide spatial management approach that is arguably the world's most sophisticated and extensively implemented example of marine zoning.' Olsson *et al.* (2008), referring to the 2003 Zoning Plan and the way the GBR was managed, wrote: 'These bold management changes comprise a rare example of an ecosystem-based approach . . . '

Arkema *et al.* (2006) concluded 'These achievements are largely due to the GBRMPA's development of specific scientific and socioeconomic goals, use of adaptive management, and its willingness to involve the public, adopt transparency, and consult with multiple user groups.'

Many of the reasons why the GBR is a good working example of the EBM approach relate to how management has evolved and adapted, and despite the jurisdictional complexities, continues to be well integrated (e.g. complementary legislation for all State and Federal waters) with good cooperation with most sectors.

Zoning is undoubtedly an important management tool for effective EBM. However to remain effective, it must be periodically reviewed, especially considering the enormous changes over the 40 years since the GBR Marine Park came into effect; these include:

- rapidly changing patterns of use;
- technological change;
- social-economic changes;
- political changes;
- and most importantly, recognizing marine ecosystems are dynamic natural systems subject to a myriad of environmental changes.

Any successful management regime must be adaptable and be able to incorporate such changes as new information becomes available (for example, connectivity as discussed in McCook *et al.*, 2008) or as circumstances change. Irrespective of whether a change in marine management results from new data, 'in-the-field' experience, or as a result of external circumstances, all management practices must be periodically reviewed and updated where appropriate.

A recent legislative requirement now requires a comprehensive report on the status of and outlook for the GBR every five years. The first GBR Outlook Report was released in 2009, providing a clear and transparent assessment of the values and emerging risks facing the GBR, as well as an assessment of the effectiveness of management. The format is repeatable, impartial, forward-looking and presents the findings in a very readable format (Dobbs *et al.*, 2011); the second GBR Outlook Report was released in August 2014 (GBRMPA, 2014).

Given all the pressures facing the GBR, what is its likely future?

The GBR remains one of the world's best managed coral reef ecosystems; however while it is likely to survive better under the pressure of accumulating risks than many other coral reefs, the current long-term outlook for the GBR is poor. The most recent Outlook Report (GBRMPA, 2014) concluded:

> Even with the recent management initiatives to reduce threats and improve resilience, the overall outlook for the Great Barrier Reef is poor, has worsened since 2009 and is expected to further deteriorate in the future. Greater reductions of threats at all levels, Reef-wide, regional and local, are required to prevent the projected declines in the Great Barrier Reef and to improve its capacity to recover.

The overall health of the GBR has declined significantly since European settlement and there is increasing evidence that its resilience is being seriously eroded. The primary pressures facing the GBR today are (GBRMPA, 2014):

- Climate change – this is the most serious threat facing the GBR and is likely to have far-reaching consequences for the future. Predictions of climate change impacts include continuing sea level and sea temperature rises, and increased acidification of the ocean. More severe extreme weather including cyclones is also predicted.
- Declining water quality due to catchment runoff – agricultural practices in the GBR catchment are slowly improving with reduced nutrient and sediment loads entering the GBR through run-off. However, there is likely to be a significant lag time before measurable water quality improvements are achieved in the GBR.
- Loss of coastal habitats due to development – clearing and modifying coastal habitats that support the GBR are likely to continue to present a very high risk, especially to inshore biodiversity; e.g. through the loss of connectivity between coastal and marine environments. Coastal development, and particularly port operations and further port developments, are likely to have impacts, especially if large amounts of capital and maintenance dredging are required.
- Outbreaks of crown-of-thorns starfish are likely to continue over forthcoming decades, contributing further to coral mortality.

- A small number of impacts from some fishing activities – while there have been some improvements in the management of fishing in the GBR, unsustainable fishing practices continue across all fisheries (some more so than others), causing impacts on target species and on other species of conservation concern.

The comprehensive GBR Strategic Assessment (GBRMPA, 2013) also concluded that without additional management intervention, there is a high risk of further declines in the condition of biodiversity and heritage values and the community benefits they support.

However, in the face of increasing pressures, the management aspects of the GBR that are the most effective are:

- a sound governance/legislative framework, including complementary State/Federal legislation;
- ecosystem-level management, including management influence over a wider context than just the federal marine park;
- integrated management across relevant Federal and State agencies;
- widespread consensus that the GBR is important, with many industries that depend upon its health recognizing that it is worth conserving; and
- specific research and monitoring programmes providing appropriate information for more effective management (Day and Dobbs, 2013).

Conclusion

Today, a comprehensive suite of ecosystem-based management and MSP arrangements help to achieve positive environmental outcomes for the GBR. Guided by the principle of balancing conservation and sustainable use, the GBRMPA has developed a multiple-use management regime that aims to allow reasonable use while protecting the health of the Marine Park and the GBR World Heritage Area for future generations.

The multiple-use zoning network provides high levels of protection in no-take zones and very small no-go zones for one-third (117,000 km^2) of the Marine Park. The design of these zones maximizes the protection of biodiversity while minimizing the impacts on all other users, including fishers. The zoning network governs all human activities, providing high levels of protection for specific areas, while still allowing other uses.

A variety of other MSP tools are also applied as additional layers to complement the underlying Zoning Plan; these include statutory Plans of Management in key areas, site plans, special management areas and other spatial provisions (e.g. Defence Training Areas, shipping areas, agreements with Traditional Owners).

MSP is a fundamental tool which helps to achieve effective marine conservation in the GBR. However MSP is only part of the multi-layered EBM approach in both the marine and terrestrial realms which collectively protect and manage the GBR; this approach, including the zoning network representative of all known biodiversity in the GBR, is now recognized as one of the most comprehensive approaches in the systematic protection of marine biodiversity and marine conservation in recent decades. Widespread recognition of the planning process used by GBRMPA for its 2003 Zoning Plan has led to numerous international, national and local awards.

Despite the complexities outlined in this chapter, the integrated governance and management model that has been functioning over the past 40 years across the GBR has proven to be effective and until recently was widely regarded as 'best practice' by most marine and coastal managers influencing many other marine conservation efforts around the world.

It is important to recognize, however, that what has worked in the GBR may not necessarily work elsewhere and may need to be modified in other marine situations (see Day, 2011, pp. 62–63). For example, the introduction of coordinate-based zone boundaries that has proven effective in the GBR is not likely to be appropriate in some developing countries.

Other MPAs around the world have different management models and objectives. It is therefore important to consider the specific political, economic, social, and managerial context of the GBR when translating the lessons from the GBR to other areas.

Note

1 Thanks to Dr Daud Hassan (UWS), Dr Richard Kenchington (UOW), Prof. Helene Marsh (JCU) and Adrian Arias (JCU) for comments on drafts of this chapter and for many useful insights. Figure 6.1 was derived after discussions with members of the National Center for Ecological Analysis and Synthesis (NCEAS) working group on Ocean Ecosystem-based Management.

References

Alvarez-Romero, J.G., Pressey, R., Ban, N.C., Vance-Borland, K., Willer, C., Klein, C.J. and Gaines, S.D. (2011) 'Integrated Land-Sea Conservation Planning: the Missing links', *Annual Review of Ecology, Evolution and Systematics*, 42, pp. 381–409.

Arkema, K.K., Abramson, S.C. and Dewsbury, B.M. (2006) 'Marine ecosystem-based management: from characterization to implementation', *Frontiers in Ecology and the Environment*, 4(10), pp. 525–532.

Australian Government (2015) Great Barrier Reef Marine Park Act (1975). Available at: http://www.comlaw.gov.au/Details/C2015C00168 (accessed 21 April 2015)

Brodie, J., Waterhouse, J. (2012) 'A critical review of environmental management of the "not so Great" Barrier Reef' *Estuarine, Coastal and Shelf Science* [DOI: 0.1016/j.ecss.2012.03.012].

Day, J.C. (2002a) 'Zoning: Lessons from the Great Barrier Reef Marine Park', *Ocean and Coastal Management*, 45, pp. 139–56.

Day, J.C. (2002b) 'Marine Park Management and Monitoring: Lessons for Adaptive Management from the Great Barrier Reef' in Soren Bondrup-Nielsen, Neil Munro,

Gordon Nelson, J.H. Martin Willison, Tom Herman and Paul Eagles (eds) *Managing Protected Areas in a Changing World* (Proc. 4th Int. Conf. Science & Management of Protected Areas, May 2000), Waterloo, Wolfville, Canada.

Day, J.C. (2008) 'The need and practice of monitoring, evaluating and adapting marine planning and management: lessons from the Great Barrier Reef', *Marine Policy* 32, pp. 823–31.

Day, J.C. (2011) 'Protecting Australia's Great Barrier Reef', *Solutions* 2(1), pp. 56–66. Available: http://www.thesolutionsjournal.com/node/846 (accessed 29 September 2014).

Day, J.C. and Dobbs, K. (2013) 'Effective governance of a large and complex cross-jurisdictional marine protected area: Australia's Great Barrier Reef', *Marine Policy*, 41, pp. 14–24.

Day, J.C., Fernandes, L., Lewis, A. and Innes, J, (2004) 'RAP: An Ecosystem Level Approach to Biodiversity Protection Planning', *Proc. ITMEMS*: Manila, Philippines, March 2003.

Day. J. C., Dudley, N., Hockings, M., Holmes, G., Laffoley, D., Stolton, S. and Wells, S. (2012) 'Guidelines for applying the IUCN Protected Area Management Categories to Marine Protected Areas', Gland, Switzerland: IUCN. 36 pp.

Deloitte Access Economics (2013) *Economic contribution of the Great Barrier Reef 2011–12*, prepared for the Great Barrier Reef Marine Park Authority, Townsville, Australia, Table 7.1 on p. 31: http://www.gbrmpa.gov.au/__data/assets/pdf_file/0006/66417/Economic-contribution-of-the-Great-Barrier-Reef-2013.pdf

Dobbs, K., Day, J.C., Skeat, H., Baldwin, J., Malloy, F., McCook, L., *et al.* (2011) 'Developing a long-term outlook for the Great Barrier Reef, Australia: A framework for adaptive management reporting underpinning an ecosystem-based management approach', *Marine Policy* 35 (2), pp. 233–40 [DOI: 10.1016/j.marpol.2010.10.007].

Ehler, C. and Douvere, F. (2007) *Visions for a Sea Change: Report of the First International Workshop on Marine Spatial Planning. Intergovernmental Oceanographic Commission and Man and the Biosphere Programme.* IOC Manual and Guides, n. 48, IOCAM Dossier, n. 4, Paris, UNESCO.

Fernandes, L., Day, J.C., Lewis, A., *et al.* (2005). 'Establishing Representative No-Take Areas in the Great Barrier Reef: Large-Scale Implementation of Theory on Marine Protected Areas', *Conservation Biology*, 19 (6), pp. 1733–44.

Fernandes, L., Day, J.C., Kerrigan, B., Breen, D., De'ath, G., *et al.* (2009) 'A process to design a network of marine no-take areas: Lessons from the Great Barrier Reef', *Ocean & Coastal Management*, 52, pp. 439–47 [DOI 10.1016/j.ocecoaman.2009.06.004].

GBRMPA (nd) Spreadsheet of Zoning Coordinates (Excel spreadsheet). Available at: http://www.gbrmpa.gov.au/__data/assets/excel_doc/0016/8503/GBRMP_coords_GDA94.xls (accessed 19 December 2014).

GBRMPA (2012) *Informing the Outlook for Great Barrier Reef Coastal Ecosystems*, Great Barrier Reef Marine Park Authority, Townsville, Commonwealth of Australia

GBRMPA (2013) *Strategic Assessment Report – Draft for Public Comment*, Great Barrier Reef Marine Park Authority, Townsville, Commonwealth of Australia.

GBRMPA (2014) *Great Barrier Reef Outlook Report 2014*, Great Barrier Reef Marine Park Authority, Townsville, Commonwealth of Australia.

Harrison, H.B., Williamson, D.H., Evans, R.D., Almany, G.R., Thorrold, S.R., Russ, G.R., Feldheim, K.A., Van Herwerden, L., Planes, S., Srinivasan, M., Berumen, M.L. and Jones, G.P. (2012) 'Larval export from marine reserves and the recruitment benefit for fish and fisheries', *Current Biology*, 22(11), pp. 1023–28.

IUCN (1981) *World Heritage Nomination – Technical Review, Great Barrier Reef.* International Union for Conservation of Nature and Natural Resources, July 1981. Available: *http://whc.unesco.org/archive/advisory_body_evaluation/154.pdf* (accessed 19 December 2014).

Kenchington, R.A. and Day, J.C. (2011) 'Zoning, a fundamental cornerstone of effective Marine Spatial Planning: lessons learnt from the Great Barrier Reef, Australia', *J. Coastal Conservation*, 15 (2), pp. 271–8. [DOI: 10.1007/s11852-011-0147-2].

Lewis, A., Day, J.C., Fernandes, F., Lowe, D. and Slegers, S. (2007) 'Analytical tools – what they can, and cannot do, when developing MPA networks', pp. 524–6, in J.C. Day, J. Senior, S. Monk and W. Neal (eds), *Proceedings of First International Marine Protected Areas Congress*, October 2005 (IMPAC1 2005), Geelong, Victoria, Australia.

McCook, L.J., Almany, G.R., Berumen, M.L., Day, J.C., Green, A.L., Jones, G.P., *et al.* (2008) 'Management under uncertainty: guide-lines for incorporating connectivity into the protection of coral reefs', *Coral Reefs*, [DOI 10.1007/s00338-008-0463-7].

Merrie, A. and Olsson, P. (2014) 'An innovation and agency perspective on the emergence and spread of Marine Spatial Planning', *Marine Policy*, 44, pp. 366–74.

Olsson, P., Folke, C. and Hughes, T.P. (2008) 'Navigating the transition to ecosystem-based management of the Great Barrier Reef, Australia', *PNAS* 105(28), pp. 9489–94 [DOI: 10.1073/pnas.0706905105].

Pressey, R., Mills, M., Weeks, R. and Day, J.C. (2013) 'The plan of the day: Managing the dynamic transition from regional conservation designs to local conservation actions', *Biological Conservation*, 166, pp. 155–69.

Queensland State Archives (1974) *Archives Series ID 20162*, Reports of the Royal Commission Into Exploratory and Production Drilling for Petroleum in the Area of the Great Barrier Reef.

Ruckelshaus, M., Klinger, T., Knowlton, N. and DeMaster, D.P. (2008) 'Marine ecosystem-based management in practice: scientific and governance challenges', *BioScience*, 58(1), pp. 53–63.

Russ, G.R., Cheal, A.J., Dolman, A.M., Emslie, M.J., Evans, R.D., Miller, I., Sweatman, H. and Williamson, D.H. (2008) 'Rapid increase in fish numbers follows creation of world's largest marine reserve network', *Current Biology*, 18(12), R514–R515. [DOI: 10.1016/j.cub.2008.04.016].

Chapter 7

Marine spatial planning in the Baltic Sea

Hermanni Backer

Introduction

This chapter is dedicated to the marine spatial planning (MSP) cooperation in the northern European Baltic Sea. It will briefly describe the geographic setting, followed by an overview of the existing regionally specific international laws, the current status of MSP and related international cooperation as well as reflecting on selected regional topics. The chapter will end with general remarks on transboundary MSP and international law in the Baltic Sea region.

The Baltic Sea

The Baltic Sea is a nearly enclosed marginal sea of the Atlantic Ocean. The sea is currently bordered by (the EU members) Denmark, Estonia, Finland, Germany, Latvia, Lithuania, Poland and Sweden as well as the Russian Federation. A Russian enclave, Kaliningrad, is sandwiched between Poland and Lithuania in the south-eastern corner of the sea (Figure 7.1).

The Baltic Sea covers 392,978 km^2, roughly the surface area of Japan or twice the combined surface of the Great Lakes of North America, while its catchment area, or extent of land from which rivers and pollution flow to the sea, is four times that size (Leppäranta and Myrberg, 2009). The catchment extends also to countries without coastline in the Baltic Sea, including clockwise from the east, Belarus, Ukraine, Slovakia, Czech Republic and Norway (Figure 7.1).

The Baltic Sea coasts, at least in the northern parts, are relatively sparsely inhabited. Recent estimates are not available but based on the relatively stable situation during the last two decades (Hannerz and Destouni, 2006; Sweitzer *et al.*, 1996), around 85 million people live in the catchment area. Around 15 million (18 per cent) live closer than 10 km from the coastline (Sweitzer *et al.*, 1996). The five largest coastal cities are currently St Petersburg (5 million), Copenhagen, Stockholm, Riga and Helsinki (0.6 million) (City of Helsinki, 2015).

The seabed consists of a series of distinct basins, a few hundred meters deep, with shallower areas between. Some of these basins, such as the Gulf of Riga or the Bothnian Sea and Bay of Bothnia (together forming the Gulf of Bothnia) create ecological sub-systems within the Baltic Sea, relevant also for MSP (Figure 7.1).

Figure 7.1 Overview map of the Baltic Sea with its drainage/catchment area, including the two largest rivers, nearby sea areas and the location of five largest cities and remaining capitals indicated. K.-G. = Kattegat, G.o.R. = Gulf of Riga. The Russian territory between Poland and Lithuania is Kaliningrad, up to the Second World War known as Königsberg.

Regional international law relevant for MSP

As elsewhere in the world, MSP in the Baltic Sea is not governed by a single targeted regional instrument under international law. Instead, planning at sea is dependent on, and takes place within, a complex set of marine and maritime rights and obligations under UNCLOS and other relevant international law (e.g. Maes, 2008).

Due to the overarching aims of MSP, a large number of different international legal instruments of specific regional nature are involved, ranging from bilateral border agreements to special regional measures under MARPOL and SOLAS conventions of the International Maritime Organization (IMO), regional fisheries agreements and the 1992 Helsinki Convention, the regional treaty on the marine environment. This section aims to highlight some of these regional instruments in the Baltic Sea, with a particular focus on spatial regulation.

Maritime borders and border treaties

As the distance between the opposing coasts is commonly less than 100 nautical miles, the Baltic Sea surface consists, in terms of jurisdiction, of national waters and adjacent exclusive economic zones (EEZ) with no natural high seas in between (Figure 7.2, page 140).

Maritime borders in the region were relatively well settled in the early 1990s (Franckx, 2012); however, the dissolution of the Soviet Union during the first years of the 1990s resulted in the re-unification of East and West Germany and the re-emergence of the independent States of Estonia, Latvia and Lithuania. As a result, unsettled maritime border sections were re-created particularly along the south-eastern and eastern coasts.

Most of these sea borders and tri-junction points have since been confirmed or established, including the Estonia–Latvia border (Anon., 1996) and the Lithuania-Russia border (in force 2003). Two remaining unsettled borders have been negotiated by diplomatic means but not actually ratified, namely the agreement between Latvia and Lithuania (Anon., 1999a) as well as that between Estonia and Russia (Anon., 2014a). A remaining unsettled border section is the one between Denmark and Poland, south and south-east of the islands of Bornholm.

Helsinki Convention (1974, revised 1992)

Of the existing regional treaty law in force in the Baltic Sea, the Helsinki Convention (HELCOM, 1992, 1974) has perhaps the most direct relevance to MSP.

Due to the enclosed nature of the sea, the environmental degradation from land- and sea-based sources has advanced rapidly in the Baltic Sea since the 1950s (Elmgren, 1989, 2001). As a result of considerable public attention, and a period of favourable Cold War diplomatic climate, the Convention on the Protection of the Marine Environment of the Baltic Sea Area (known as the Helsinki Convention) was adopted by the seven (at the time) coastal countries in 1974 (HELCOM, 1974). The Helsinki Convention provided also for the establishment of the Helsinki Commission (HELCOM) as an international legal entity.

The original area to be protected and restored by the Helsinki Convention and HELCOM did not include internal waters landward of the baseline of the Contracting Parties,[1] mainly due to security concerns by the Soviet Union

(Fitzmaurice, 1996). Towards the Atlantic, the application area was defined as south of the Skaw parallel in the Skagerrak at 57° 44.43'N. In 1992, the area to be protected was enlarged to include internal waters of the Baltic Sea countries. This was done as part of a new, updated Convention ratified by the current nine coastal states and also the European Union.

The current 1992 Helsinki Convention covers a wide range of MSP-related issues within its remit, including shipping (art. 8, 10 and 11 on dumping), pleasure craft (art. 9), response to accidental pollution (art. 13 and 14), Environmental Impact Assessment (EIA) of projects (art. 7), exploitation of sea-bed resources (art. 12), nature conservation (art. 15) and information to the public (art. 17 and 18). As an example, in Article 15 the parties agree to take 'all appropriate measures to "conserve natural habitats and biological diversity", "protect ecological processes"' and, perhaps most importantly in the MSP context, 'to ensure the sustainable use of natural resources'.[2]

The wide remit of the 1992 Helsinki Convention, especially Article 15, was at the time highlighted (Birnie, 1996, pp. 355–6) as an indication of the global push towards a more holistic ecological approach to marine management by bringing related fisheries and wildlife conventions into closer relationship with marine pollution prevention conventions. This idea had emerged from the 1992 United Nations Conference on Environment and Development (UNCED) and developed within the United Nations Food and Agricultural Organization (FAO) and the Environmental Programme (UNEP) (Birnie, 1996, pp. 355–6).

Based on the revised 1992 Helsinki Convention including the new Article 15, as well as the earlier HELCOM experience, both with biodiversity protection and maritime traffic measures, the coastal countries established a process of area-based protection in the 1990s. Examples include recommendations on protecting coastal strip (HELCOM, 1994a), establishing a network of Baltic Sea protected areas (HELCOM, 1994b) and protection of biotopes (HELCOM, 2000), including a list of threatened biotopes.

By the turn of the millennium this 'spatial turn' had been further fertilized with ideas of overarching management approaches. This is exemplified by documents like the HELCOM Recommendation 24/10 of 2003 on 'Implementation of integrated marine and coastal management of human activities in the Baltic Sea area' (HELCOM, 2003). It calls the signatories to organize and implement an 'offshore management process' that brings together private and public stakeholders, referred to as MSP today. Since 2003 these HELCOM developments were part of an ongoing process to implement ecosystem-based management of human activities (HELCOM and OSPAR, 2003), as well as the EU Marine Strategy Framework Directive (EU, 2008) within the Baltic Sea region (Backer *et al.*, 2010).

Regional dimensions of international shipping regulations

Spatial regulation of shipping in the Baltic Sea took a leap forward in the 1960 revision of the Safety of Life at Sea (SOLAS) Convention (SOLAS, 1960), which explicitly referred to ships' routeing measures for safety of navigation, a topic later expanded in the SOLAS revision of 1974.

In the Baltic Sea, these developments were followed closely and a number of routeing measures to prevent accidents in the Gulf of Finland and Northern Baltic Proper were adopted by the Inter-Governmental Maritime Consultative Organization (IMCO) (present International Maritime Organization, IMO) in 1968 (IMCO, 1968), only a year after the world's first traffic separation scheme in Dover Straits.

Measures in the Baltic Sea adopted in 1968 include 'Off Kallbadagrund Lighthouse', 'Off Hogland (Gogland) Island', 'Off Porkkala Lighthouse', 'Off Hankoniemi Peninsula', 'Off Kopu Peninsula', 'Off Gotland Island' and 'Off Öland Island' (IMCO, 1968). Such measures were initially voluntary but were later made mandatory (IMCO, 1971) and defined in greater detail (IMCO, 1973a). During the 1980s, IMO decisions also allowed routeing measures based on environmental justifications.

The Baltic Sea is also a special area of International Convention for the Prevention of Pollution from Ships (MARPOL) (IMO, 1973b) Annexes I (oil), IV (sewage from passenger ships), V (garbage) and VI (airborne emissions of SOx). Excluding Russian Federation waters, the Baltic has been designated by IMO as a particularly sensitive sea area (PSSA) in 2005 (IMO, 2005), a status without direct effects but which has been used to push for new shipping measures in the region.

Even if many of the decisions regarding Baltic Sea shipping are taken within IMO, the work on drafting proposals and implementing measures on clean and safe shipping, as well as response to pollution incidents, takes place regionally mainly within the maritime-related working groups of HELCOM, in place since the Interim Commission of 1970s (Anon., 1975, pp. 4–5).

Fisheries agreements and cooperation

Spatial regulation of fishing in the Baltic Sea has been less widespread until recently. One early example of international spatial fishing regulation dates back to 1932 in the narrow Öresund between Denmark and Sweden where bans on towed fishing gear, such as trawls, were imposed due to heavy traffic (Anon., 1932; Svedäng, 2010).

The regional fisheries commission, International Baltic Sea Fisheries Commission (IBSFC), established with the 1973 Gdansk Convention (Anon., 1973) was discontinued on 31 December 2005. Even if IBSFC mainly set catch quotas it also enabled area-based fisheries closures. More recently, the EU multi-annual plan for the cod stocks in the Baltic Sea has closed off larger areas of importance for cod spawning in the southern Baltic Sea seasonally (EU, 2007a).

Today the overall regional fisheries management regime in the Baltic Sea, including spatial measures, is somewhat unique, as the European Union (EU) member countries have, according to the EU treaty, delegated powers in fisheries matters to the EU. Regional intergovernmental cooperation and negotiations on fisheries takes place currently within no less than five main bodies.

In 2009, the EU and the Russian Federation concluded a new agreement on fisheries and living marine resources of the Baltic Sea (Anon., 2009a), establishing the Joint Baltic Sea Fisheries Committee, a bilateral fisheries body, in order to fill the gap left by the closure of the IBSFC in 2005. Within the EU system, BALTFISH, a regional cooperation body established in 2013 (Anon., 2013), makes regional proposals on fisheries measures to be considered and adopted by the decision-making body consisting of the EU Council of fisheries ministries.

Scientific advice on the status of fisheries stocks is provided by the International Council for the Exploration of the Seas (ICES) (Anon., 1964). Further, the HELCOM group on ecosystem-based sustainable fisheries, originally established in 2008, involves environmental and fisheries authorities of all Baltic Sea states and the EU as well as interest groups for fisheries–environment negotiations. Another EU body, the Baltic Sea Regional Advisory Council (BSRAC) provides stakeholder advice on management of fisheries in the Baltic Sea.

1991 UNECE convention on transboundary EIA and 2003 Protocol on SEA

In an effort to ensure the sustainability of infrastructure developments the United Nations Economic Commission for Europe (UNECE) Convention on Environmental Impact Assessment in a Transboundary Context (UNECE, 1991), or the Espoo Convention, and its SEA protocol (Anon., 2003) are important MSP-related agreements in the region. Even if not covering the Russian Federation, the Baltic Sea contracting parties have discussed maritime and land-based projects as well as MSP itself within the main bodies but also within regional Baltic Sea cooperation seminars (UNECE, 2012). It should also be noted that even if the Helsinki Convention has an article on EIA (art. 7) the more specific provisions of 1991 UNECE Convention are commonly used instead.

The Great Belt Fixed Link Bridge over the Great Belt in Denmark, opened in 1997, is one of the major maritime construction projects of transboundary importance since the Kiel channel (Kaiser Wilhelm Kanal) was opened in 1895[3] (Boczek, 1996). The bridge was later followed by the Öresund link (opened 2010), the St Petersbug Flood Prevention Facility Complex (opened 2011) and the Nordstream gas pipeline between Russia and northern Germany (opened 2011). The construction of another major project, the Fehmarn Belt Fixed Link tunnel, originally planned as a bridge, is expected to start in 2021.

Wind power is another rapidly emerging field of infrastructure developments in the region. According to a regional study from 2012, around 20 gigawatts (GW) of wind power is planned or already constructed in the Baltic Sea region. Poland and Finland had 760 megawatts of consented projects, while Sweden, Germany and Denmark have operational offshore wind farms, with more planned (BASREC, 2012a). The same study estimated that 40 GW of offshore wind capacity is possible in the Baltic Sea, when taking into account estimates on known environmental and other constraints (BASREC, 2012b).

As 40 GW of wind power has been estimated to occupy 6,700 km^2 (Anon., 2014b, p. 25), more than twice the surface area of Gotland Island, it is no surprise that wind power development, potential or actual, is one of the important drivers of MSP in the region.

Major infrastructure developments have also raised international tensions. As an example, Finland raised a case against Denmark in the International Court of Justice on the grounds that Finnish-built mobile offshore drilling units would not be able to pass beneath the planned Great Belt bridge (ICJ, 1991). Also the Nordstream gas pipeline across the Baltic raised some opposition from some coastal countries but was difficult to argue against as it was based on rights to EEZ seabed, as conferred by art. 79 of the United Nations Convention on the Law of the Sea (UNCLOS).

2014 MSP Directive of the European Union

Even if not traditional international law, the MSP Directive of the European Union (EU, 2014) is currently the strongest transnational legal instrument in the field of marine planning applicable to the EU Member States in the region. As all the coastal countries except the Russian Federation are, since 2003, members of the European Union (EU), the Directive will be a major catalyst for implementing planning in the Baltic Sea region during the coming five years. The Directive requires the EU Member States in the Baltic and elsewhere to have MSP legislation in place by 2016 (art. 15) and to establish maritime spatial plans at the latest by 2021 (art. 4, 15) ultimately in order to promote sustainable growth of the European maritime economy (art. 1).

The EU MSP Directive was initiated by the EU maritime policy (EU, 2007b) but is also partly a descendant of earlier spatial planning cooperation in the EU context such as the European Spatial Development Perspective (ESDP) (Anon., 1999b), Territorial Agenda (Anon., 2007) and their concepts including 'territorial cohesion' (Faludi, 2007).

Overview of MSP in the Baltic Sea region

The focus of this section will be on describing the current status of national planning at sea and various forms of regional cooperation on MSP in the Baltic Sea region.

National MSP activities

During the last two decades the coastal countries of the northern European Baltic Sea region have been active in MSP, both in terms of national work as well as transboundary cooperation (Backer, 2011; Zaucha, 2014, pp. 5–46). Concrete developments towards comprehensive planning of sea space in the region, eventually to be called MSP, started within research projects after the turn of the millennium (Zaucha, 2014, p. 11). As elsewhere, planning at sea has been catalysed by an interest in the development of offshore wind power as well as hopes for a more efficient implementation of environmental policies and sustainable development (Nolte, 2010).

The first explicit MSP plans in the region were the ones for the German Territorial Seas (TS) in the Federal State of Mecklenburg-Vorpommern (2005) followed by the Federal State of Schleswig Holstein (2010) as well as for the Exclusive Economic Zone (EEZ) by the German Federal Government (Anon., 2009b), the first EEZ plan in force in Europe. Also many other coastal countries have by now adopted legislation and made clear decisions to develop plans for their sea areas (Figure 7.2) (HELCOM-VASAB MSP WG, 2014a; Zaucha, 2014). Examples include Sweden, where legislation was adopted in 2014 with a designated authority[4] established in 2011, tasked to develop MSP plans for both TS and EEZ. Estonia, Latvia, Lithuania and Poland have taken steps to implement planning of their sea areas. In the remaining countries Denmark, Finland and Russia, MSP is also under development, even if somewhat more in a preparatory phase (HELCOM-VASAB MSP WG, 2014a; Zaucha, 2014).

In addition to national MSP developments, the transboundary or international dimensions of planning at sea have received considerable attention in the region. Regular intergovernmental cooperation on MSP, involving the competent national ministries and authorities, has been in place since 2010 within a dedicated regional working group on MSP called the HELCOM-VASAB MSP WG. Further, exploratory joint transboundary planning or MSP, extending across the sea areas of two or more countries, has been explored within cooperation projects in three sub-areas of the Baltic Sea (Figure 7.2).

HELCOM-VASAB MSP working group

The break-up of the Soviet Union and the end of the Cold War in the 1990s opened up the region for new initiatives on cooperation, also within spatial planning on land. One of the initiatives emerging from this period is 'Visions and Strategies in the Baltic Sea' (VASAB), a regional cooperation forum of spatial planning ministries established 1992 in Karlskrona, Sweden (Vasab, 1992). As was typical of the organizations established during that period, support in the transition from socialist to democratic and market economy framework was one of the original tasks of VASAB (Vasab, 1992).

The VASAB process around MSP was initiated during a meeting in 2001 of the region's spatial planning ministers, where the outcome called for extending spatial planning into the offshore direction (Zaucha, 2014). As a result of projects and other work, a set of recommendations on MSP was endorsed by the next meeting of VASAB ministers in 2005 and spatial planning at sea was raised to being one of the organization's priorities (Zaucha, 2014). These developments

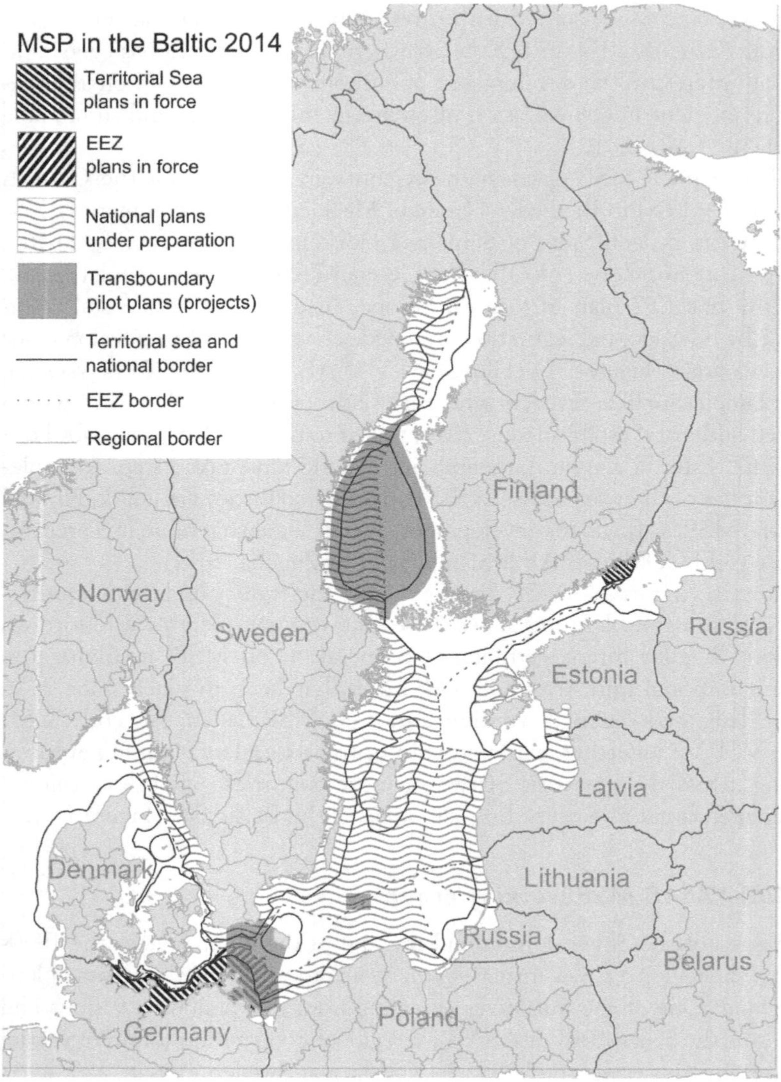

Figure 7.2 Status of Maritime Spatial Planning in the Baltic Sea region in December 2014. Drawn based on the HELCOM-VASAB MSP WG (2014a) and Zaucha (2014, p. 26). Please note that regional and municipal land use plans in Finland and Sweden cover in theory the TS adjacent to the planning area, but in Finland the regional phase plan of Kymenlaakso (in force November 2014), included for the first time explicit attention to the entire marine area of the region. Depicted maritime borders are from HELCOM GIS (www.helcom.fi). Please note that some of the EEZ and TS borders depicted have been agreed but not actually ratified, including those between Latvia and Lithuania and Estonia and Russia.

took place in parallel with the work to implement a holistic ecosystem-based approach and MSP within HELCOM.

In 2010, the two organizations HELCOM and VASAB established a joint initiative, the HELCOM-VASAB MSP working group, which remains the key intergovernmental forum for transboundary MSP dialogue and developments in the region (Backer, 2011; Zaucha, 2014). Within the group, the competent national authorities of the coastal countries and the EU have negotiated and adopted a set of joint regional principles on MSP (HELCOM&VASAB, 2010), partially fulfilling a related regional commitment (HELCOM, 2007). The group has also discussed a number of important topics including legal aspects and MSP-related data needs as well as the ecosystem approach in the MSP context.

The group has additionally drafted a regional road map to MSP implementation by 2021, which was adopted in 2013 on a political level by the countries and the EU both within VASAB and HELCOM (HELCOM&VASAB, 2013). Key milestones of the roadmap include, besides planning itself, a set of three regional guidelines on how to implement the ecosystem approach, transboundary consultations as well as public and stakeholder participation in MSP processes (Table 7.1).

Another important dimension for the regional group is the EU MSP Directive adopted in 2014 (EU, 2014). Since the establishment of the group it has been a platform for the regional exchange of views on MSP during the policy process and negotiations leading to the Directive (2009–2014). The group also enables regional dialogue called for by the Directive (art. 11 and 12), if so decided by the coastal countries and the EU.

The joint MSP group has been designated as the action leader for the EU Strategy in the Baltic Sea Region (EU SBSR) (EU, 2009), an overall effort to strengthen the European dimension of regional work. In this latter role, the group provides, for example, recommendations for funding of MSP relevant EU projects in the region.

Nordic cooperation

For Denmark, Finland and Sweden, an expert group and a wider network on MSP, established in 2010 under the Nordic cooperation based on the 1962 Helsinki Treaty (Anon., 1962), has provided another regional forum to develop views on MSP. Even if the cooperation covers only a part of the Baltic and involves also Nordic countries in the north-east Atlantic,[5] it is an important reference framework for the three Baltic Sea members.

On the landward planning field such Nordic cooperation has a long pedigree. Nordplan (The Nordic Institute for Studies in Urban and Regional Planning), a joint institution aiming at exchanging and developing best practices in spatial (urban and regional) planning between Nordic countries, was established back in 1968. This centre for Nordic cooperation on spatial planning was active until 1997 when it was replaced by Nordregio, an institution more focused on research than education or policy development.

Table 7.1 Regional Baltic MSP Roadmap 2013–2020 (summary timetable) (HELCOM& VASAB, 2013).

Tasks of the Regional Baltic MSP Roadmap 2013–2020	*Deadline*
Share basic, relevant and available MSP-related information utilizing existing processes.	As soon as possible.
Promote the creation and sharing of MSP relevant Baltic Sea regional datasets.	As soon as possible.
Promote the education and professional development of MSP planners.	As soon as possible.
Initiate and draw lessons from practical sub-regional experiences of coherent MSP.	As soon as possible.
Identification of competent national MSP contacts (focal points).	2013
Baltic Sea regional *Guidelines on the application of Ecosystem Approach in transnationally coherent MSP* adopted.	2015
Baltic Sea regional *Guidelines on transboundary consultations and cooperation in the field of MSP* adopted.	2015
Baltic Sea regional *Guidelines on public participation for MSP with transboundary dimensions* adopted.	2015
Prepare a future-oriented report on marine and maritime activities and developments of Baltic Sea regional importance.	2015.
Assessment on the implementation of this Roadmap.	2016, 2018 and 2020
National frameworks for coherent MSP in place.	2017
Apply Baltic Sea regional *Guidelines on the application of Ecosystem Approach in transnationally coherent* MSP.	2018
Apply Baltic Sea regional *Guidelines on transboundary consultations and cooperation in the field of MSP.*	2018
Apply Baltic Sea regional *Guidelines on public participation for MSP with transboundary dimensions.*	2018
Maritime spatial plans throughout the Baltic Sea Region which are coherent across borders and apply the ecosystem approach.	2020

Other regional cooperation

In addition to the national, EU, Nordic and HELCOM-VASAB MSP work, there is also much work on MSP in the Baltic Sea region, which takes place without an explicit basis in national, international or European law. Particularly, after the break-up of the Soviet Union in the early 1990s, a large number of cooperation structures without a legal base have been established, illustrating the lively cooperation typical of the region.

Non-treaty regional cooperation includes, on the ministerial or other national political level, VASAB but also for example the Council of the Baltic Sea States (CBSS), involving mainly foreign ministries and the Baltic Sea Parliamentary Conference (BSPC), involving members of national parliaments. Similar cooperation of sub-national actors includes the Union of Baltic Sea Cities (UBC) involving cities as well as the Baltic Sea States Sub-regional Cooperation (BSSSC) and the Conference of Peripheral Maritime Regions Baltic Sea Commission (CPMR-BSC) both involving sub-national ('regional') actors.

Expert cooperation is also widespread in the Baltic Sea and includes the International Council for the Exploration of the Seas (ICES) involving marine scientists from the Baltic and North-East Atlantic, the Baltic Sea Hydrographic Commission (BSHC) of the International Hydrographic Organisation (IHO) involving hydrographic offices, and the Baltic Ordnance Survey Board (BOSB) involving navy mine clearance experts. In addition to such public sector cooperation, various other maritime industries and NGOs have their own cooperation structures and the implementation of various time-bound MSP projects create ephemeral regional groupings.

Transboundary MSP case studies

Besides international dialogue and policy developments, the countries in the region have also carried out a number of joint projects to concretely test MSP (Backer, 2011; Zaucha, 2014). Such initiatives have provided a means to explore MSP prior to legally binding national planning activities are initiated, as called for by the EU MSP Directive (EU, 2014) or national processes (Zaucha, 2014, pp. 28–46).

One example of the three transboundary initiatives in the region (Figure 7.2), the Plan Bothnia project (Backer and Frias, 2012) was completed in 2012. It was an exploratory pilot MSP initiative in the Bothnian Sea region, specifically the northern part of the Baltic Sea (Figure 7.1). With the involvement of the responsible planning ministries in Finland and Sweden, planners, experts and stakeholders of the project gathered background information, future plans and scenarios for different maritime activities including traffic (e.g. Pekkarinen and Repka, 2014) and wind power, and turned such material into MSP plan drafts. The project ended with a pilot plan (Figure 7.3) covering both Finland and Sweden, as a source of inspiration for more binding national developments (Backer and Frias, 2012).

Plan Bothnia, and the two similar transboundary project plans for MSP completed in the Baltic Sea (the Middle Bank and Pomeranian Bay/Arkona Basin) finalised with pilot plans (Zaucha, 2014). However, perhaps more importantly, these projects have enabled the involved institutions and countries to start thinking of issues, processes and possible other forms of concrete transboundary MSP in region, but also beyond.

One lesson learned from the Plan Bothnia project is that the relatively short history of international collaboration on MSP as well as the exotic nature of maritime activities for most traditional land use planners, but perhaps also for politicians and general public involved in planning decisions, puts special requirements to new innovations in international law, practical planning techniques and communication/visualisation efforts (Backer and Frias, 2012).

Of the two countries involved in the Plan Bothnia initiative, Sweden has since adopted national legislation in 2014 and is drafting three national MSP plans for

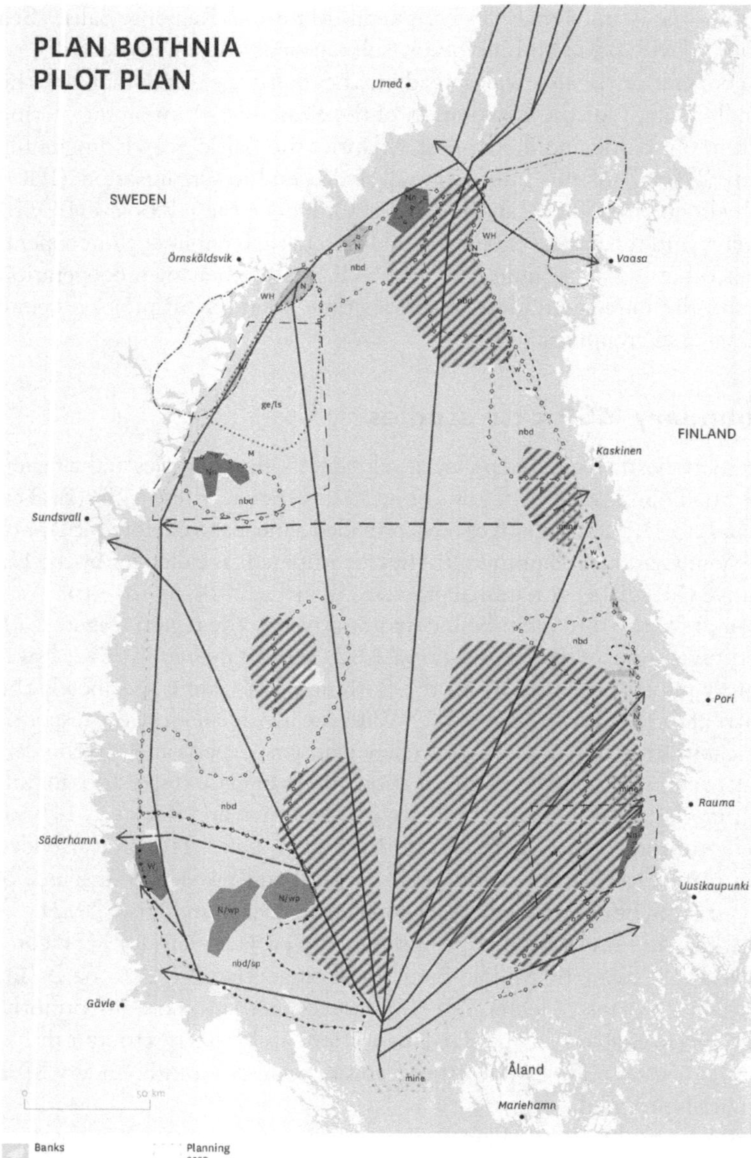

Figure 7.3 Plan Bothnia pilot MSP plan covers TS and EEZ of both Finland and Sweden (Backer and Frias, 2012). Arrows depict important shipping routes (dashed for potential future route), F: Fisheries areas, N: Nature protected areas, W: wind power (overlaps with natural value, dashed for potential), M: Military, nbd/sp: fish spawning and nursery area: WH: Unesco natural World Heritage, ge/ls: landscape special area related to the world heritage.

its sea areas (EEZ and TS), one for the western sea areas facing Denmark, the Baltic Sea Proper as well as the Gulf of Bothnia. The Swedish plan for the Gulf of Bothnia will cover the Plan Bothnia project area but, as it will be a national plan, the transboundary dimensions of the drafting process are not a primary concern. Finland has not yet initiated planning on the EEZ but is working to have an MSP system in place by 2016 as called for by the EU MSP Directive. Even if a more formal joint transboundary planning for the pilot area is not in the horizon, Finland has already been involved by Sweden for initial discussions and will likely be consulted further during the drafting of the Swedish plan.

Reflections on transboundary MSP in the Baltic

Transboundary cooperation on MSP in the Baltic Sea region has so far been about joint research projects, seminars, as well as establishing a formal and transparent intergovernmental dialogue within the joint HELCOM-VASAB working group. In the latter context, the coastal countries and the EU have exchanged information as well as developed and agreed on overarching policy documents (HELCOM&VASAB, 2013, 2010), with 'soft' normativity. Many of these activities have been linked to the development and future implementation of the 2014 EU MSP Directive. Other regional bodies have also had a valuable role in developing the transboundary dimensions of MSP in the region.

In the near future the drafting and implementation of the three guidelines called for by the regional MSP roadmap (HELCOM&VASAB, 2013) on ecosystem approach, transboundary consultations and public, as well as stakeholder, participation in planning processes, respectively will provide opportunities to develop further these MSP themes. Further, the development of regional spatial data services, needed to advance transboundary dialogue on concrete MSP issues, will remain an active field of regional engagement.

Ecosystem approaches

Calls to use the ecosystem approach in MSP, to enable the inclusion of marine environmental concerns in the planning and management of infrastructure developments, fisheries and shipping, have been among the key global arguments to implement MSP (Douvere, 2008; Kidd *et al.*, 2011). In the Baltic, these calls have been related to the decisions of the coastal countries to implement ecosystem approaches within the work to implement the 1992 Helsinki Convention (Backer *et al.*, 2010; HELCOM and OSPAR, 2003). Also the EU MSP Directive gives the ecosystem-based approach an important role.

Within the HELCOM-VASAB working group, the concept has received formal acceptance on the headline level as part of the regional MSP principles (HELCOM&VASAB, 2010) and via the drafting of a targeted technical document (HELCOM-VASAB MSP WG, 2014b). However, defining the concrete function of the ecosystem approach in MSP remains a difficult topic. One likely reason is that with its environmental emphasis, the concept raises to the surface latent power struggles between different professional groups as well as administrations, both national and within the EU Commission. The parallel and potentially conflicting (Qiu and Jones, 2013) implementation of the EU Marine Strategy Framework Directive, including its concept of 'Good Environmental Status' (Mee *et al.*, 2008), and the EU MSP Directive, in its partial role as a vehicle of economic growth and development, tends to emphasize this polarization.

However, as environmental concerns are increasingly part of mainstream public and political opinion, such tensions are perhaps imaginary. Further, a pragmatic definition of the ecosystem approach as a set of concrete procedures for the use and inclusion of ecosystem information in the drafting of plans, as highlighted in a separate table of the mentioned HELCOM-VASAB document on the ecosystem approach, might help to make the concept more interesting for planners.

Transboundary consultation and dialogue

While the existing regional approach with projects and soft policy development has its role in transboundary consultation and dialogue on MSP, it is clear that the regional cooperation would be strengthened by more early dialogue on concrete national plans under drafting.

So far the coastal countries have not, at least not in detail, presented their concrete MSP plans at the HELCOM-VASAB meetings but focused on projects and overall policy dialogue. Clarifying structures to be used for regional implementation of the EU MSP Directive would probably also focus on transboundary dialogue in the region.

The existing international legal framework, and the SEA protocol of the 1992 UNECE EIA Convention, have a relatively high minimum threshold for transboundary consultation of spatial plans. It requires only consultation with anticipated parties that could be significantly affected by transboundary impacts, and not earlier than before actual adoption. In addition, Russia has not ratified either the Convention or the Protocol.

Besides national planning activities, the administrations of the various countries have also explored bi- or multilateral planning within transboundary pilots like Plan Bothnia. At least theoretically, such plans could in the future be not only consulted, but actually developed jointly and adopted as sub-regional agreements, even as formal Memorandums of Understanding (MoUs) or treaty law. However, it is clear that such transboundary negotiations with more 'binding' end results are likely to emerge, if at all, only after the first rounds of national MSP developments.

Public consultation

One of the key findings of the Plan Bothnia initiative was that legitimacy and democratic anchoring of MSP plans require that particular attention is put on transparent and clear presentation of the background information and the rationale behind decisions leading to the final plan. This is essential as MSP processes involve distribution of marine space, a collective property, to private stakeholders.

Despite the awareness of the pitfalls of expert rule in planning (Jay, 2010), the balancing counterpower, democratic anchoring and legitimacy of MSP has received little attention in the Baltic and MSP literature at large. The main focus in terms of consultations has been on the direct involvement of interest groups and stakeholders, not citizens, in planning processes (Pomeroy and Douvere, 2008). If taken to the extreme, this provides for a MSP which runs the risk of actually weakening the democratic control and strengthening the influence of strong interest groups (Bengs, 2005).

MSP data

Spatial planning needs spatial data, which is collected digitally through Geographical Information Systems (GIS). While such spatial information related to MSP is starting to be relatively widely available for national use, regional data requires additional compilation efforts. As work on generating and improving access to such regional GIS data has been recognized as a priority field to regional MSP, it is likely to receive attention during the coming years.

Currently region-wide data is hosted and made openly available via GIS services of HELCOM, ICES and the IHO BSHC (hydrographical data). European data services such as those of the European Environment Agency or the European Marine Observation Data network (EMODnet) are also available but include mainly the same information as the regional services and do not cover Russia. Other databases exist but their contents are not distributed openly for various reasons.

Final remarks

Spatial planning is an activity with roots in efforts to reduce the negative effects of urban growth during the industrial revolution (Hall, 2002). The activity feeds on the desire, and need, of public authorities to collectively steer future developments in our neighbourhoods, cities, regions or even entire nations (Hall, 2002). Even if backed by rational arguments, the direction of this steering is ultimately based on the worldviews and political convictions of those in power.

Also in the context of Baltic Sea regional cooperation, where nine coastal countries are involved in a dazzling number of cooperative initiatives and processes, MSP has been heralded as a way to make concrete joint visions of unity and bring direction to future spatial developments in the entire region (Backer *et al.*, 2010; Gee *et al.*, 2011; Zaucha, 2014).

Such calls to bring coherence and rationality to the Baltic Sea regional cooperation via MSP are related to the desires among some scholars of international law to create a fixed hierarchy for international law, in other words its constitutionalization. Such desires have emerged from the perhaps exaggerated (Koskenniemi and Leino, 2002) concerns regarding the fragmentation of the normativity of international law (e.g. Weil, 1983). Even if appealing on the surface, these ideas raise follow-up questions such as who exactly should define the rationality to be applied, the rules and objectives of the game (Koskenniemi and Leino, 2002).

In heated discussions on transboundary planning in the Baltic Sea region, the dual face of planning as theory, as reflected in academic writings or overarching regional policy documents, and planning as a concrete practice is easily forgotten. While the former is relatively free to explore new utopian visions of planning, the latter (actual planning) tends to be a rather sobering process, steered to a large part not by idealism and theoretical constructs but by status quo, and the interests of powerful economic and political actors (Bengs, 2005). Koskenniemi (2005) has formulated similar tendencies as the unavoidable balance between international law as a manifestation of utopian ideals (such as democracy, human rights or sustainable development) and as an apology to actual state practice. Like international lawyers, MSP practitioners in the region will unavoidably be squeezed between the two.

It is, nevertheless, clear that the regionally specific treaty law in the Baltic Sea captures only a part of the political desires influencing transboundary MSP in the region. The need to protect the Baltic Sea marine environment, and thus to ensure the environmental sustainability of development, is relatively well developed in terms of formal treaty obligations via the 1992 Helsinki Convention. As described, the international law related to fisheries and shipping is also relatively well developed in the Baltic Sea region.

The notion of a dedicated regional agreement on MSP has also been raised by some commentators (Zaucha, 2014). However, these calls have so far not received support by the coastal countries. Further, the 2014 EU MSP Directive, providing a comparable transboundary legal base for MSP in all countries except Russia, might have removed some of the underlying rationale.

In the short term, it seems likely that MSP cooperation in the Baltic Sea will take its current forms of soft normativity, within the existing fora and based on the existing regional complex of international law. However, in the longer term, transboundary MSP with 'harder' independent normativity, such as bilateral joint transboundary plans, might also be developed – if it is seen as desirable by the coastal countries. However, even without such a clear international law dimension, planning at sea has a role in helping the region to imagine, and steer toward, a more sustainable maritime future.

Acknowledgements

Sincere thanks to the editors for endless patience with the manuscript, to Ulf Bergström for providing material on fisheries closure in the Sound and to Carsten Jensen for providing material on the history of routeing measures in the Baltic Sea.

Notes

1 According to the United Nations Convention of the Law of the Seas (UNCLOS) (Art. 3–16) the maritime border of a coastal country, defining the outer limit of the territorial sea under national jurisdiction, may extend at most 12 nm outward from the baseline. Baseline is defined as the low water line of a coast or by connecting low water lines of outermost features (such as islands, peninsulas and reefs) with straight lines.
2 Article 15, Nature conservation and biodiversity: The Contracting Parties shall individually and jointly take all appropriate measures with respect to the Baltic Sea Area and its coastal ecosystems influenced by the Baltic Sea to conserve natural habitats and biological diversity and to protect ecological processes. Such measures shall also be taken in order to ensure the sustainable use of natural resources within the Baltic Sea Area. To this end, the Contracting Parties shall aim at adopting subsequent instruments containing appropriate guidelines and criteria.
3 The Kiel channel provides an alternative to using the Danish sounds as a seaway connection between the Baltic and the North Seas.
4 Swedish Agency for Marine and Water Management (SWaM)
5 Norway, Iceland and the Danish dependencies, Faroe island and Greenland

References

Anon. (1932) 'Kommissionen med Danmark angående fiskeriförhållandena i det till Sverige och Danmark gränsande farvattnen.' (Joint commission with Denmark concerning the fisheries in waters of Sweden and Denmark) Stockholm, 31 December 1932, in Swedish.

Anon. (1962) 'Treaty of Cooperation between Denmark, Finland, Iceland, Norway and Sweden (the Helsinki Treaty)', signed in Helsinki on 23 March 1962 and entered into force on 1 July 1962, the most recent amendments entered into force on 2 January 1996. http://www.norden.org/avtal/helsingfors/uk/helsinki_agreement.pdf.

Anon. (1964) 'Convention for The International Council for the Exploration of the Sea' (Copenhagen, 12 September 1964).

Anon. (1973) 'Convention on Fishing and Conservation of the Living Resources in the Baltic Sea and Belt' (signed at Gdansk on 13 September 1973, entered into force on 28 July 1974).

Anon. (1975) 'Convention of the Protection of the Marine Environment of the Baltic Sea Area, Report of the Second Meeting of the Interim Commission' (Helsinki 8–11 December 1975).

Anon. (1996) 'Agreement between the Republic of Estonia and the Republic of Latvia on the Maritime delineation in the Gulf of Riga, the Strait of Irbe and the Baltic Sea (concluded 12 July 1996, in force 10 October 1996).

Anon. (1999a) 'Agreement between the Republic of Latvia and the Republic of Lithuania on the delimitation of the Territorial Sea, Exclusive Economic Zone and Continental shelf in the Baltic Sea' (agreed on 9 July 1999, not in force).

Anon. (1999b) 'ESDP European Spatial development Perspective Towards balanced and sustainable development of the territory of the European Union' (agreed at the informal Council of Ministers responsible for Spatial Planning in Potsdam, May 1999), Office for Official Publications of the European Communities, Luxembourg; 87 pp. ISBN 92-828-7658-6.

Anon. (2003) 'Protocol on Strategic Environmental Assessment to the Convention on Environmental Impact Assessment in a transboundary context' (Kiev 21 May 2003).

Anon. (2007) 'Territorial Agenda of the European Union: towards a more competitive and Sustainable Europe of Diverse Regions' (agreed on the occasion of the Informal Ministerial Meeting on Urban Development and Territorial Cohesion in Leipzig on 24/ 25 May 2007).

Anon. (2009a) 'Agreement between the European Community and the Government of the Russian Federation on cooperation in fisheries and the conservation of the living marine resources in the Baltic Sea' (concluded 28 April 2009 in Brussels) *Official Journal of the European Union* L129, pp. 2–7.

Anon. (2009b) 'Anlage zur Verordnung über die Raumordnung in der deutschen ausschließlichen Wirtschaftszone in der Ostsee' (AWZ Ostsee-ROV) vom 10. Dezember 2009, Raumordnungsplan für die deutsche ausschließliche Wirtschaftszone in der Ostsee (Textteil und Kartenteil). Bundesgesetzblatt (Anlageband, G 5702) I.

Anon. (2013) 'Memorandum of Understanding: Principles and working methods of the Baltic Sea Fisheries Forum' (BALTFISH) signed 13 December 2013 in Brussels, Belgium.

Anon. (2014a) 'The Estonian-Russian Border Treaty between the republic of Estonia and the Russian Federation' (agreed 17 February 2014, not in force).

Anon. (2014b). *North Sea 2050 Spatial Agenda*, Ministry of Infrastructure and the Environment, co-production with Ministry of Economic Affairs (Netherlands). 81 pp. www.noordzeeloket.nl (last accessed 20 April 2015)

Backer, H. (2011) 'Transboundary maritime spatial planning: a Baltic Sea perspective'. *Journal of Coastal Conservation*, 15, pp. 279–89.

Backer, H. and Frias, M. (eds.) (2012) *Planning the Bothnian Sea: Outcome of Plan Bothnia – a transboundary Maritime Spatial Planning pilot in the Bothnian Sea*, Finepress, Turku, 153 pp.

Backer, H., Leppänen, J.-M., Brusendorff, A.C., Forsius, K., Stankiewicz, M., Mehtonen, J., Pyhälä, M., Laamanen, M., Paulomäki, H., Vlasov, N., Haaranen, T. (2010) 'HELCOM Baltic Sea Action Plan: a regional programme of measures for the marine environment based on the Ecosystem Approach', *Marine Pollution Bulletin* 60 (5), pp. 642–49.

BASREC (2012a) 'Conditions for Deployment of Wind Power in the Baltic Sea Region: Analysis part II Strategic outline offshore wind promotion', 78 pp. basrec.net (last accessed 20 April 2015).

BASREC (2012b) 'Conditions for Deployment of Wind Power in the Baltic Sea Region: Analysis part I Enabling studies', 186 pp. lisehenningsson.com (last accessed 20 April 2015).

Bengs, C. (2005) 'Planning Theory for the Naive?' *European Journal of Spatial Development* (nordregio.se/EJSD Debate and Miscellaneous, July 2005), 10 pp.

Birnie, P.W. (1996) 'The new Helsinki Convention: background and commentary' in: Platzöder, R.& V., P. (eds) *The Baltic Sea: New Developments in National Policies and International Cooperation*, Kluwer Law International, The Hague, pp. 346–59.

Boczek, B. (1996) 'Law and Politics in the Baltic Sea Area: A historical perspective' in: Platzöder, R. and V.P. (eds) *The Baltic Sea: New Developments in National Policies and International Cooperation*, Kluwer Law International, The Hague, pp. 39–47.

City of Helsinki (2015) 'Facts about Helsinki 2014', 22 pp. www.hel.fi/tietokeskus (last accessed 20 April 2015).

Douvere, F. (2008) 'The importance of marine spatial planning in advancing ecosystem-based sea use management', *Marine Policy* 32, pp. 762–71.

Elmgren, R. (1989) 'Man's Impact on the Ecosystem of the Baltic Sea: Energy Flows Today and at the Turn of the Century', *Ambio* 18, pp. 326–32.

Elmgren, R. (2001) 'Understanding Human Impact on the Baltic Ecosystem: Changing views in recent decades', *Ambio* 4–5, pp. 222–231.

EU (2007a), Council Regulation (EC) No 1098/2007 of 18 September 2007 establishing a multiannual plan for the cod stocks in the Baltic Sea and the fisheries exploiting those stocks, amending Regulation (EEC) No 2847/93 and repealing Regulation (EC) No 779/97.

EU (2007b) COM(2007) 575: 'An Integrated Maritime Policy for the European Union'.

EU (2008) Directive 2008/56/EC of the European Parliament and the Council of 17 June 2008: 'Establishing a framework for community action in the field of marine environmental policy' (Marine Strategy Framework Directive), *Official Journal of the European Union* L164/19.

EU (2009) COM (2009) 248 final: 'Communication from the Commission to the European Parliament, The Council, The European Economic and Social Committee and the Committee of the Regions concerning the European Union Strategy for the Baltic Sea Region'.

EU (2014) Directive 2014/89/Eu of the European Parliament and of the Council of 23 July 2014 establishing a framework for maritime spatial planning.

Faludi, A. (2007) 'Making sense of the territorial agenda of the European Union', *European Journal of Spatial Planning* (Refereed Articles, November 2007, no. 25). 22 pp (last accessed 20 April 2015).

Fitzmaurice, M. (1996) 'The 1974 Helsinki Convention on the Protection of the Marine Environment of the Baltic Sea' in: Platzöder, R. and V. P. (eds) *The Baltic Sea: New Developments in National Policies and International Cooperation*, Kluwer Law International, The Hague, pp. 312–29.

Franckx, E. (2012) 'Maritime Delimitation in the Baltic Sea: What Has Already Been Accomplished?' *International Journal on Marine Navigation and Safety of Sea Transportation* 6 (3) pp. 437–42.

Gee, K., Kannen, A. and Heindrichs, B. (2011) 'BaltSeaPlan Vision 2030: Towards the Sustainable Planning of Baltic Sea Space' (a report of the EU project 'Baltseaplan') 48 pp. (last accessed 20 April 2015).

Hall, P. (2002) *Urban and regional planning* (4th edition) Routledge, London and New York, p. 237.

Hannerz, F. and Destouni, G. (2006) 'Spatial characterization of the Baltic Sea drainage basin and its unmonitored catchments', *AMBIO: A Journal of the Human Environment*, 35, pp. 214–219.

HELCOM (1974) Convention on the Protection of the Marine Environment of the Baltic Sea Area, 1974 (Helsinki Convention, 22 March 1974 Helsinki, in force 3 May 1980).

HELCOM (1992) Convention on the Protection of the Marine Environment of the Baltic Sea Area (Helsinki 9 April 1992, in force 17 January 2000).

HELCOM (1994a) Recommendation 15/1: Protection of the Coastal Strip. (Adopted 8 March 1994.)

HELCOM (1994b) Recommendation 15/5: System of coastal and marine Baltic Sea Protected Areas (BSPA). (Adopted 10 March 1994.)

HELCOM (2000) Recommendation 21/4: Protection of heavily endangered or immediately threatened marine and coastal biotopes in the Baltic Sea area. (Adopted 20 March 2000.)

HELCOM (2003) Recommendation 24/10: Implementation of integrated marine and coastal management of human activities in the Baltic Sea area. (Adopted 25 June 2003.)

HELCOM (2007) Recommendation 28E/ 9: Development of broad-scale marine spatial planning principles in the Baltic Sea area. (Adopted 15 November 2007.)

HELCOM, OSPAR (2003) Annex 5: Statement on the Ecosystem Approach to the Management of Human Activities, in: Outcome of the First Joint Ministerial Meeting of the Helsinki and OSPAR Commissions (JMM) Bremen 25–26 June 2003.

HELCOM&VASAB (2010) Baltic Sea broad-scale maritime spatial planning (MSP) principles. Adopted in 2010 by countries in the region and the EU Commission as members of both HELCOM and VASAB in December 2010 (Annex 3, Minutes of HELCOM HOD 34/2010).

HELCOM&VASAB (2013) Regional Baltic Maritime Spatial Planning Roadmap 2013–2020 (adopted by the 2013 HELCOM Ministerial Meeting on 3 October 2013 in Copenhagen, Denmark).

HELCOM-VASAB MSP WG (2014a) National Maritime Spatial Planning developments (HELCOM-VASAB MSP WG 9-2014, document 2-2).

HELCOM-VASAB MSP WG (2014b) Document on the ecosystem-based approach and MSP (HELCOM-VASAB MSP WG Online intersessional meeting on EBA & MSP document, 2-1 Rev1).

ICJ (1991) Case concerning passage through the Great Belt (Finland v. Denmark). Request for the indication of provisional measures order of 29 July 1991.

IMCO (1968) Resolution A. 161 (Es. IV) Recommendation on establishing traffic separation schemes and areas to be avoided by certain classes of ships.

IMCO (1971) Assembly Resolution A.228 (VII) Observance of traffic separation schemes. (Adopted 12 October 1971.)

IMCO (1973) Assembly Resolution A.284 (VIII) Routeing systems. (Adopted 20 November 1973.)

IMO (1973) International Convention for the Prevention of Pollution from Ships (MARPOL). (Adopted on 2 November 1973 in London, UK.)

IMO (2005). Resolution MEPC 136 (53) Designation of the Baltic Sea area as a particularly sensitive sea area. (Adopted on 22 July 2005 in London, UK.)

Jay, S. (2010) 'Built at sea: Marine management and the construction of marine spatial planning', *Town Planning Review*, 81, pp. 173–91.

Kidd, S., Maltby, E., Robinson, L., Barker, A. and Lumb, C. (2011) 'Chapter 1: The Ecosystem Approach and Planning and Management of the Marine Environment', in *The Ecosystem Approach to Marine Planning and Management*, Earthscan Publications Ltd, pp. 1–33.

Koskenniemi, M. (2005) *From Apology to Utopia: The structure of international legal argument* (reissue with new epilogue), Cambridge University Press, Cambridge, p. 683.

Koskenniemi, M. and Leino, P. (2002). 'Fragmentation of International Law? Postmodern Anxieties', *Leiden Journal of International Law* 15, pp. 553–79.

Leppäranta, M. and Myrberg, K. (2009) *Physical Oceanography of the Baltic Sea*, Springer-Praxis, Chichester, p. 378.

Maes, F. (2008) 'The international legal framework for marine spatial planning', *Marine Policy* 32, pp. 797– 810.

Mee, L.D., Jefferson, R.L., Laffoley, D. d'A. and Elliott, M. (2008) 'How good is good? Human values and Europe's proposed Marine Strategy Directive', *Marine Pollution Bulletin* 56, pp. 187–204.

Nolte, N. (2010) Nützungsansprüche und Raumordnung auf dem Meer. *HANSA International Maritime Journal*, 9, pp. 79–81.

Pekkarinen, A. and Repka, S. (2014) 'Maritime Transport in the Gulf of Bothnia 2030', *AMBIO: A Journal of the Human Environment* 43, pp. 791–800.

Pomeroy, R. and Douvere, F. (2008) 'The engagement of stakeholders in the marine spatial planning process', *Marine Policy* 32, pp. 816–22.

Qiu, W. and Jones, P.J.S. (2013) 'The emerging policy landscape for marine spatial planning in Europe', *Marine Policy* 39, pp. 182–90.

SOLAS (1960) International Convention for the Safety of Life at Sea, done at London 17 June 1960, entered into force: 26 May 1965.

Svedäng, H. (2010) 'Long-term impact of different fishing methods on the ecosystem in the Kattegat and Öresund' (report for European Parliament's Committee on Fisheries), Parliament of the European Union. www.europarl.europa.eu/studies (last accessed 20 April 2015).

Sweitzer, J., Langaas, S. and Folke, C. (1996) 'Land use and population density in the Baltic Sea drainage basin: a GIS database', *Ambio* pp. 191–98.

UNECE (1991) Convention on transboundary environmental impact assessment in a transboundary context done at Espoo (Finland), on 25 February 1991 (http://www.unece.org/env/eia/eia.htm).

UNECE (2012) Sixth Seminar on cooperation on the EIA Convention in the Baltic Sea Region (20–21 September 2012, Tallinn Estonia): Minutes.

Vasab (1992) Conclusions of the First Conference of Ministers for Spatial Planning and Development (Karlskrona, Sweden, 20–21 August 1992).

Weil, P. (1983) 'Towards relative normativity in international law?' *American Journal of International Law* 77, pp. 413–442.

Zaucha, J. (2014) *The Key to Governing the fragile Baltic Sea: maritime spatial planning in the Baltic Sea and the way forward*, VASAB Secretariat, p.110. ISBN 978-9934-14-165-2.

Chapter 8.1

Transboundary maritime spatial planning across the French–Belgian maritime borders

Past and future cooperation

Betty Queffelec and Frank Maes

Introduction

Cross-border activities, such as fisheries, shipping, nature conservation and offshore wind energy, are essential drivers for Marine Spatial Planning (MSP). However, until now, MSP remains a national policy implemented by one country, even if neighbouring countries are also conducting MSP with comparable objectives. Cross-border MSP is a challenge for the European Union (EU) too, which has to cope with multiple national borders across its maritime space. MSP in Member States (MS) is currently attracting the attention of the European Commission (EC) that views 'cross-border cooperation and consultation' as a principle of MSP to 'ensure coherence of plans across ecosystems'.[1] In 2009, the EC organized four workshops on MSP, highlighting cross-border issues as topical. It also funded two pilot projects on MSP: MASPNOSE (Maritime Spatial Planning in the North Sea see: https://www.wageningenur.nl/en/show/Maspnose-Maritime-spatial-planning-in-the-North-Sea.htm) for the North Sea and Plan Bothnia for the Baltic Sea, both focusing on cross-border challenges, opportunities and constraints.[2] Taking into account this focus, it comes as no surprise that DG Mare (European Commission Directorate-General for Maritime Affairs and Fisheries) justified its initiative to develop draft legislation concerning MSP as a means to provide a 'framework for efficient cross-border cooperation and the rational management of the European maritime space'.[3] Following this objective, the EC proposed a Directive establishing a framework for MSP and Integrated Coastal Zone Management (ICZM) in 2013.[4]

Based on a case study in the framework of the TransMaSP research project (Transboundary Maritime Spatial Planning see: http://www.transmasp.ugent.be/transmaspnl.html), with focus on the French–Belgian maritime border, this project aimed to contribute to the analysis of cross-border cooperation in MSP.[5] In this area (see Figure 8.1.1), where there is a substantial amount of human activities such as maritime transport, tourism, and fisheries, the two countries share the same sand banks and its rich biodiversity. Nevertheless, they have a different governance approach and state structure. France is a centralized state with close to 11,000,000 km^2 of sea under its jurisdiction while Belgium is a federal state governing only a small part of the North Sea (3,457 km^2) (Maes *et al.*, 2013a).

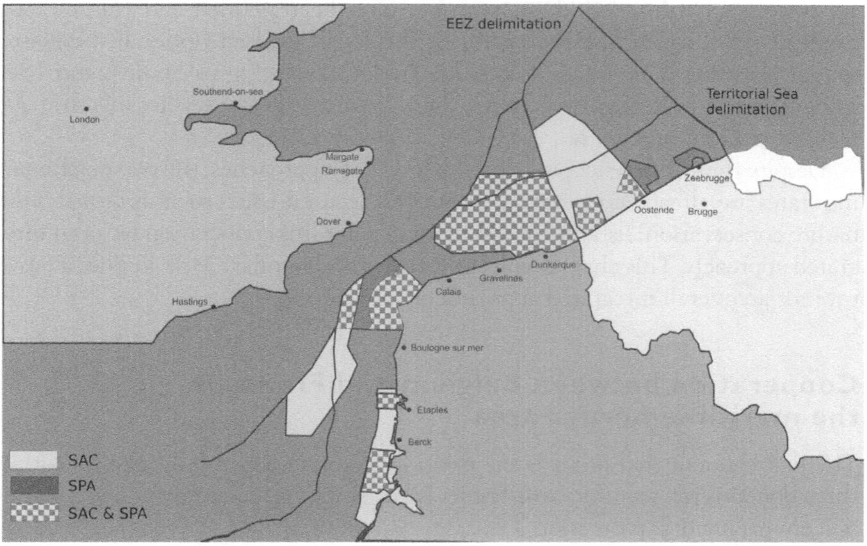

Figure 8.1.1 **French-Belgian case study area with Natura 2000 site at sea.**

In terms of MSP processes, the two countries have developed a rather different approach. MSP in Belgium is initially implemented by a Master Plan covering the Belgian part of the North Sea. The plan allocates marine space for specific maritime uses[6] and was driven by the need to reallocate sand and gravel extraction, to allocate zones for offshore wind farms (2003) and to designate Natura 2000 marine protected areas (2005). In 2012, an additional large area of the Belgian part of the North Sea was designated as a Natura 2000 area.[7] The initial Master Plan is an example of zoning plans, since the plan was not the result of a transparent process for adaptation and stakeholder participation (Douvere *et al.*, 2007; Maes *et al.*, 2013b). Although participation took place at a bilateral level, with a selection of stakeholders (Plasman, 2008), transparency was missing. In July 2012, a legal basis for MSP was adopted, including the obligation for stakeholder participation, a clear planning process, a strategic environmental assessment reporting and consultation with neighbouring countries. A Royal Decree of 20 March 2014 concluded the process for a revised Belgian MSP. Instead of a Master Plan, Belgium now has a comprehensive MSP that is legally enforceable, future orientated and has an adaptive six-year revision process.[8] The legal basis is the law on the protection of the marine environment and not legislation regulating economic activities at sea. Conversely, France started by developing an overall legal framework. It foresees a Littoral and Marine Strategy at national level, complemented by maritime front documents specifying it at a sub-national level. Advisory bodies have been set up: the Sea and Littoral National Council at the national level and the Maritime

Front Councils at a sub-national level. At the same time, some sectoral processes are ongoing. Offshore wind energy zones have been defined and Natura 2000 zones at sea have been designated. At the local level an optional integrated spatial planning tool already exists, the *Schéma de mise en valeur de la mer* (Sea Enhancement Scheme), which is a legal framework for developing strategic plans at sea (Trouillet *et al.*, 2011; de Cacqueray, 2011).[9]

Despite these differences in contexts and MSP approaches, the two neighbouring states are already cooperating on various sectoral issues such as cross-border nature conservation, fisheries and shipping. So far this cooperation lacks an integrated approach. This chapter will show that transboundary MSP implies a move towards an overall integrated approach of cooperation.

Cooperation between Belgium and France in the maritime border area

The first element that arises is the existing sectoral cooperation, mainly within three domains relevant for cross-border MSP: shipping and safety at sea, fisheries and environmental protection.[10]

Shipping and safety at sea

Due to the high intensity of shipping traffic in the Strait of Dover and a strong competition between ports in the Hamburg–Le Havre range, including the port of Dunkerque in France and Zeebrugge, Antwerp and Ghent in Belgium, shipping and safety at sea are major issues in the Belgian–French border area (Dauvin, 2008).

Concerning maritime safety there is a long and effective tradition of cooperation between the governments and between their respective stakeholders. This cooperation is mainly organized at an international level within the International Maritime Organization (IMO) or by implementing IMO Conventions, in particular with respect to search and rescue, managing and monitoring maritime traffic,[11] exchange of information on ship movements and cooperation in case of accidents.[12] At the regional North Sea level, the 1969 Bonn Agreement focused on cooperation in case of pollution from ships, dealing with prevention and detection of operational pollution (airborne surveillance) and assisting each other in case of shipping accidents.[13] At a bilateral level, cooperation in common exercises is developed through the Manche Plan (1978), firstly between France and the UK, followed by Belgium, the Channel Islands and Ireland. Nowadays the EU has developed extensive legislation on the matter of pollution prevention, ship tracking and cooperation in case of accidents. As a result of accidents in or near the waters of EU MS, such as the 1999 Erika and 2002 Prestige accidents, three packages were developed to improve maritime safety legislation (Liu and Maes, 2009) and the European Maritime Safety Agency monitor its implementation[14] (Groenleer, 2010).

Fisheries

Since the 1970s, fisheries have been mainly an EC competence. The Treaty on the Functioning of the European Union repeats the exclusive competence of the EU concerning the conservation of marine biological resources under the Common Fisheries Policy (CFP)[15] with some shared fisheries' competences with MS.[16] Mostly ruled at EU level, a system of exceptions allows MS to partly regulate fisheries in their territorial sea. Community fishing vessels benefit from an equal access to waters and resources in all Union waters, defined as 'the waters under the sovereignty or jurisdiction of the Member States, with the exception of the waters adjacent to the territories listed in Annex II of the Treaty, which refers to overseas countries and territories.'[17] Territorial seas are another exception.[18] Indeed, in the sea area up to 12 nautical miles from the coast, MS are allowed to limit fishing, taking into account two exceptions: neighbouring rights and historical rights.[19] The 2013 CFP Regulation codifies historical rights in its Annex I. Accordingly, French fishing vessels have the right to fish herring in the zone from 3 to 12 nautical miles off the Belgian part of the North Sea. In the same way Belgian fishing vessels have the right to fish demersal species and scallops in the zone between 6 and 12 nautical miles off the French–Belgian frontier to the east of the *Département Manche*.[20] Moreover, the Netherlands hold rights without species limitation in these zones.

In addition, fisheries faced temporal uncertainties with the 2013 CFP reform,[21] while increasing claims for sea use to fully or partially exclude fisheries in zones with wind energy production. Shipping and fishing are prohibited in a safety zone of 500 metres measured from the outer limit of the Belgian offshore wind energy concession zones,[22] as indicated by coordinates.[23] These coordinates have been published in 2000 and changed in 2011.[24] Only in exceptional cases is shipping allowed in the offshore wind concession zones, such as for navy and governmental vessels, vessels contracted by the operators of offshore wind mills for maintenance works, vessels contracted for the maintenance of cables and pipelines, vessels used for scientific research as well as all other vessels, in case of *force majeure*, that may be in distress or to save human beings only.[25]

Conflicts regularly arise between fishermen from those countries based on gear incompatibility, especially while they target the same species. Annually, at the beginning of the spring, such conflicts occur at the French–Belgian border mainly between French, Belgian and Dutch fishermen targeting sole with different types of gear.

A Belgian–French Fisheries Commission, created by a 1975 bilateral agreement on seasonal fisheries[26] meets annually with representatives of fishermen and fisheries administrations to solve fisheries' problems. Although the agreement only applies to sprat and winter herring fisheries, the consultations in this forum evolved towards other fishery issues. The agreement and the regular meetings became a very useful forum for fisheries stakeholders to discuss and to find solutions for problems arising in the border zone. Due to its limited scope, the meetings allow its members to address, in detail, practical questions that appear to be complementary to the North Sea Regional Advisory Council (NSRAC) created by the EU to implement the CFP.[27] However, the bilateral Commission's main limitation is the absence of Dutch fishermen as stakeholders. Dutch fishermen are very active in this border zone and are often involved in the problems raised. Their participation would be an added value. They have been invited to join the Commission, but for the time being they refused, arguing that language problems with French representatives would impede an effective dialogue. This shows how difficult it is to involve stakeholders from outside the geographical scope of cooperation, although active in the zone of cooperation.

Environmental protection

For a long time, marine environmental protection between France and Belgium has been stimulated by cooperation through the framework of the former 1974 Paris Convention, followed by the 1992 Convention for the Protection of the Marine Environment of the North-East Atlantic, known as the OSPAR Convention, and recently by the 2008 Marine Strategy Framework Directive (MSFD).[28] To some extent, the MSFD refers directly to 'existing regional institutional cooperation structures, including those under regional sea conventions' such as OSPAR.[29] Concretely, MS have to develop, at the national level, marine strategies to reach the objectives of the MSFD, in particular to achieve or maintain a good environmental status in the marine environment by 2020. This regional and sub-regional cooperation could help ensure coherence and coordination.[30] The MSFD includes the Belgian part of the North Sea and the maritime part of northern France in the same sub-region: the Greater North Sea, including the English Channel.[31] This sub-region is consistent with OSPAR region II. Regional institutional cooperation structures remain optional since the MSFD stipulates that MS should use it 'where practical and appropriate'. Furthermore, the MSFD does not oblige MS to develop a common plan of action for a marine region or sub-region as such. If they decide not to develop such a common plan, each MS will be able to present its national part to the EC. Finally, the cooperation commitment itself remains rather weak. Indeed, MS only need to 'endeavour to follow a common approach'.[32]

Additionally, the EU is supporting technical cooperation. Following the first step of the MSFD calendar to implement the plans of action, each MS had to develop its initial assessment(s) to determine a good environmental status for the waters concerned and to establish a series of environmental targets and associated indicators by 15 July 2012. At the EU level, a Common Implementation Strategy for MSFD was developed based on the following process: (1) regular meetings of the national marine directors; (2) a marine strategy coordination group, including MS, neighbouring countries, relevant international organisations and stakeholders; (3) a committee gathering only MS; and (4) three working groups dedicated respectively to good environmental status, data, information and knowledge exchange as well as economic and social assessment.[33]

At the regional sea level, OSPAR can be a platform to implement the MSFD.[34] OSPAR develops activities especially to this end (i.e. the Intersessional

Correspondence Group for the Implementation of the Marine Strategy Framework Directive workshops on MSFD biodiversity descriptors)[35] and has as an overall framework, the 'OSPAR Regional Implementation Framework for the EU Marine Strategy Framework Directive – MSFD Road Map'(2010).[36]

In contrast, cross-border cooperation is not really addressed in the EC Birds and Habitats Directives. Coordination between MS is only mentioned in the Habitat Directive regarding research[37] while the EC is in charge of coordination to ensure the coherence of the Natura 2000 network.[38] The Directives do not contain an explicit coordination or cooperation obligation concerning the adoption of transboundary conservation measures.[39] However, in the Belgian–French maritime border coordination takes place. Special Areas of Conservation under the Habitats Directive have been designated at each side of the border: the *Bancs des Flandres* (112,919 ha, including a part in the EEZ) and *the Dunes de la plaine maritime flamande* (4425 ha, including both the terrestrial and maritime parts) on the French side; and the extension of the Trapegeer-Stroombank zone[40] at the Belgian side (100,994 ha, including the largest part in the EEZ), now called the Flemish Banks. In 2012 this area was legally designated as a special area for conservation (SAC) under the Habitats Directive[41] covering an area of more than 1,099 km^2 or nearly one-third of the Belgian part of the North Sea (see Figure 8.1.1). Additionally, France designated a Special Protection Area *Bancs des Flandres* (117,167 ha covering the same surface as the *Bancs des Flandres* SAC and part of the *Dunes de la Plaine maritime flamande* SAC surface area) under the Birds Directive. Both states are at the beginning of a process to develop management plans for these zones. A first cross-border meeting took place in March 2011 between institutions in charge of the Belgian and French Natura 2000 maritime zones. This first step mainly allowed the countries to inform each other about their processes, and further cooperation is foreseen. Moreover, the management of Natura 2000 sites should be discussed in a broader perspective within the framework of OSPAR. This cooperation through OSPAR is complementary to the cooperation presently ongoing. As for fisheries, the need for different levels of cooperation in the same marine region is clearly apparent. A larger scope should yield a general vision, which should be completed by small-scale cooperation on specific and detailed issues arising in the maritime border areas.

Finally, the importance of a transboundary environmental impact assessment (EIA) in cross-border cooperation should be highlighted because this is a valuable way to implement the aims of MSP (Maes, 2008; Backer, 2011). The EU adopted an EIA Directive in 1985 that already considered transboundary impacts[42] and was further developed in the Directive 2011/92[43] to comply with the 1991 Espoo Convention on Environmental Impact Assessment in a Transboundary Context.[44] In 2001, the EU adopted a Directive on the assessment of the effects of certain plans and programmes on the environment in 2001.[45] In 2003, a Protocol to the Espoo Convention on Strategic Environmental Assessment (SEA) was adopted in Kiev.[46] Belgium, France and the EU ratified the Convention, and the EU ratified the Protocol. Information supply and consultation in a transboundary SEA process can be improved, in particular regarding maritime areas. The Flemish Region developed an Integrated Master Plan for coastal safety and proposed coastal adaptation measures to climate change effects. The Plan is the policy basis for taking protective measures against erosion and flooding. On 1 September 2009, the Flemish authorities sent the environmental and security incidence assessment of this Plan to French local authorities.[47] However, some obstacles in the consultation process arose. First, since this procedure is rarely implemented, the administration did not fully master it. Some delays subsequently occurred in the document delivery to the relevant French service (DREAL[48]). Moreover, the report is a large document entirely written in Dutch. The French service could only proceed with an informal translation of the main elements of the study. The language issue remained an obstacle to an in-depth analysis of the document and the process was very time consuming. As a result, the deadline to present comments to the Flemish authorities was too short and France was not able to forward observations. Lack of regular cooperation partly explains these difficulties.

Assessment of cooperation

It can be concluded that maritime border cooperation between France and Belgium/Flanders is case-by-case driven and based on specific common needs to ensure maritime safety, protect environmental quality and implement European or international commitments. Consequently, cross-border cooperation is often set up as a reaction to concrete difficulties that have to be solved. As a result, this cooperation remains mainly sectoral. The major added value of cross-border cooperation in MSP lies in its integrated approach (Koivurova, 2009). Interviews and the questionnaire used for the TransMaSP project revealed that most of the basic issues, between French and Belgian/Flemish services, were resolved away from formal procedures such as through informal communication (mostly email or phone).[49] This implies that civil servants have a basic understanding of their neighbour's administrative structures and procedures as well as staying in regular contact with their colleagues, on the other side of the border, for information sharing and updates related to ongoing processes. New needs lead to the development of cooperation, such as in the case of the informal meeting set up to cope with the designation of new Natura 2000 areas. A congested maritime space, like the Belgian–French border, is a good example of where a common vision on shipping, nature conservation and fisheries would be appropriate. In order to achieve this, an effective transboundary MSP should build on past experiences and move towards an integrated cooperation for transboundary MSP.

Moving towards an integrated cooperation

Considering existing cooperation, the selection of an appropriate scale for an integrated planning approach can be difficult. The example of the Belgian–French fisheries commission, in which Dutch representatives are not represented, is an example of this problem (see as described above). On the other hand, cooperation at the macro-regional and sea-basin levels in order to achieve an ecosystem approach should not erase the special added value of local maritime cooperation. Actually, some concrete day-to-day or local issues can benefit from small-scale cross-border cooperation.[50]

Various decision-making scales can be complementary to one another and are a necessary condition to develop an efficient transboundary approach in MSP. Even solving a specific sectoral problem usually implies using different decision-making levels. As a result, the solution lies in strongly inter-linked structures and instruments used for transboundary MSP, from informal forums to specific international conventions. This allows for the capitalisation of previous cooperation to create a multi-scale network for transboundary MSP. According to each specific context, states will develop specific instruments that will become crucial nodes in the network. However, the coherence of an integrated cooperation in MSP remains dependent on good communication and inter-linkage in the network. The considered instruments can be an informal forum for an integrated approach, a European Grouping for Territorial Cooperation (EGTC), regional seas conventions, international agreements with local or specific focus, or a new EU Directive concerning MSP.

Informal forum for an integrated approach

The easiest option to organize cross-border cooperation, including stakeholders' participation, is to set up an informal forum. A major advantage of an informal forum is its flexibility. The role of Interreg projects can be highlighted. Integrated maritime cooperation is part of the European Community's strategic guidelines on economic, social and territorial cohesion, 2007–2013.[51] Within the EU Integrated Maritime Policy, an integrated maritime cooperation should remain part of the EU cohesion policy for the period 2014–2020 and regarded as an investment priority.[52]

The main constraint of informal forums is the risk of lack of continuity. Indeed, if it is linked to a particular project funding, the end of the project can lead to the end of the cooperation. But this is not always the case. Some informal or project-based cooperation continued on its own. After several experiences of informal French–Belgian cross border cooperation, the partners decided to continue their cooperation focusing on a more global approach. They set up the West-Vlaanderen/Flandre-Dunkerque platform with the support of Interreg. They have formalized their cooperation on 29 November 2004 in the Furnes official commitment declaration and on 9 June 2005 they set up a permanent conference, gathering elected representatives from the various partners. All along this cooperation, Interreg projects have been developed between partners, to support the day-to-day cooperation. A step further was taken in 2006 during the permanent conference in De Panne with the proposal to evolve towards an EGTC (European Grouping for Territorial Cooperation).

European Grouping for Territorial Cooperation (EGTC)

EGTC is a European cooperation structure developed within the framework of the EU Territorial Cohesion Policy of EU Regulation 1082/2006.[53] This structure was created under pressure of border regions asking for a framework for efficient cooperation. Indeed, they experienced technical barriers in their transboundary cooperation, especially due to different national laws and procedures.[54] Spinaci (2009) states that 'EGTC was designed to facilitate the implementation of programmes and projects co-financed by the structural funds', but he also acknowledges that it is not limited to it as it can 'carry out actions relating to Community policies other than structural policy' (Spinaci, 2009). For the French–Belgian coastal border area, the West-Vlaanderen-Flandre-Dunkerque-Côte d'Opale EGTC was set up in 2009.

From a technical point of view, EGTC is a legal body, with its own budget and the ability to employ staff. Its territorial application and its competences are defined in the Agreement by which an EGTC is established. But, as recalled by the Regulation, 'the powers exercised by regional and local authorities as public authorities, notably police and regulatory powers, cannot be the subject of a convention'.[55] The EU evaluation of EGTC implementation is globally positive except for some technical issues mainly occurring during the setting-up stage. The EGTC appears to be a flexible cooperation tool, efficient in coping with different national laws and procedural issues.[56]

A major added value of EGTC lies in its ability to develop multi-level cooperation.[57] Indeed, MS, regional authorities, local authorities and bodies governed by public law can be members of an EGTC. This feature is especially valuable to conduct integrated policies across various governance levels. Lack of cohesion between competent authorities is a major obstacle to achieve such policies and this is further amplified in a transboundary context (Queffelec and Maes, 2013). As such, the West-Vlaanderen-Flandre-Dunkerque-Côte d'Opale EGTC gathers most of the authorities competent for its territory: States (France and the Federal State of Belgium), Regions (Nord Pas-de-Calais and the Flemish government[58]), local authorities (for France: Départements of Nord and Pas-de-Calais; Dunkerque urban community; 'Moulins de Flandre' and 'Coeur de Flandre' pays; for Belgium: West Flanders Province; West-Vlaamse intermunicipal;) and two local publically funded organisations (Urbanism and Development Agency of Flanders Region – AGUR and ERSV West-Vlaanderen on behalf of Resoc Westhoek). Due to the presence of competent authorities within a given cross-border area, EGTC has a good potential for dealing with transboundary issues in MSP. It can promote a coherent implementation of authorities' competences by supporting a regular dialogue and is consistent with the EU Territorial Cohesion Policy on maritime matters. The Galicia North Portugal EGTC already plans to develop projects concerning maritime issues[59] and West-Vlaanderen-Flandre-Dunkerque-Côte d'Opale EGTC has set up a working group dedicated to maritime cooperation.

From a technical point of view, EGTCs are flexible enough to encompass large areas too, such as the Amphictyony EGTC linking Mediterranean islands from France to Greece (Spinaci, 2009). However, considering transboundary MSP at this scale, the framework of regional seas conventions can be considered more appropriate.

Regional seas conventions

Dedicated to the marine environment, the regional seas conventions are well-established frameworks embracing large geographic areas in which states can discuss their policy priorities. They have still an important role in stimulating and coordinating a marine environmental policy. The North-East Atlantic Sea is covered by the OSPAR Convention. Its Commission aims to develop its capacities to support the implementation of MSP. A comparable dynamic can be seen within the Helsinki Convention on the protection of the Baltic Sea. In 2003, the first joint ministerial meeting of the OSPAR and Helsinki Commissions (OSPARCOM and HELCOM) already mentioned MSP as a tool for managing human activities at sea.[60] Several major OSPAR policy documents refer to MSP. Its 'Quality Status Report 2010',[61] the Bergen Statement of the 2010 OSPARCOM ministerial meeting[62] and the North-East Atlantic Environment Strategy consider MSP as a tool for integrated management of human activities.[63] This strategy advocates measures developed by OSPARCOM to support transboundary cooperation and consultation. The Commission set up an Intersessional Correspondence Group dedicated to MSP. This group works especially on a joint spatial map of the southern North Sea to identify transboundary issues and a draft OSPAR recommendation on MSP for which a consultation procedure was proposed as a point of departure to further develop mechanisms for transnational cooperation.[64]

The OSPAR interest towards MSP is not an isolated case. A similar process is commonly led by HELCOM and Vision and Strategies around the Baltic Sea (VASAB), gathering ministers responsible for spatial planning and development.[65] As decided in the HELCOM Baltic Sea Action Plan, they have commonly developed MSP principles,[66] and the Fifth Conference of Ministers Responsible for Spatial Planning and Development in the countries of the Baltic Sea region has adopted the Wismar Declaration on transnational spatial planning and development policies for the Baltic Sea region 2010.[67]

The framework of regional sea conventions presents some benefits to transboundary cooperation in MSP. They already exist and do not require a new dedicated institution. Moreover, the involvement of regional sea conventions in the implementation of the MSFD, which mention MSP, increases that potential. However, these instruments and bodies can be seen as too large a forum to address specific transboundary issues. It will need some complementary means to enhance cooperation in bilateral and multilateral agreements within a smaller geographical scope. Moreover, some authors consider that MSP should be a 'neutral' tool, whereas the purpose of regional sea conventions is environmental conservation only (Schaefer and Barale, 2011). Even if, in the context of the EU, cooperation is increasingly developed through EU legislation, international agreements are still used and EU legislation can even refer to them for its implementation. This is the case for the Water Framework Directive (WFD).[68]

The major advantage of developing international agreements with a local or specific focus is the ability to design tailor-made cooperation that can include a large variety of obligations ranging from weak to strong commitments and to establish bodies able to monitor the implementation of those obligations (e.g. secretariat and scientific committees). However, legal agreements appear less flexible than policy agreements (e.g. North Sea Declaration, trilateral Wadden Sea Declaration), although much depends on the mandate given to the institutions set up by the agreement. The French–Belgian Fisheries Commission extended its scope to adapt to new issues without amending the agreement.

Policy cooperation

Transboundary MSP cooperation is mainly bilateral and cooperation is focusing on the exchange of information, the preparation of planning, the development of future visions, the organization of stakeholder participation and how to adapt to new situations (i.e. cooperation between civil servants in which also scientists need to be involved). This cooperation can be adequately dealt with by means of bilateral or trilateral memoranda of understanding (MoUs) that do not require ratification and are flexible instruments to cope with new situations. An example of a successful memorandum is the Paris Memorandum of Understanding on Port State Control in Europe.[69] Combined with a MoU or separately, a political commitment such as a ministerial declaration as a basis for cooperation is often an added value.

A policy agreement is the choice made in the trilateral Wadden Sea cooperation.[70] This cooperation is based on ministerial declarations establishing a framework for cooperation: a permanent secretariat and regular meetings. This is a long-term international cooperation, which began 30 years ago with the Joint Declaration on the Protection of the Wadden Sea in 1982. Trilateral governmental conferences regularly meet every two to three years, as part of a secretariat that was set up in 1987 and afterwards a Wadden Sea Forum for stakeholders was created (Moser and Brown, 2007). The Wadden Sea Plan is one of the only existing examples of transboundary MSP.

The proposed MSP/ICZM EU Directive

Following the 'Roadmap on Maritime Spatial Planning: Achieving Common Principles in the EU', the EC DG MARE proposed to develop a legislative proposal concerning MSP called the 'Proposal for a legislative action of the

European Parliament and Council setting a framework for Maritime Spatial Planning'.[71] Several options have been considered 'from no action to detailed legislative measures'.[72] To assess available options, the EC launched a stakeholder consultation through a questionnaire on MSP and ICZM where 255 responses were received. The results showed that 154 respondents currently consider cross-border cooperation in MSP as moderately difficult or difficult. However, they largely advocate cross-border cooperation in MSP. Almost half of the respondents support the establishment of a 'platform for MSP cooperation in each sea basin'. From the results of this consultation, cross-border cooperation appears to be a 'central element' requiring further action from the EC.

As a result, on 12 March 2013, EC published a proposal for a Directive establishing a framework for MSP and ICZM widely focusing on cross-border cooperation.[73] This is a framework directive based on EU sectoral competencies regarding fisheries, energy, transport and the environment.[74] Sectors such as the trans-European network, tourism and cooperative administration could have completed the list. Moreover, the EU competence in contributing to territorial coherence could have been used as a legal basis for an integrated approach on the coastal zone and at sea.[75] However, it is obvious that the EC wants to avoid interfering with national competences on planning issues.[76] To this aim, article 2.3 of the draft Directive states that 'The provisions of this Directive shall be without prejudice to Member States' competences for town and country planning'. However, it seems that the EC has a different approach concerning sea planning when mentioning that MS shall establish and implement a MSP or plans.[77] Furthermore 'maritime spatial plans shall contain at least a mapping of marine waters which identifies the actual and potential spatial and temporal distribution of all relevant maritime activities' (art. 7). Although it seems at first glance that MS are not obliged to develop a legal basis for their MSP, article 18 nevertheless contains a duty for MS to transpose the draft Directive through laws, regulations and administrative provision. The EU draft Directive focuses on minimum operational requirements for transboundary cooperation, such as the establishment of a process to ensure cooperation between MS and between sectoral stakeholders in order to assess transboundary effects of MSP of MS (art. 6 (2) c) and to ensure well-coordinated and coherent plans and management strategies that cover a larger area than the one under national jurisdiction of one MS (art. 12.1). The Commission will have an oversight on this, while reporting will have to take place every six years (art. 15). The draft Directive further pays attention to the issue of data collection and exchange of information (art. 10). This is a critical issue that arose constantly in the interviews and focus groups during the TransMaSP project. Everyone agreed that there is a need for more and better data as well as for data sharing among neighbouring states. Indeed, developing MSP requires good data sets on the state of the marine environment, activities and legislation. These data sets are usually incomplete, not transparent, not accessible or not exchangeable, for example due to language difficulties, lack of protocols, data sharing formats and guidelines. Moreover, as summarized by the EC, 'Finding out who holds the data is already a major challenge. Obtaining them can take weeks of negotiation. Putting them together to provide a complete picture can be a nightmare.'[78] This is a problem for all stakeholders, including administrations and scientists.[79] Certain European Directives, and in particular the WFD and the MSFD, oblige MS to complete a number of their data sets. Furthermore, the INSPIRE Directive establishing an Infrastructure for Spatial Information in the European Community is enhancing sharing and diffusion of spatial data.[80] In addition, within the framework of 'Marine Knowledge 2020'[81] the EU is supporting the European Marine Observation and Data Network (EMODnet) which offers a common platform to gather marine data.[82] But this very promising process is still beginning and faces resistance with respect to data sharing.[83] As a basis for transparency, data sharing should be improved since comprehensive information on environment and sea use management is crucial for decision-making and for effective stakeholder participation. However, even if the proposal states that MS shall collect data and exchange information, it does not detail the way to process this data, except for making 'use, as far as possible, of instruments and tools developed under the Integrated Maritime Policy' (art. 10). The EC is granted the power to further adopt provisions on data sharing and data interface in surplus of the requirements of the INSPIRE and the Marine Strategy Framework Directives (art. 16 1(a)).

Finally, providing a binding commitment to cooperate, while leaving flexibility concerning the means of cooperation, the proposed MSP/ICZM Directive is a good way of improving transboundary cooperation, with the focus on an integrated approach of maritime activities and to develop a comprehensive and common vision on sea uses that affect or might affect the maritime border areas of MS.

Conclusion

French–Belgian cooperation for the management of certain maritime activities clearly indicates a willingness to cooperate when transboundary issues are at stake. This cooperation is mainly on a sectoral basis (i.e. fisheries, nature conservation, shipping) and often *ad hoc* or problem solving, but less forward looking. Although there are broader frameworks (such as EU, OSPAR, IMO) to cooperate, bilateral cooperation still remains the practice to deal with local cross-border issues. Some bilateral cooperation has a formal legal basis, such as the fisheries commission, while others are part of a particular policy choice (Natura 2000). In contrast to Qiu and Jones (2013), who advocated for non-binding EU legislation on MSP, an EU Directive will better ensure transboundary cooperation on MSP among MS. Indeed, despite the incentives of the MSP roadmap, a strong stimulus for integrated cooperation is clearly lacking today. At the same time, the proposed Directive on MSP/ICZM leaves MS to decide on how to cooperate.

This cooperative process should be seen as a node linking existing sectoral cooperation and informal networks towards a framework suitable for an integrated approach of all sectors relevant for transboundary MSP. A transition from sectoral cooperation towards an integrated approach of all sectors relevant for MSP requires a flexible formal basis, which can be found in two cooperation instruments that highlight local specificities. The EGTC would be a suitable structure, in particular to link ICZM with MSP with the potential to include local, regional and national authorities. Otherwise, if third parties should have access to MSP cooperation in the Belgian-French maritime border due to their involvement or interests in certain activities such as fisheries, MPA network, shipping and offshore wind energy, a MoU would be the most suitable instrument. A MoU is flexible in terms of adoption (no ratification required) and its objectives to be achieved (easy amendment procedure). As a starting point, a bilateral MoU can be adopted, while leaving room for inviting third parties as observers for matters affecting their interests. Several MoUs between states bordering the same regional sea would contribute to cooperation on transboundary MSP, as stated in the draft EU Directive on MSP/ICZM, while leaving the competences of MS regarding their town and country planning untouched. Stakeholder participation in a transboundary MSP process is a major challenge that can be dealt with in a MoU between neighbouring states or in an EGTC.

Acknowledgment

This study was developed in the framework of the TransMaSP project, standing for Transboundary Maritime Spatial Planning, funded by a Marie Curie Fellowship Grant, Intra-European Fellowships for career development (IEF). See: http://www.transmasp.ugent.be/nl

Notes

1 Communication from the Commission, 'Roadmap for Maritime Spatial Planning: Achieving Common Principles in the EU', COM (2008) 791 final, p. 14. Available at the following address: http://ec.europa.eu/governance/impact/planned_ia/docs/2011_mare_017_maritime_spacial_planning_en.pdf

2 See: http://ec.europa.eu/maritimeaffairs/spatial_planning_en.html

3 The 2011/MARE/017 roadmap document gives some elements of possible answers. The aim of the initiative is described as follows: '(i) Ensure that Member States provide a stable, reliable and future-oriented integrated planning framework to optimise the use of marine space to benefit economic development and the sustainable use of the marine environment. (ii) Ensure that in doing so, Member States apply a common approach in order to facilitate cross-border maritime spatial planning.' The EU level is justified because 'Yes, action should be taken by the EU to ensure that national systems link up with each other in a way that provides a framework for efficient cross-border cooperation and the rational management of the European maritime space'.

4 European Commission, Proposal for a Directive of the European Parliament and of the Council establishing a Framework for Maritime Spatial Planning and Integrated Coastal Management, COM(2013)133, 12 March 2013.

5 TransMaSP stands for Transboundary Maritime Spatial Planning and was a project funded by a Marie Curie Fellowship Grant, Intra-European Fellowships for career development (IEF). See: http://www.transmasp.ugent.be/nl

6 Communication from the Commission, 'Roadmap for Maritime Spatial Planning: Achieving Common Principles in the EU', op. cit.

7 *Arrêté royal du 16 octobre 2012 modifiant l'arrêté royal du 14 octobre 2005 créant des zones de protection spéciale et des zones de conservation spéciales dans les espaces marins sous juridiction de la Belgique*, *Moniteur Belge 5 novembre 2012*, p. 66465.

8 *Loi du 20 juillet 2012 modifiant la loi du 20 janvier 1999 visant la protection du milieu marin dans les espaces marins sous la juridiction de la Belgique, en ce qui concerne l'organisation de l'aménagement des espaces marins*, *Moniteur Belge 11 septembre 2012*, p. 56962; *Arrêté royal du 20 mars 2014 relatif à l'établissement du plan d'aménagement des espaces marins*, *Moniteur Belge28 mars 2014*, p. 26936.

9 Art. 57 Law n°83-8 of 7 January 1983 *relative à la répartition des compétences entre les communes, les départements, les régions et l'Etat.*

10 Even if offshore wind energy is usually a hot topic for MSP, the stakes in this respect are low at the Belgian–French border. In the Belgian part of the North Sea, offshore wind energy is planned and implemented in the East along the border with the Netherlands while there are no zones designated for offshore wind energy in the North of France next to Belgium. Although offshore wind energy is considered important in both countries, it does not appear to be a transboundary issue in this maritime frontier zone.

11 MRAG, 'Legal aspects of Maritime Spatial Planning: Final report', report to DG Maritime Affairs & Fisheries, 2008, p. 86, Appendices, p. 16.

12 Convention on Maritime Search and Rescue (SAR) adopted 27 April 1979, entered into force 22 June 1985, 1405 *UNTS* No. 23489 (as amended); Convention for the Safety of Life at Sea (SOLAS) adopted 1 November 1974 entered into force 15 May 1980, 1184 *UNTS* No. 1861 (as amended); Convention on Oil Pollution, Preparedness, Response and Cooperation (OPRC) adopted on 30 November 1990, entered into force on 15 May 1995, 30 ILM 733.

13 An agreement for cooperation in dealing with pollution of the North Sea by oil was adopted in Bonn on 9 June 1969. It was revised through the agreement adopted on 13 September 1983, entered into force 1 September 1989, extending its scope and thus adding to its title 'and other harmful substances' OJEC L188 of 16/07/1984, p. 9 (amended by the Decision of 21 September 2002 by the Contracting Parties to enable the Accession of Ireland to the Agreement).

14 Regulation (EC) No 1406/2002 of the European Parliament and of the Council of 27 June 2002 establishing a European Maritime Safety Agency OJ L 208, 5.8.2002, pp. 1–9;

15 Art. 3.1.d). Consolidated version of the Treaty on the Functioning of the European Union, OJEU C 83, 30.3.2010, pp.47–199 (TFUE). Belgium and the Eastern part of North France belong to zone IVc while the West of the North of France belongs to zone VIId.

16 Art. 4.2.d). TFEU.

17 Art.4 1. 1.) Council Regulation (EC) no 1380/2013 of the European Parliament and of the Council of 11 December 2013 on the Common Fisheries Policy, amending Council Regulations (EC) No 1954/2003 and (EC) No 1224/2009 and repealing Council Regulations (EC) No 2371/2002 and (EC) No 639/2004 and Council Decision 2004/585/EC OJ L 354, 28/12/2013, p. 22–61.

18 Art. 5.1 Council Regulation (EC) no. 1380/2013, *op. cit.*
19 Art. 5.2 Council Regulation (EC) no. 1380/2013, *op. cit.*
20 Annex I Council Regulation (EC) no. 1380/2013, *op. cit.*
21 EC, Proposal for a Regulation of the European Parliament and of the Council on the Common Fisheries Policy COM(2011) 425 final, 13 July 2011.
22 See concession zones at http://www.mumm.ac.be/EN/Management/Atlas/map.php?WindmillsCurrent.
23 *Arrêté royal du 11 avril 2012 établissant une zone de sécurité autour des îles artificielles, installations et ouvrages pour une production d'énergie à partir de l'eau, des courants et des vents dans les espaces marins sous la juridiction de la Belgique*, Moniteur Belge *1 juin 2012*, p. 31377.
24 *Arrêté royal du 3 février 2011 modifiant l' arrêté royal du 20 décembre 2000 relatif aux conditions et à la procédure d'octroi des concessions domaniales pour la construction et l'exploitation d'installations de production d'électricité à partir de l'eau, des courants ou des vents dans les espaces marins sur lesquels la Belgique peut exercer sa juridiction conformément au droit international de la mer*, Moniteur Belge *17 février 2011*, p. 11741.
25 Art. 5 *Arrêté royal du 11 avril 2012 établissant une zone de sécurité autour des îles artificielles, installations et ouvrages pour une production d'énergie à partir de l'eau, des courants et des vents dans les espaces marins sous la juridiction de la Belgique*, Moniteur Belge *1 juin 2012*, p. 31378.
26 *Décret n°76-205 du 24 février 1976 portant publication de l'échange de lettre des 30 septembre et 23 octobre 1975 entre la France et la Belgique relatif à l'exercice des pêches saisonnières dans les eaux territoriales belges et françaises. Journal officiel du 1° mars 1976, p. 1401, JORF du 2 mars 1976 page 1401.*
27 Council Decision 2004/585/EC of 19 July 2004 establishing Regional Advisory Councils under the Common Fisheries Policy OJEU, L 256 , 03/08/2004, p. 0017–0022.
28 Directive 2008/56/EC of the European Parliament and of the Council of 17 June 2008 establishing a framework for community action in the field of marine environmental policy (Marine Strategy Framework Directive), OJ L 164, 25.6.2008, pp. 19–40.
29 Art. 6 Marine Strategy Framework Directive.
30 Art. 5.2 and 6 Marine Strategy Framework Directive.
31 Art. 4.1 Marine Strategy Framework Directive.
32 Art. 5 Marine Strategy Framework Directive.
33 See http://ec.europa.eu/environment/water/marine/implementation_en.htm
34 Informal Meeting of Water and Marine Directors of the European Union, Candidate and EFTA Countries, Budapest, 26–27 May 2011, Final Synthesis, 9p., p. 2.
35 See the OSPAR website: http://www.ospar.org/
36 http://www.ospar.org/documents/dbase/publications/p00501_MSFD%20Roadmap.pdf
37 Art. 18 Council Directive 92/43/EEC of 21 May 1992 on the conservation of natural habitats and of wild fauna and flora, OJ L 206, 22.7.1992, p. 7 (Habitats Directive).
38 Art. 4.3 Directive 2009/147/EC of the European Parliament and of the Council of 30 November 2009 on the conservation of wild birds OJ L 20, 26/01/2010, p. 7–25 (Birds Directive) and art. 4 and 5 of the Habitat Directive.
39 The Birds Directive mentions 'coordination' for measures and research, which belong to EC, but don't state about cooperation. Al. 8 of its preamble states that for the conservation of birds and their habitats: 'Such measures must also take account of migratory species and be coordinated with a view to setting up a coherent whole.' 'Member States shall send the Commission all relevant information so that it may

take appropriate initiatives with a view to the coordination necessary to ensure that the areas provided for in paragraphs 1 and 2 form a coherent whole which meets the protection requirements of these species in the geographical sea and land area where this Directive applies' (article 4.3) and 'Member States shall send the Commission any information required to enable it to take appropriate measures for the coordination of the research and work referred to in paragraph 1.' (art. 10 al. 2).

40 See this zone at http://www.mumm.ac.be/EN/Management/Atlas/map.php?MarineProtectedAreas

41 *Arrêté Royal du 16 octobre 2012 modifiant l'arrêté Royal du 14 octobre 2005 créant des zones de protection et des zones de conservation spéciales dans les espaces marins sous juridiction de la Belgique*, *Moniteur Belge 5 novembre 2012*, p. 66465.

42 Art. 7 Council Directive 85/337/EEC of 27 June 1985 on the assessment of the effects of certain public and private projects on the environment OJ L 175, 5.7.1985, pp. 40–48

43 Directive 2011/92/EU of the European Parliament and of the Council of 13 December 2011 on the assessment of the effects of certain public and private projects on the environment, OJ L 26, 28.1.2012, pp. 1–21.

44 Convention on Environmental Impact Assessment in a Transboundary Context adopted in Espoo, 25 February 1991, entered into force on 10 September 1997. As a matter of interest, the International Agreement on the Scheldt, the so-called *Accord de Gand* 4.4, deals with EIA too, as well as the OSPAR Convention but in a limitative way, art. 21.1 (MRAG, 2008).

45 Directive 2001/42/EC of the European Parliament and of the Council of 27 June 2001 on the assessment of the effects of certain plans and programmes on the environment *OJ L 197, 21.7.2001*, pp. 30–37.

46 Protocol on Strategic Environmental Assessment adopted in Kiev, 21 May 2003, entered into force on 11 July 2010.

47 Representatives from the State at the local and regional levels.

48 *Direction Régionale de l'Environnement, de l'Aménagement et du Logement* (Regional direction for the environment, development and housing).

49 Interviews and questionnaire have been developed in the framework of the TransMaSP project.

50 Workshop 5 cooperation maritime conference 2007 'Cross-border territories day-to-day Europe' http://www.espaces-transfrontaliers.org/en/themes/theme_maritime.html.

51 Council Decision 2006/702/EC of 6 October 2006 on Community strategic guidelines on cohesion, OJ L 291, 21.10.2006, pp. 11–32.

52 'The development and implementation of macro-regional and sea-basin strategies (within the thematic objective of enhancing institutional capacity and an efficient public administration) especially through macro-regional and sea-basin strategies': COM/2011/0611 final Proposal for a Regulation of the European Parliament and of the Council on specific provisions for the support from the European Regional Development Fund to the European territorial cooperation goal.

53 Regulation (EC) No 1082/2006 of the European Parliament and of the Council of 5 July 2006 on a European grouping of territorial cooperation (EGTC), OJUE L 210 of 31.7.2006.

54 COM(2011) 462 final report from the commission to the European Parliament and the Council on 'The application of the Regulation (EC) No 1082/2006 on a European Grouping of Territorial Cooperation (EGTC)' 12 p., p. 2.

55 Preamble al. 13 Regulation (EC) No 1082/2006 of the European Parliament and of the Council of 5 July 2006 on a European grouping of territorial cooperation (EGTC) OJ L 210, 31.7.2006, pp. 19–24.
56 Based on the feedback of first implementations, a revision of the Regulation is planned. See: COM/2011/0610 final Proposal for a Regulation of the European Parliament and of the Council amending Regulation (EC) No. 1082/2006 of the European Parliament and of the Council of 5 July 2006 on a European grouping of territorial cooperation (EGTC) as regards the clarification, simplification and improvement of the establishment and implementation of such groupings.
57 COM(2011) 462 final *op. cit.*
58 Flemish Region and Community.
59 See: http://www.gnpaect.eu/index.php?componente=noticias&arch=index&id=232
60 OSPAR-HELCOM, Statement on the ecosystem approach to the management of human activities, first joint ministerial meeting of the Helsinki and OSPAR Commissions (JMM). Bremen, Germany, 25–26 June 2003.
61 OSPAR Commission, Quality Status Report 2010, 177p, especially p. 92 http://qsr2010.ospar.org/en/media/chapter_pdf/QSR_complete_EN.pdf
62 Bergen Statement, Ministerial Meeting of the OSPAR Commission, Bergen: 23–24 September 2010, available at the following address: http://www.ospar.org/html_documents/ospar/news/ospar_2010_bergen_statement.pdf
63 Strategy of the OSPAR Commission for the Protection of the Marine Environment of the North-East Atlantic 2010–2020 adopted by the agreement 2010-03 in 2010, Bremen available at the following address: http://www.ospar.org/html_documents/ospar/html/10-03e_nea_environment_strategy.pdf
64 Terms of Reference for ICG Marine Spatial Planning (ICG-MSP), OSPAR Convention for the Protection of the Marine Environment of the North East Atlantic, Meeting of the Environmental Impact of Human Activities Committee (EIHA) The Hague: 16–20 April 2012 available at the following address: http://www.ospar.org/zip/SZ20120518-174001-2663/download.zip
65 See the Mandate for the joint, co-chaired Working Group on Maritime Spatial Planning between HELCOM and VASAB; minutes of the Joint HELCOM-VASAB Maritime Spatial Planning Working Group First Meeting Helsinki, Finland, 21–22 October 2010, Annex 2, available at the following address: http://meeting.helcom.fi/web/bsap/5
66 Baltic Sea Broad-Scale Maritime Spatial Planning (MSP) Principles, available at the following address: http://meeting.helcom.fi/web/bsap/5
67 Wismar Declaration on transnational spatial planning and development policies for the Baltic Sea Region to 2010, Fifth Conference of Ministers Responsible for Spatial Planning and Development in the Countries of the Baltic Sea Region held under the chairmanship of the German Federal Minister for Transport, Building and Housing in Wismar on 21 September 2001, available at the following address: http://www.vasab.org/?id=36
68 Directive 2000/60/EC of the European Parliament and of the Council of 23 October 2000 establishing a framework for Community action in the field of water policy, *OJEC* L.327, p. 1.
69 See http://www.parismou.org/
70 See http://www.waddensea-secretariat.org/
71 Proposal for a legislative action of the European Parliament and Council setting a framework for Maritime Spatial Planning (2011/MARE/017), October 2010, available

at the following address: http://ec.europa.eu/governance/impact/planned_ia/docs/2011_mare_017_maritime_spacial_planning_en.pdf

72 Ibid.

73 European Commission, Proposal for a Directive of the European Parliament and of the Council establishing a Framework for Maritime Spatial Planning and Integrated Coastal Management, *op. cit.*

74 EU competences regarding the Common Fisheries Policy (art. 43 al. 2); transport (art. 4 al. g, 91 al. 1 and 100 al. 2); environment (art. 4 al. e and 192 al. 1); and energy (art. 4 al. i and 194 al. 2). Shared competences with member states regarding fisheries, excluding the conservation of marine biological resources (art. 4 al. d), trans-European networks (art. 4 al. h and 170), supporting competence regarding tourism (art. 6 al. g and 195 al. 2) or cooperative administration (art. 6 d and 197 al. 2).

75 Art. 175 TFEU.

76 Ibid.

77 Art. 4 of the Proposal for a Directive of the European Parliament and of the Council establishing a Framework for Maritime Spatial Planning and Integrated Coastal Management.

78 EC, Note for the attention of Integrated Maritime Policy Member States Expert Group – Roadmap for European Marine Observation and Data Network (EMODnet), Ref. Ares(2012)275043 – 08/03/2012, p. 2. Available at the following address: http://ec.europa.eu/maritimeaffairs/policy/marine_knowledge_2020/documents/roadmap_en.pdf

79 Ibid.

80 Directive 2007/2/EC of the European Parliament and of the Council of 14 March 2007 establishing an Infrastructure for Spatial Information in the European Community (INSPIRE).

81 Communication from the Commission to the European Parliament and the Council 'Marine Knowledge 2020: marine data and observation for smart and sustainable growth' COM (2010) 461 final, 8 September 2010; 3139th environment Council meeting Brussels, 19 December 2011.

82 Regulation (EU) No 1255/2011 of the European Parliament and of the Council of 30 November 2011 establishing a Programme to support the further development of an Integrated Maritime Policy, OJ L 321, 05/12/2011, pp. 1–10.

83 See for instance the 'ur_EMODnet biology: Final maintenance report', May 2012, available at the following address: https://webgate.ec.europa.eu/maritimeforum/content/2824

References

Backer, H. (2011) 'Transboundary maritime spatial planning: a Baltic Sea perspective', *Journal of Coastal Conservation*, vol. 15, no. 2, pp. 279–89.

Cacqueray, M. D. (2011) *La planification des espaces maritimes en France métropolitaine: un enjeu majeur pour la mise en œuvre de la Gestion Intégrée de la Mer et du Littoral*, PhD, University of Brest.

Dauvin, J C. (2008) 'The Main Characteristics, Problems, and Prospects for Western European Coastal Seas', *Marine Pollution Bulletin*, vol. 57, pp. 22–40.

Douvere, F., Maes, F., Vanhulle, A. and Schrijvers, J. (2007) 'The role of marine spatial planning in sea use management: The Belgian case', *Marine Policy*, vol. 31, no. 2, pp. 182–91.

Groenleer, M., Kaeding, M. and Versluis, E. (2010) 'Regulatory governance through agencies of the European Union? The role of the European agencies for maritime and aviation safety in the implementation of European transport legislation', *Journal of European Public Policy*, vol. 17, no. 8, pp. 1212–30.

Koivurova, T. (2009) 'A Note on the European Union's Integrated Maritime Policy' *Ocean Development & International Law*, vol. 40, no. 2, pp. 171–83.

Liu, N. and Maes, F. (2009) 'The European Union's Role in the Prevention of Vessel-source Pollution and Its Internal Influence' *The Journal of International Maritime Law*, vol. 15, no. 5, pp. 411–22.

Maes, F. (2008) 'The international legal framework for marine spatial planning', *Marine Policy*, vol. 32, no. 5, pp. 797–810.

Maes, F., Cliquet, A., Van Gaever, S., Lescrauwaet, A.K., Pirlet, H. and Verleye, T. (2013a) 'The Marine Science–Policy Interface', in Lescrauwaet, A.K., Pirlet, H., Verleye, T., Mees, J., Herman, R. (eds), *Compendium for Coast and Sea: integrating knowledge on the socio-economic, environmental and institutional aspects of the Coast and Sea in Flanders and in Belgium*, Oostende, pp. 288–95. Available at http:// www.compendiumcoastandsea.be

Maes, F., Vanhulle, A. and Lescrauwaet, A.K. (2013b) 'Marine Spatial Planning', in Lescrauwaet, A.K., Pirlet, H., Verleye, T., Mees, J., Herman, R. (eds). *Compendium for Coast and Sea: integrating knowledge on the socio-economic, environmental and institutional aspects of the Coast and Sea in Flanders and in Belgium*, Oostende, pp. 261–73. Available at http:// www.compendiumcoastandsea.be

Moser, M. and Brown, A. (2007) 'Trilateral Wadden Sea Cooperation External Evaluation Report', p. 79. Available at the following address: http://www.waddensea-secretariat.org/news/Evaluation/Wadden%20Sea%20Evaluation%20Report%20Final070621.pdf

Plasman, I. C. (2008) 'Implementing marine spatial planning: A policy perspective', *Marine Policy*, vol. 32, no. 5, pp. 811–15.

Qiu, W. and Jones, P.J.S. (2013) 'The emerging policy landscape for marine spatial planning in Europe' *Marine Policy*, vol. 39, pp. 182–90.

Queffelec, B. and Maes, F. (2013) 'Improving Sea-Land Management by Linking Maritime Spatial Planning and Integrated Coastal Zone Management – French and Belgian Experiences', *Ocean Yearbook*, vol. 27, pp. 147–70.

Schaefer, N. and Barale, V. (2011) 'Maritime Spatial Planning: Opportunities & Challenges in the Framework of the EU Integrated Maritime Policy', *Journal of Coastal Conservation*, vol. 15, pp. 237–45.

Spinaci, G. and Vara-arribas, G. (2009) 'The European Grouping of Territorial Cooperation (EGTC): New Spaces and Contracts for European Integration?' *EIPASCOPE*, no. 2, pp. 5–13.

Trouillet, B., Guineberteau, T., de Cacqueray, M. and Rochette, J. (2011) 'Planning the sea: The French experience. Contribution to marine spatial planning perspectives', *Marine Policy*, vol. 35, no. 3, pp. 324–34.

Chapter 8.2

Transboundary marine spatial planning in the Irish Sea

Stephen Jay

Introduction

The Atlantic region of Europe can be defined as the Atlantic seaboard nations of western Europe and their marine territories, including their extensive exclusive economic zones (EEZ) and continental shelf areas. The region's marine area broadly coincides with the north-east Atlantic as defined by OSPAR, the regional sea convention which represents these nations (Alexander, 2004; OSPAR, undated). In addition, island territories, especially of Portugal and Spain, extend the marine interests of the region further into the northern mid-Atlantic; this is becoming more evident with current applications for extensions of the continental shelf (Suárez de Vivero, 2013), representing, perhaps, a renewed 'Atlanticism', in the wake of former western, maritime expansion (Suárez de Vivero and Rodriguez Mateos, 2014).

The European Commission has identified the north-east Atlantic (NEA) as a regional sea, and through policy has given it more prominent attention by the development of an Atlantic Strategy, with a specific Action Plan, as part of the Commission's blue growth agenda (Commission of the European Communities (CEC), 2011, 2012, 2013). However, this strategy only includes the five Member States facing the open ocean, and not those facing just the North Sea; the North Sea is generally regarded as a separate entity as far as maritime policy is concerned (European Commission, undated).

The NEA is a geographically diverse region; it spans northern and southern Europe and includes continental and island nations as well as a wide range of sea areas, from semi-enclosed shelf seas to the deep ocean. It is the European sea area with the strongest oceanic characteristics, especially as far as the five Atlantic Strategy nations and Norway are concerned. The pattern of nation states within the region creates a complex network of transboundary areas at sea. EEZs have been established throughout the region. These generally extend into the north Atlantic from the full 200 nautical miles (nm) limit, set under the United Nations Convention on the Law of the Sea (UNCLOS), with further continental shelf areas in some cases, creating a large marine hinterland for Atlantic nations. However, not all international maritime borders have been agreed in the region.

Some European Atlantic nations have established their own statutory systems of maritime (or marine) spatial planning (MSP) over the last decade, namely Belgium, Germany, the Netherlands, Norway, Portugal and the United Kingdom (Jay *et al.*, 2013). The others will follow with the adoption of the MSP Directive (2014/89/EU) establishing a framework for maritime spatial planning (European Parliament & Council, 2014). These systems generally include provisions to carry out cross-border consultation when preparing a plan for an area with an international maritime border. For instance, the UK has recently completed a plan for its East Offshore area involved consultation with neighbouring North Sea nations (HM Government, 2014). The Directive places a specific requirement on Member States to cooperate in coordinating their plans in a marine region, such as the Atlantic, taking into account transnational issues.

However, transboundary cooperation to date has been of a voluntary and non-binding nature. One such example is a project co-funded by the European Commission which involved two transboundary planning exercises in the Atlantic region, as described below. This was one of a series of projects exploring cooperation in MSP between EU Member States. (The scope of this project was limited to one or more cross-border sea areas situated within the European Atlantic, thus excluding the North Sea and Norway.) This project, called Transboundary Planning in the European Atlantic (TPEA, undated), involved not just scientific institutions, but also government authorities with responsibility for coastal management or MSP, with the intention that the project's outputs could potentially contribute to the development of transboundary MSP, even though they were non-statutory in nature.

TPEA focused on two pilot areas in the southern and northern waters of the NEA, one in the Gulf of Cadiz between Portugal and Spain, and the other in the Irish Sea between Ireland and Northern Ireland (UK). The transboundary exercise was conducted over 18 months, ending in mid-2014. In this section, the focus is on some key features of the project and their wider implications for transboundary MSP with a particular focus on the Irish Sea pilot area.

The difficulties of defining a transboundary area

MSP introduces a stronger spatiality to maritime governance, with the focus on arranging uses and interests into more coordinated geographical patterns (Ehler and Douvere, 2007). It presupposes clearly defined areas for which plans can be drawn up, following terrestrial planning practice. But this is more problematic at sea than on land, for a number of reasons. Firstly, there are fewer, or less clearly established administrative boundaries of the kind that usually form the basis for terrestrial plan areas. Secondly, the environment is more graded and shifting than on land, with fewer natural or human features to suggest where plan boundaries might lie. Thirdly, many maritime activities are mobile and less well disposed to being contained within plan areas or specific sites (Jay, 2013).

These difficulties are not insurmountable and, within the context of national MSP, plan boundaries are being drawn up (generally on a much larger scale than for terrestrial plans) and being given legal standing for the purposes of MSP. These may simply represent the whole or a large part of national waters, as in the case of mainland Portugal's marine plan, or an EEZ, as in the case of Germany's federal marine plan. Where national waters are subdivided, the definition of plan areas typically represents a compromise, taking into account such things as legal zoning of the sea (such as the border between territorial waters and the EEZ), broad environmental or ecosystem distinctions (as defined, for example, under the EU's 'Marine Strategy Framework Directive') and broad patterns of use (such as areas heavily used for shipping). In the UK, for instance, ten marine plan areas have been defined for English waters, following a consultation process in which considerations of these particularities in marine planning were taken into account (Department for Environment, Food and Rural Affairs, 2011).

However, these difficulties are heightened further within transboundary contexts. The logic of transboundary MSP is that it should be based on cross-border areas within which matters of shared concern are considered, such as the impacts of maritime activities spreading across a border, or the potential for mutual benefits from planned activities. But, considering the three points above, firstly, it is unlikely that there would be administrative boundaries to help with defining such areas (Jay, 2010). Even where new boundaries have been established for the purpose of national-level MSP, as in English waters, these may not assist in encapsulating in a meaningful way areas of transboundary influence. It would also be difficult to attribute legal standing to any such transboundary area, no matter how defined, of a kind equivalent to that which has been established for national marine plans. This would require some form of special agreement, which the nations concerned might be reluctant to come to, not least as it might be seen as undermining national sovereignty as far as the part of the transboundary area falling within each nation's territory is concerned.

Secondly, trying to accommodate ecosystem dynamics and, thirdly, containing mobile maritime activities may prove even more problematic when defining transboundary rather than national plan areas (Jay, 2012). It is true that part of the rationale for transboundary MSP is that it offers the opportunity to do precisely this; 'artificial' national borders can be transcended and cross-border considerations can be taken into account more effectively (Gilliland and Laffoley, 2008). But translating this aim into practice by establishing plan areas specifically with transboundary dynamics in mind is no simple matter. The starting-point for this approach is to assume that transboundary activities can have impacts (either negative or positive) on each side of a border. The transboundary area may, therefore, be drawn in such a way as to capture the extent of those impacts. However, effects are likely to diminish with distance from their source; there is no clear-cut point at which they cease to have transboundary relevance (Figure 8.2.1). Also, the range of the impacts from one activity will not be the same as that from another. For example, the visual effect of an offshore wind array is likely to be more limited in scope than the migration of pollution from an industrial outfall (Figure 8.2.2). Moreover, impacts may vary in their direction, reach and intensity with changing conditions, such as currents, weather and the seasons; no stable line can accurately represent the shifting limits of transboundary influence. So a simply-drawn transboundary area is unlikely to accommodate the variable and multi-scalar consequences of maritime activities in a satisfactory manner. In one of its pilot areas, the TPEA project attempted to deal with these challenges in the following way.

The Irish Sea: a graded transboundary area

The focus of attention in TPEA's northern pilot area was the transboundary area in the Irish Sea between Ireland and Northern Ireland (UK). Ireland does not yet have an MSP system, but is developing its marine policy and some technical capacity for MSP (Inter-Departmental Marine Coordination Group, 2012). Within Northern Ireland, the Department of the Environment has statutory responsibility for preparing a marine plan for its waters. Since the 1998 Belfast Agreement, Ireland and Northern Ireland have sought opportunities for cooperation on matters of shared interest, often expressed in terms of 'all-Ireland' or 'the island of Ireland', phrases which emphasize the shared geography of the two jurisdictions (Murray, 2004). It is in the context of cooperation that institutions on both sides of the border worked together in the TPEA project. This included the government department with responsibility for preparing a marine plan in

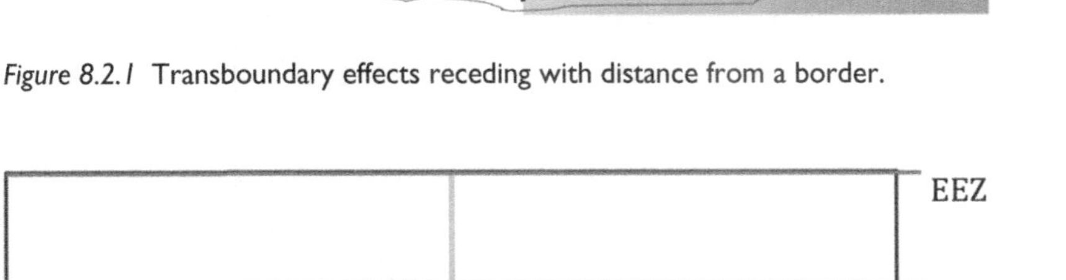

Figure 8.2.1 Transboundary effects receding with distance from a border.

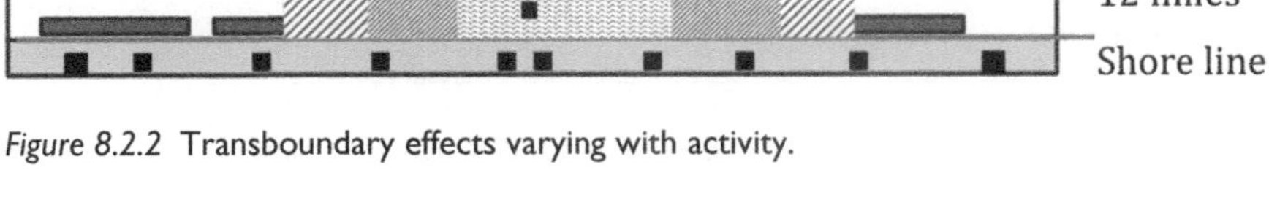

Figure 8.2.2 Transboundary effects varying with activity.

Northern Ireland (Department of the Environment) and a research institution with maritime specialism in Ireland (Coastal and Marine Research Centre, University College Cork), with advisory support from Marine Institute, an Irish government agency. The University of Liverpool, UK, was also a partner in this part of the project.

The pilot area was broadly defined as extending from the international land border on the east coast extending into the Irish Sea. A number of considerations were taken into account in defining the precise limits of the pilot area, reflecting the complications of establishing meaningful transboundary areas as discussed above.

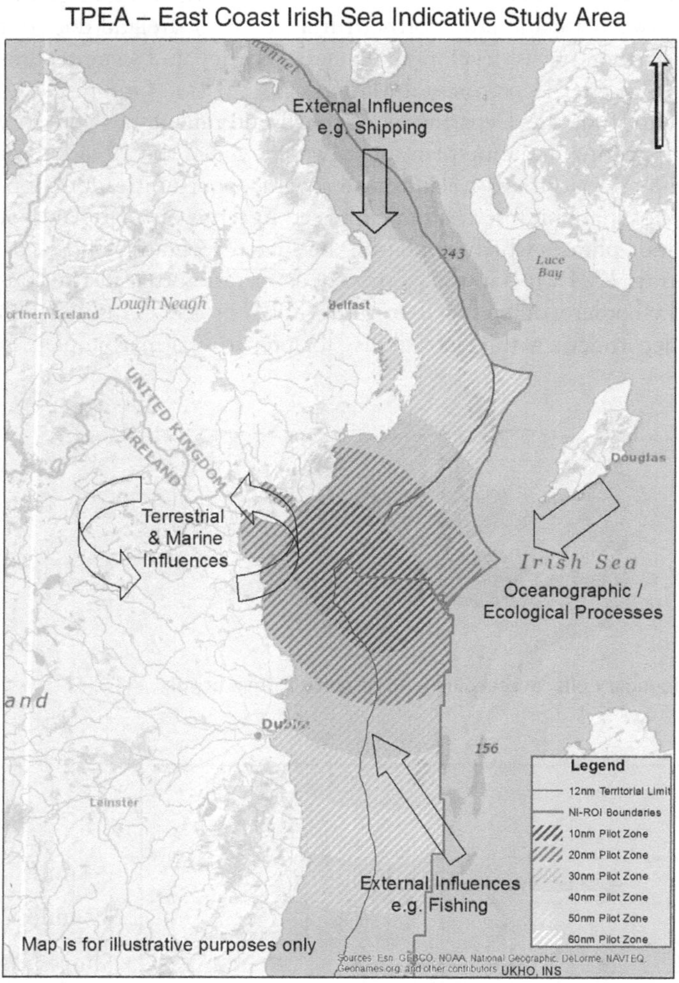

Figure 8.2.3 Transboundary area between Ireland and Northern Ireland.

- International border considerations. The land border terminates at a sea lough (Carlingford Lough). Beyond the 12 nm territorial sea limit there is a boundary between the UK and Ireland that defines the contiguous zone, however, no boundary exists linking the land boundary to the territorial limit. For the purposes of the project a pragmatic approach was adopted, using an imaginary centre line running directly from the axis point where the territorial limit meets the contiguous zone to the end of the land border.
- Other jurisdictional considerations. The outer limit of the pilot area respected the jurisdictional reach of the two jurisdictions, as defined under UNCLOS. Both have territorial waters and/or an EEZ, which adjoin the waters of other Irish Sea jurisdictions (Wales, England, Isle of Man, Scotland). As the focus was on bilateral exchange between Ireland and Northern Ireland, the pilot area was given a hard boundary at these limits, and did not include the other Irish Sea territories.
- A graded approach to transboundary effects. Zones of decreasing intensity extending out from the central area were indicated with different shading at intervals of 10 nm. These zones were intended not to indicate calculated bands of transboundary effects (relating, for example, to varying combinations of different activities), but simply to represent the principle of diminishing effects in an approximate way. Similarly, wider influences from outside the pilot area were suggested by the use of arrows.
- Extension of the pilot area along the coast away from the central zone. It was judged that this should extend to include the maritime and coastal influence of the major coastal cities of Dublin and Belfast in Ireland and Northern Ireland respectively, so the pilot area extended 60 nm in each direction along the coast. Although the TPEA project demonstrated defined boundaries, it was also mindful that beyond these boundary limits there are influences that have significant impacts on transboundary areas, such as oceanic processes, and large-scale transient marine activities such as shipping.
- Landward limit. The pilot area focused mainly on the marine environment. However, it was recognized that land–sea interactions are integral to transboundary MSP, and were kept in mind throughout the project.

So the definition of the pilot areas was a combination of hard borders where necessary for jurisdictional and governance reasons, and softer gradations embodying diminishing transboundary effects and other geographical considerations. The process of determining the extent of pilot areas was a matter of understanding the factors described above and extensive discussion between all parties. It involved not applying pre-set rules, but judging the most appropriate approach for the case in hand. This represents a flexible approach, in line with the European Commission's Roadmap principle for MSP, 'using MSP according to area and type of activity' (CEC, 2008, p. 9).

This flexible and discretionary approach to drawing the boundaries of planning areas is also in keeping with a current trend in terrestrial planning. There are a number of plans that have recently been prepared for areas that do not correspond to administrative boundaries and do not have clearly defined edges. Conventional boundaries, such as between municipalities or even nations, are regarded as unnecessary constraints to the ideas being proposed, and so are overridden in favour of new assemblages of territory that are more suited to the matters in hand. Examples include, in fact, strategies for the two jurisdictions on the island of Ireland, which extend their scope, to a greater or lesser extent, across the border between them (Murray, 2004; Walsh and Knieling, 2013). Moreover, there is a reluctance to define these new territories by tightly-drawn boundaries; instead, the edges are often depicted as fuzzy, blurring into surrounding areas with the potential for expanding further into them, and with arrows and other symbols representing connections with areas beyond the immediate scope of the plan (Haughton *et al.*, 2010). These are generally strategic-level plans in which broad priorities for development for large areas are being set out, with an interest in things like transport corridors, regional development, ecosystem integrity and settlement patterns, where inter-territorial cooperation is regarded as the key to success. They demonstrate a greater emphasis on relations across conventional boundaries, and lead to the creation of new 'soft' spaces with the emphasis upon further change and adaptability.

Interestingly, the first generation of European marine plans are being prepared on a similar geographical scale to these terrestrial strategies, with the emphasis on broad patterns of sea use rather than discrete siting of activities (Calado *et al.*, 2010; Jay *et al.*, 2012). Transboundary MSP obviously correlates to the transnational dimension expressed in some of these strategies. In addition, the graded approach in the TPEA pilot area described above echoes the transition in 'soft space' plans away from the main centre of interest to more peripheral areas, as represented by fuzzy edges, arrows and so on. It would seem that there is considerable scope for exploring the links between the parallel evolution of spatial plans in these terrestrial and marine contexts. Indeed, there may already be some cross-over, as terrestrially focused plans extend (fuzzily and uncertainly, perhaps) into sea space. Similarly, plans which are primarily marine cannot avoid considering the landward connections and dependencies of maritime activities, although typically with some unwillingness to attribute terrestrial issues with the same sense of significance.

Transboundary institutional working

Having selected the pilot area, the transboundary MSP exercise consisted of a number of steps focused around three main elements of MSP:

1 Data (D): spatial data for natural conditions and human activities, collected from various sources, inputted to a Geographical Information System (GIS) and represented on maps.
2 Governance (G): an understanding of the legal, policy and regulatory frameworks relating to marine and coastal issues in the area in question.

3 Stakeholders (S): gaining the participation of sectoral interests and wider communities, and understanding their perspectives on planning the area in question.

The assumption was that each of these elements is of equal importance in MSP, and that outcomes should be based upon drawing together these three sets of knowledge. Figure 8.2.4 illustrates how MSP might thus be conceptualized within a particular jurisdiction.

Within a transboundary setting, each of these elements takes on an added dimension. It is not just a matter of gathering information on these elements in relation to a particular area, but of dealing with the inter-relation of these elements across international borders (Figure 8.2.5). This introduces additional complexities and calls for a greater level of coordination, as follows.

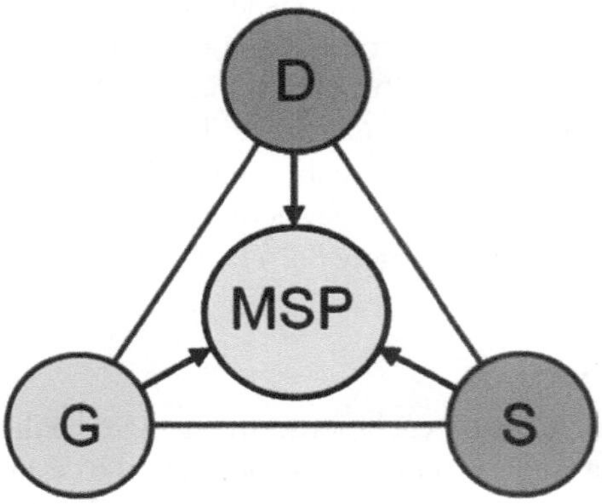

Figure 8.2.4 MSP incorporating data, governance and stakeholder perspectives.

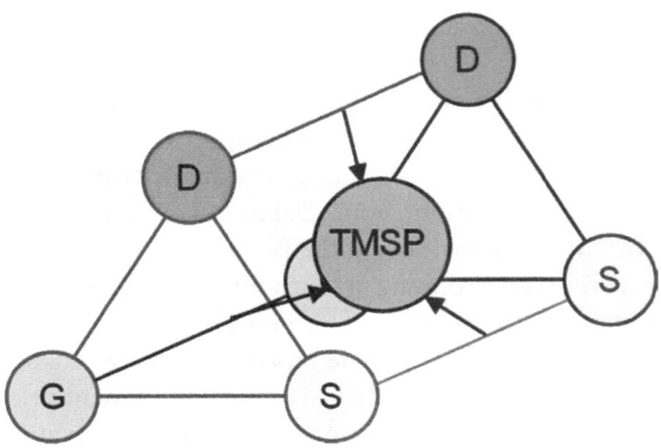

Figure 8.2.5 Inter-relation of elements of MSP in transboundary MSP.

Data

Spatial data for MSP is typically drawn from a disparate range of sources, and inputted into a common GIS, with different forms of data being harmonized as much as possible. The challenges involved in integrating data are multiplied in a transboundary setting, as data will probably be drawn together from different national sources, and must 'speak' to each other, so that, for example, pipeline data on one side of a border meets pipeline data on the other side, and the pipeline is represented as continuous.

In TPEA, data was gathered from UK and Irish sources, to cover a range of maritime and coastal conditions and activities, including natural heritage, fisheries and cables and pipelines (TPEA, 2014). This involved challenges which are typical to MSP as a whole, such as gaining access rights to data, gathering data in a suitable form for input to a common GIS, ensuring that data is of sufficient quality, and so on (TPEA, 2013). Additional challenges were presented in the transboundary context. For example, data for offshore energy was drawn from different national sources, including governmental and commercial bodies, and was harmonized to the best extent possible (Figure 8.2.6). On the other hand, some datasets were already available on an all-Ireland basis, such as recreational data, and some on a Europe-wide basis, such as for seabed habitats. It was then possible to compile a 'composite map' of key activities, demonstrating some of the pressures for the area as a whole (Figure 8.2.7).

Governance

Governance frameworks involve legislation, regulations, strategies and policy for environmental protection and maritime economies as they relate to a marine area, taking into consideration various levels of governance from the local to the international. In a transboundary setting, the governance frameworks for respective jurisdictions must be set alongside each other, and an understanding reached about where the frameworks are in step and reinforce each other, and where there are differences. For example, expectations for nature conservation between nations may be similar or may vary.

In TPEA, governance information was similarly drawn together within each jurisdiction. This covered legislation and policy from the national level downwards. For example, the Irish national strategy on the maritime economy (Inter-Departmental Marine Coordination Group, 2012) will shape marine policy in Ireland and is an important step in achieving the present Government's commitment to expand the Irish ocean economy and attaining the target to double the ocean economy (O'Mahony *et al.*, 2014). This and the UK's marine policy statement (HM Government *et al.*, 2011) set the broad context for cross-border cooperation. A range of strategies and plans then suggest development priorities for certain sectors and localities in both jurisdictions, with regard, for example, to tourism, renewable energy and coastal management. An analysis was carried out

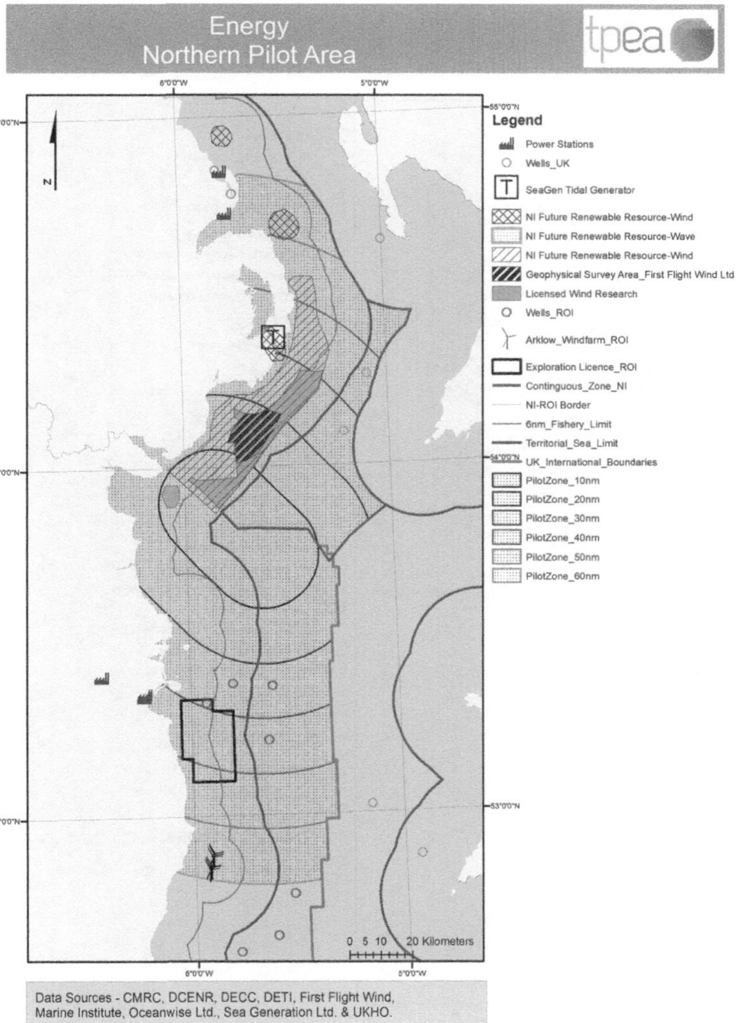

Figure 8.2.6 Energy activities in the northern TPEA pilot area.

to see where common themes and priorities relevant to the transboundary area were being put forward in the two jurisdictions. For instance, it became clear that there are common commitments to marine renewable energy and aquaculture in both jurisdictions. As in the case of data collection, all-Ireland initiatives were also recognized, such as the inter-governmental Marine Coordination Group. Again, this illustrates the importance of drawing upon wider transboundary initiatives already taking place.

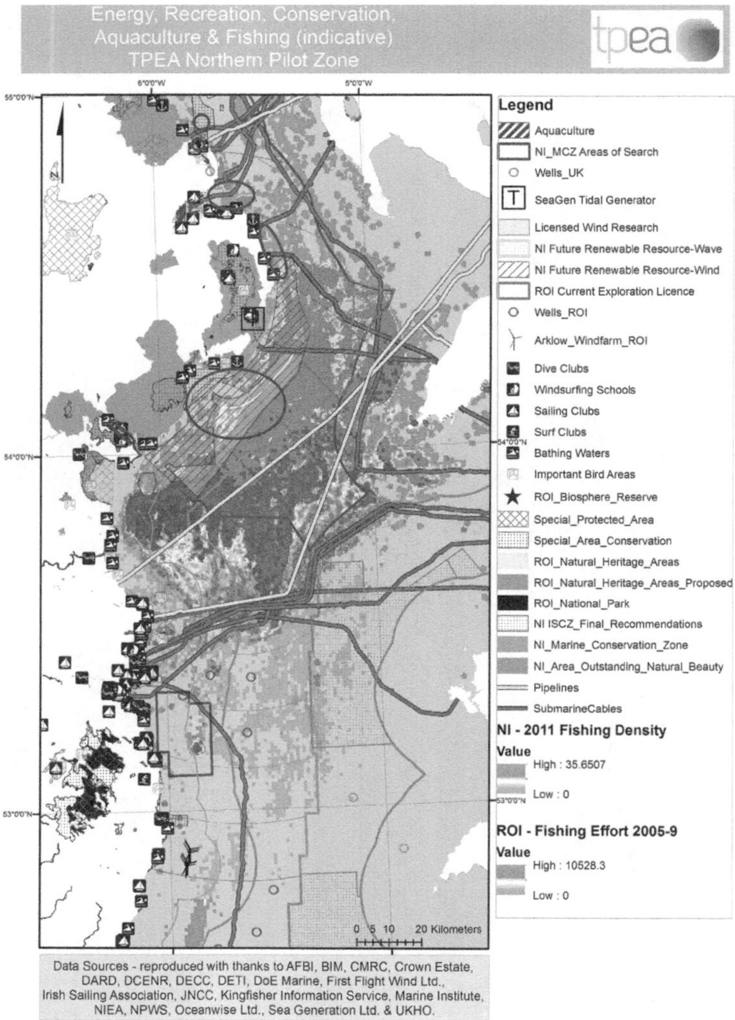

Figure 8.2.7 Composite map for the northern TPEA pilot area.

Stakeholders

Stakeholder engagement generally involves giving interested parties the opportunity to contribute their knowledge and to shape MSP outcomes through consultation, workshops, public meetings, and so on. Stakeholders will typically have different views and expectations; the MSP process may involve facilitating greater understanding between participants. In a transboundary setting, these dynamics are likely to be magnified, with a greater range of different backgrounds and aims, which may be related to jurisdictional priorities, and greater effort may need to be made in facilitating dialogue and working towards cooperation across a border.

In TPEA, stakeholder participation in the project was primarily encouraged through a series of workshops giving participants the opportunity to comment on the transboundary MSP process. They were invited in order to gain a representation of maritime sectoral interest, such as fishing, leisure and conservation, and of different levels of governance, from the local to the national. Importantly, equal participation was sought from each jurisdiction, and some participants represented all-Ireland interests, such as for the shared sea lough at the border. The workshops were also designed to maximize discussion between participants from the two jurisdictions, so that common issues could be explored bilaterally, and emphasis was placed on developing mutual understanding in the discussions.

Conclusions

Taking a transboundary approach to MSP introduces further complexities to what is already the challenging endeavour of extending the principles of spatial planning to the unfixed, open and mobile setting of the sea. Establishing meaningful areas for planning purposes, integrating data for marine conditions and activities, coming to an understanding of relevant policy priorities and gaining stakeholder input are all more demanding when more than one jurisdiction is involved and when the focus of attention is on cross-border, rather than national, waters and interests. In sea areas with very dynamic marine characteristics, such as the European Atlantic, the interchanges between jurisdictional waters may be particularly strong and far-reaching, adding further to the potency of transboundary effects and the need for cross-border cooperation.

There are generally no legal requirements for carrying out MSP on a transboundary scale, apart from statutory responsibilities to consult or cooperate with neighbours in some MSP systems. However, in Europe, a number of EU-funded projects, including TPEA, has led to some experience of transboundary MSP at a non-statutory level, facilitating exchange between institutions in adjoining Member States. These have demonstrated particularly the need, firstly, for gathering, sharing and portraying (using GIS) relevant data across jurisdictions and, secondly, for engaging with stakeholders in understanding concerns and developing planning priorities for shared sea areas (Backer and Frias, 2012; Gee *et al.*, 2011). TPEA has further emphasized these points, but has added an equal need to analyse and synthesize the marine-related policy frameworks that are in place for the jurisdictions concerned, as a means of highlighting the policy concerns to which transboundary MSP should respond and contribute.

The fundamental lesson from this project is that taking a transboundary approach requires sustained attention to inter-relations in all aspects of planning. This is necessary at several levels, including:

- scientific and technical, in order to facilitate effective data gathering and representation over areas with variable data units, from a wide range of national and other sources;
- political and administrative, in order to enable exchange between different jurisdictions' institutions of governance and to coordinate their policy priorities;
- social and cultural, in order to foster good working relationships between stakeholders and other participants representing different jurisdictions.

Developing the capacity for cross-border cooperation is needed at all stages of planning in transboundary contexts. It is important to ensure fair representation of interests from the different jurisdictions involved, sharing tasks equitably and with participants working together to an agreed programme and learning from each other's contribution. Mechanisms need to be set up for sharing information, such as online file sharing, and integrating spatial data, such as a shared database and GIS, which may raise technical challenges, such as harmonising data from disparate sources and covering different areas. Particular attention must be paid to cross-border perspectives, with time and care being given to understanding each other's policy concerns, to finding areas of shared interest and recognizing where differences and difficulties remain, which may not be resolved in the current planning cycle. Developing shared objectives may be a helpful way of expressing what can be achieved in a transboundary context. Planning outputs need to be carefully agreed by all parties, with regard to any jurisdictional sensitivity that may exist, and with a willingness to negotiate and compromise on statements where necessary. Consideration must also be given to the resource needs for a transboundary exercise; although cross-border working inevitably requires additional time and human and financial resources, it should be carried out efficiently, preferably in conjunction with jurisdictions' existing MSP processes. Finally, transboundary MSP cannot be divorced from wider processes of cooperation and negotiation between neighbouring jurisdictions. It can benefit from, and contribute to, other initiatives and strategies, not just marine-related, by which agents of governance are already strengthening links across borders and becoming socially, economically and environmentally more inter-related.

Acknowledgements

This section has been written on behalf of the Transboundary Planning in the European Atlantic team, especially partners from Ireland and the UK, with particular thanks to Cathal O'Mahony and Sarah Twomey from University College Cork, Gerard McClarey, Andrew McGreevy and Aoibheann Rooney from Department of the Environment Northern Ireland, and Kira Gee and Sue Kidd from the University of Liverpool. Partners from Portugal and Spain are also gratefully acknowledged for their contribution to the wider project exemplified in this section of this chapter (see http://www.tpeamaritime.eu). The project was co-funded by the European Commission (project MARE/2012/08).

References

Alexander, L. (2004) 'The North Atlantic', in Smith, H. (ed.) *The Ocean: Key Issues in Marine Affairs*, Kluwer, London, pp. 215–30.

Backer, H. and Frias, M. (eds.) (2012) *Planning the Bothnian Sea: Key Findings of the Plan Bothnia Project*, Helcom, Helsinki.

Calado, H., Ng, K., Johnson, D., Sousa, L., Phillips, M. and Alves, F. (2010) 'Marine spatial planning: Lessons learned from the Portuguese debate', *Marine Policy*, vol. 34, pp. 1341–1349.

Commission of the European Communities (CEC) (2008) *Roadmap for Maritime Spatial Planning: Achieving Common Principles in the EU*, COM 791, CEC, Brussels.

CEC (2011) *Developing a Maritime Strategy for the Atlantic Ocean Area*, COM 782, CEC, Brussels.

CEC (2012) *Blue Growth: Opportunities for Marine and Maritime Sustainable Growth*, COM 494, CEC, Brussels.

CEC (2013) *Action Plan for a Maritime Strategy in the Atlantic area Delivering Smart, Sustainable and Inclusive Growth*, COM 279, CEC, Brussels.

Department for Environment, Food & Rural Affairs (2011) *A Description of the Marine Planning System for England*, Defra, London.

Ehler, C. and Douvere, F. (2007) *Visions for a Sea Change, Report of the First International Workshop on Marine Spatial Planning, Intergovernmental Oceanographic Commission and Man and the Biosphere Programme*, UNESCO, Paris, 83 pp.

European Commission (undated) *European Atlas of the Seas* http://ec.europa.eu/maritime affairs/atlas/seabasins/northsea/index_en.htm (accessed 11.08.14).

European Parliament & Council (2014) 'Directive 2014/89/EU of the European Parliament and of the Council of 23 July 2014 establishing a framework for maritime spatial planning', *Official Journal of the European Union*, vol. L 257, pp. 135–45.

Gee, K., Kannen, A. and Heinrichs, B. (2011) *BaltSeaPlan Vision 2030: Towards the Sustainable Planning of Baltic Sea Space*, BaltSeaPlan, Hamburg.

Gilliland, P. and Laffoley, D. (2008) 'Key elements and steps in the process of developing ecosystem-based marine spatial planning', *Marine Policy*, vol. 32, no. 5, pp. 787–96.

Haughton, G., Allmendinger, P., Counsell, D. and Vigar, G. (2010) *The New Spatial Planning: territorial management with soft spaces and fuzzy boundaries*, Routledge, London.

HM Government (2014) *East Inshore and East Offshore Marine Plans*, Department for Environment, Food & Rural Affairs, London.

HM Government, Northern Ireland Executive, Scottish Government & Welsh Assembly Government (2011) *UK Marine Policy Statement*, The Stationary Office, Norwich.

Inter-Departmental Marine Coordination Group (2012) *Harnessing our Ocean Wealth: An Integrated Marine Plan for Ireland*, Inter-Departmental Marine Coordination Group, Dublin.

Jay, S. (2010) 'Built at Sea: marine management and the construction of marine spatial planning', *Town Planning Review*, vol. 81, no. 2, pp. 173–91.

Jay, S. (2012) 'Marine space: manoeuvring towards a relational understanding', *Journal of Environmental Policy and Planning*, vol. 14, no. 1, pp. 81–96.

Jay, S. (2013) 'From sectors to segments: questioning the functional zoning of the seas', *Planning Theory and Practice*, vol. 14, no. 4, pp. 509–25.

Jay, S., Klenke, T., Ahlhorn, F. and Ritchie, H. (2012) 'Early European experience in marine spatial planning: planning the German exclusive economic zone', *European Planning Studies*, vol. 20, no. 12, pp. 2013–31.

Jay, S., Flannery, W., Vince, J., Liu, W., Xue, J.G., Matczak, M., Zaucha, J., Janssen, H., van Tatenhove, J., Toonen, H., Morf, A., Olsen, E., Suárez de Vivero, J.L., Rodríguez Mateos, J.C., Calado, H., Duff, J. and Dean, H. (2013) 'International progress in marine spatial planning', in Chircop, A., Coffen-Smout, S. and McConnell, M. (eds) *Ocean Yearbook*, vol. 27, Martinus Nijhoff, Leiden, pp. 171–212.

Murray, M. (2004) 'Strategic spatial planning on the island of Ireland: towards a new territorial logic?' *The European Journal of Social Science Research*, vol. 17, no. 3, pp. 227–42.

O'Mahony, C., Kopke, K., Twomey, S., O'Hagan, A.M., Farrell, E. and Gault, J. (2014) *Integrated Coastal Zone Management in Ireland: Meeting Water Framework Directive and Marine Strategy Framework Directive targets for Ireland's transitional and coastal waters through implementation of Integrated Coastal Zone Management*, report prepared for Sustainable Water Network, unpublished document.

OSPAR (undated) *OSPAR Commission: Protecting and Conserving the North East Atlantic and its Resources*, http://www.ospar.org (accessed 11.08.14).

Suárez de Vivero, J. L. (2013) 'The extended continental shelf: a geographical perspective of the implementation of article 76 of UNCLOS', *Ocean and Coastal Management*, vol. 73, pp. 113–26.

Suárez de Vivero, J. L. and Rodriguez Mateos, J. C. (2014) 'Changing maritime scenarios: the geopolitical dimension of the EU Atlantic Strategy', *Marine Policy*, vol. 48, pp. 59–72.

Transboundary Planning in the European Atlantic (TPEA) (undated) *Transboundary Planning in the European Atlantic* http://www.tpeamaritime.eu (accessed 11.08.14).

TPEA (2014) *Pilot Area Report*, unpublished document.

TPEA (2013) *Conceptual Framework Report*, unpublished document.

Walsh, C. and Knieling, I. (2013) 'Creating a space for cooperation: soft spaces, spatial planning and territorial cooperation on the island of Ireland'. Paper presented at the AESOP-ACSP Joint Congress, Dublin, 15–19 July.

Chapter 9

Marine spatial planning in the European Union

Niko Soininen

Recent policy background and evolution of MSP in the EU

In 2006, the European Commission in its Green Paper on Maritime Policy emphasized the importance of sustainable development, mainly the importance of competitiveness and growth of the maritime industry, increasing employment and sustainable use of marine resources (Blue Growth), protection of marine environment and mitigation of and adaption to climate change (COM, 2006, 275, pp. 3–21).[1] It further emphasized the importance of a stable regulatory framework in the form of spatial planning for the marine areas as a way forward to implement these policy goals. The Commission stated that marine spatial planning (MSP)[2] should be ecosystem based and this regulatory framework should also be connected to licensing or other means of 'promoting or placing restrictions on maritime activities' (COM, 2006, 275). This emphasis on MSP, as an implementation mechanism for sustainable development, gained further support in the Blue Book of the Commission in which it stated that MSP is one of the key instruments in implementing Integrated Maritime Policy (IMP) in the EU (COM, 2007, 575).[3]

After the Green Paper and Blue Book, the Commission drafted a roadmap for the implementation of MSP in the EU. The EU-wide approach to MSP was justified by the Commission as creating coherence and integration between sectoral planning which in turn would help in addressing the problems acknowledged in the Green Paper (COM, 2008, 791). In the roadmap, the Commission recognized several key principles to implementing MSP. These included: (1) recognition of the characteristics of the area and type of activity;[4] (2) definition of objectives; (3) transparency of planning; (4) stakeholder participation; (5) coordination within the member states; (6) ensuring the legal effects of MSP; (7) cross-border cooperation and consultation; (8) incorporation of monitoring and evaluation in the planning process; (9) coherence between MSP and Integrated Coastal Management; and (10) strong data and knowledge base (COM, 2008, 791).

The aim of the roadmap was to facilitate MSP developments in the member states, encourage implementation of MSP and stimulate an EU-wide debate on the development of MSP (Schäfer, 2009). To further this aim, the

Commission sent out a questionnaire with an aim of finding out the most important characteristics of MSP in the member states. Facilitation of transboundary cooperation was seen as one of the most important aspects of MSP in the report analysing the results of the questionnaire (European Commission, 2011). Consequently, the main problems recognized by the report were the lack of transboundary MSP, incompatibility of datasets as well as the lack of joint procedures with regard to MSP. Furthermore, differences with national legislation, timing and understanding the concept of MSP were acknowledged. These transboundary issues were raised mostly within EU-member states, not so much with third party countries. A vast majority of the respondents considered MSP as a transboundary issue, while only three per cent of the respondents considered MSP to be a mainly national issue (European Commission, 2011, p. 5). Due to this, the Commission sought to enhance cross-border cooperation and facilitate common understanding of MSP (Schäfer, 2009).

After the roadmap, the Commission emphasized that the implementation of MSP would remain with the member states. This would however be supported by EU-wide coordination of MSP to secure: (1) the efficiency of MSP; (2) implementation of the EU's Blue Growth strategy by increasing legal certainty, predictability and transparency of marine planning; (3) effective implementation of EU legislation already in place; and (4) knowledge and expertise sharing (COM, 2010, 771, p. 2–3). Following these policy developments, the Commission gave a proposal on a new MSP-directive in the spring of 2013 (COM, 2013, 133). The directive was adopted in July and came into force in September 2014 (MSPD).[5]

After the adoption and entry into force of the directive, it seems timely to analyse the legal obligations set in the directive. In this chapter, I will first analyse the overall framework of MSPD and then turn to the obligations of the member states for transboundary cooperation with regard to MSP in the EU.

Legal framework for marine spatial planning in Europe

Overall framework of the directive

The MSP directive is one of the instruments designed to implement Integrated Maritime Policy in the EU. It is aimed at achieving sustainable growth and development of marine areas and sustainable use of its resources (art. 1). Consistent with the idea of sustainable development, the directive aims at economic growth and better quality of the environment simultaneously. As such, the MSPD can be seen as an implementation device for sustainable development on a general level, and for different aspects of the different sectoral policies under the IMP on a more specific level.[6] By way of doing this, marine spatial planning has also been endorsed and encouraged in different sectors (or pillars) of IMP. As its environmental pillar, the Marine Strategy Framework Directive (MSFD)[7] sets certain obligations to the member states (e.g. for the Programmes of Measures aimed at implementing the overall aim of good marine environmental status by 2020 in the EU) (MSFD, art. 13(2)). One of the instruments to be considered in the Programme is spatial and temporal distribution of marine activities.

Complementing the implementation of earlier legislative instruments MSP can be seen as paramount to the overall aim of IMP, as for instance MSFD has been criticized for accomplishing very little in terms of integration between different sectors of marine governance. Some scholars have stated that this is mainly due to the lack of specific and hard normative obligations on transboundary cooperation, exchange of information and unified criteria for achieving good environmental status under the MSFD (Markus *et al.*, 2010).[8] My question here is: what are the mechanisms which the new directive on MSP can employ to aid in this regard? Are there any hard legal obligations aimed at the member states to cooperate in the drafting of MSP, which is to implement inter alia the obligations set in the MSFD?[9]

The overall legal obligation for the member states to produce a marine spatial plan is rather strict. Art. 3(1) stipulates that each member state shall establish and implement a marine spatial plan. However, when comparing the draft directive (COM, 2013, 133) to the adopted directive, one can see that obligations relating to the spatial scale of the planning have been left out from the adopted directive. Art. 7 of the draft directive stated that 'Maritime spatial plans shall contain at least a mapping of marine waters which identifies the actual and potential spatial and temporal distribution of all relevant maritime activities . . . ' In the adopted directive this formulation was changed to read: 'When establishing and implementing maritime spatial planning, Member States shall set up maritime spatial plans which identify the spatial and temporal distribution of relevant existing and future activities and uses in their marine waters . . . '[10]

The biggest difference between the two formulations seems to be that the member states do not have an obligation to produce a map of activities in the marine areas. Furthermore, art. 4(3) states that MSPs shall be developed and produced in accordance with institutional and governance levels determined by the member states. The directive does not harmonise the scale or level of planning which can have a negative effect on the overall level of integration of sectoral policies and cooperation between member states.[11] This has a negative potential of undermining the advantages identified with MSP in general.[12]

Another important limitation becomes clear when comparing the directive proposal and the final directive. This concerns the scope and applicability of the directive. According to the directive proposal art. 2(1), the directive was set up as applying to coastal zones as well as marine waters. The width of the scope would have undoubtedly supported the implementation of the MSFD and inclusion of the land–sea interface in the development of national and transboundary MSPs within the EU. Despite these benefits, the scope was considerably narrowed down in the final form of the directive. According to art. 2(1), MSPD shall apply only to marine waters, not to coastal waters. This restriction of scope leaves one important element of MSP outside the scope of its application and can limit the EU-wide application of MSP mostly to the Exclusive Economic Zone (EEZ).[13]

Despite the two major shortcomings, MSPD sets legally binding obligations to the member states in terms of the process leading to a Europe-wide adoption of MSP.[14] This means that member states have to have MSP-legislation in force by 18.9.2016 (art. 15(1)). By that date also relevant authorities need to have been identified to the Commission. Transboundary marine spatial plans in the meaning of the directive have to be in place by March 31, 2021 at the latest. After the adoption and implementation of an MSP, the plan has to be reviewed at least every 10 years (MSPD art. 6(3)).[15] MSPs that have been drafted and implemented before the adoption of the directive will suffice provided they are in conformity with the directive (art. 3(6)).

Presently it seems that the obligations set for the member states are mainly procedural. This means that the requirements of the directive can be met by setting up a rather broad framework for planning in marine waters and the requirements for the plan itself can be fulfilled on a quite abstract level of planning. Quite a lot is left to the discretion of the member states. However, some legislation regarding planning in marine areas does have to be in place on the national level by 2016. This means that the directive does not oblige the member states to develop and implement a detailed system of planning, coupled with marine zoning, Environmental Impact Assessment and a permit system.[16] In other words, there is no strict obligation in the directive to integrate different sectors and instruments of marine governance under the umbrella of MSP.[17] It remains to be seen whether the MSPD will reap success in creating an integrated and functioning framework for MSP on an EU-level or whether it will remain a moot point in this regard.

Despite the discretion left to the member states in how to implement MSP on a national level, one can argue that MSPD does also set certain substantive requirements for national MSP legislation and national MSPs.[18] Firstly, the objectives for MSP set in the directive should have an effect on drafting and implementing national legislation in the member states. Under art. 5 of MSPD member states have to, *inter alia*, consider economic, social and environmental aspects of MSP and shall aim to contribute to the sustainable development of energy sectors at sea, of maritime transport, and of the fisheries and aquaculture sectors, and to the preservation, protection and improvement of the environment, including resilience to climate change impacts. In this line, an ecosystem-based approach is underlined as is the aim to support economic growth in the marine areas.

Secondly, in line with the objectives set in art. 5 of the directive, art. 6 sets certain minimum requirements for national MSP legislation and MSPs. According to art. 6, member states shall establish procedural steps to reach the aims set in the directive. These procedural steps have to take into consideration several substantive requirements. In line with art. 6(1) of the MSPD, this process shall:

a take into account land–sea interactions;[19]
b take into account environmental, economic and social aspects, as well as safety aspects;

c aim to promote coherence between maritime spatial planning and the resulting plan or plans and other processes, such as integrated coastal management or equivalent formal or informal practices;
d ensure the involvement of stakeholders in accordance with Article 9;
e organise the use of the best available data in accordance with Article 10;
f ensure transboundary cooperation between Member States in accordance with Article 11;
g promote cooperation with third countries in accordance with Article 12.[20]

While the procedural requirements of MSP are rather strict, at least in the sense that the member states have to be able to illustrate that the minimum requirements of art. 6 have been taken into consideration, the substantive requirements for MSP are normatively weak.[21] The directive gives some guidance on the identification of different interests in the planning area but the assignment of weight is left to the discretion of the member states (art. 5(3) of MSPD).[22] The member states are free to balance marine interests as they see fit in the confinements of other international and EU law.

With regard to the identification of relevant interests involved in the planning process, the draft directive art. 7(1) stated that an MSP has to contain at least marine interests such as shipping, fishing, nature conservation and so on. In the adopted directive, this was changed to a considerably softer formulation.[23] Under art. 8(2) of MSPD the interests included in the temporal and spatial allocation of MSP *may* include: aquaculture areas, fishing areas, installations and infrastructures for the exploration, exploitation and extraction of oil, of gas and other energy resources, of minerals and aggregates, and for the production of energy from renewable sources, maritime transport routes and traffic flows, military training areas, nature and species conservation sites and protected areas, raw material extraction areas, scientific research, submarine cable and pipeline routes, tourism and underwater cultural heritage. The only strict substantive obligation in the directive is that national MSPs have to identify the spatial and temporal distribution of marine activities in marine waters (art. 8(1) of MSPD).

Obligations on transboundary cooperation in MSP

In light of the transboundary character of marine spatial planning, the directive has adopted a cooperative approach to planning. This means that member states have a legal obligation to jointly draft and implement MSPs when the plan would have transboundary effects.[24] Art. 9(1) states that all the interested parties shall be informed of the process and relevant stakeholders and authorities have to be consulted. In this process, collection, use and sharing of data have to be organized in accordance with the Union legislation.[25] The aim of transboundary MSP can be seen in the development of common processes and standards which are seen as raising the overall quality of MSP (Schäfer and Barale, 2011).

The transboundary approach to governance of marine areas also gains normative support from the MSFD which MSP can be seen partially implementing (Schäfer, 2009). Art. 2(1) of the MSFD states that member states have to adopt a transboundary approach in aiming to achieve the good status of the marine environment set in the directive. This means that transboundary effects on the marine environment have to be taken into account when adopting national measures to reach the quality target. This means transboundary cooperation within and outside of the EU (Markus *et al.*, 2010). On a more concrete level this means establishing coordinated monitoring programmes for the ongoing assessment of the environmental status of marine waters (MSFD art. 11(1)). The overall aim of good condition of marine environment also requires that negative effects to the high seas are not caused by unilateral actions (MSFD art. 6).[26]

With regard to MSP, there are three major transboundary challenges the directive tries to tackle.[27] Firstly, the fragmentation of standards and data among sectors constitutes hardships for finding the correct data. Furthermore, there are restrictions on use and reuse of data as well as lack of precision and information (COM, 2010, 461. p. 4). The Commission has emphasized the importance of a quality-checked and easily accessible marine knowledge, which needs to be coordinated across borders (COM, 2010, 771, p. 7). The production and existence of valid data for the planning process can be seen as a pre-requirement for drafting and implementing a marine spatial plan.

Secondly, there is the problem of coordinating the planning process itself between the member states. As has been recognized by the Commission 'Communication, consultation and cooperation with neighbouring states need to take place at an early stage.' This requires identification of relevant contact points across borders and the development of a common vision for the use of the marine area in question (COM, 2010, 771, pp. 5–6). The first step of identifying relevant authorities is well covered in the directive with clear obligations and a timeline for this identification (MSPD art. 13 and 15). However, more precise mechanisms leading to the adoption and implementation of a common vision for the use of marine area are left rather vague. Art. 11 of MSPD only requires member states to cooperate ('member states bordering marine waters shall cooperate') in order to ensure that MSPs are coherent across the line.

The cooperative obligations set by the directive can be fulfilled with existing Regional Seas organizations, networks of member states' competent authorities or any other means, which meet the requirements of cooperation (art. 11(2)).[28] Furthermore, the obligation to cooperate extends beyond union boundaries. In line with art. 12, the member states shall endeavour to cooperate with third countries where possible by using existing mechanisms established under international law.[29] This lack of new forms of cooperation emphasizes the importance of existing transboundary governance bodies, such as the HELCOM-VASAB Working Group, in implementing the normative requirements of the directive.

To further transboundary cooperation, the proposed MSP-directive would have given the Commission a mandate to issue implementing acts with regard to

MSP in relevant aspects. These would have included more operational steps for the establishment and reporting of MSP. Transboundary cooperation would have been one important aspect of the implementation acts. However, in the legislative process, the Committee of the Regions was critical towards giving this wide a mandate to the Commission and moved to remove the proposed article from the directive.[30] Consequently, there is no sign of this mandate in the adopted directive. This further underlines the importance of existing organizational structures and modes of cooperation already in place.

Thirdly, cooperation with other member states further requires that there is a monitoring and reporting systems in place in each member state and all the updates and changes in national MSPs have to be communicated to the member states affected. This has to be completed within three months of the publication or revision of the plan (art. 14(1)). This obligation has a transboundary element only in the sense that even national MSPs may have to be communicated to other member states.[31] This is an *ex post facto* obligation which does not affect the planning process itself. 'Transboundary' in this context means only notification of other member states, not necessarily cooperation in the drafting and implementation of the plan. In this sense, the obligation to cooperation set in art. 14 of MSPD is substantially weaker in terms of transboundary cooperation compared to the obligations set in art. 11 discussed above.

Conclusions

One of the main issues that the new framework directive on MSP tries to tackle is transboundary cooperation in drafting and implementing marine spatial plans. These were also the problems most widely emphasized in the member states prior to the adoption of the directive (European Commission, 2011, p. 5). When comparing the directive proposal and the final directive, one can also criticize the adopted directive from this perspective. MSPD leaves the substantive implementation of marine spatial plans to member states setting primarily procedural obligations on identifying relevant authorities in each member country and cooperation between member states in situations where the MSP would have transboundary effects.

The mode and organization of cooperation is for the most part left to existing legal institutions and transboundary bodies. In this way the MSPD can be seen as complementing earlier international and EU legislation without adding much to prior legal obligations. One cannot help but to wonder: if there were problems prior to the adoption of the directive in transboundary cooperation in drafting and implementing MSPs, will they not be present within the context of the MSP-directive as well if it leaves cooperative procedures between member states for the most part as they were prior to the adoption of the MSPD? Without harmonization of the level and scale of MSP, it remains challenging to draft and implement an integrated transboundary MSP.[32]

Only time will tell whether the MSPD will aid in implementing the EU's Integrated Maritime Policy and its pillars, such as the Marine Strategy Framework

Directive. In its current state, by setting hardly any substantive obligations and even procedural obligations being in many aspects rather weak, it remains an open question. From this perspective, MSPD can only be seen as an initial step in the regulatory developments regarding MSP on the EU level.[33]

Notes

1 The key drivers on a more concrete level are maintaining and improving biological diversity and blue growth with a close connection to renewable energy, such as offshore wind energy, see Maes, Frank 'Maritime Spatial Planning: will there still be some space left for nature?' Presentation in the VVOR Conference – 20 years of Habitats Directive in Antwerp 13.12.2012. <http://www.omgevingsrecht.be/sites/default/files/habtitat1213122012/20121213-08.pdf>, accessed on 15.10.2014.

2 See on the conceptual differences between the EU and the rest of the world Chapter 1 of the book. Contrary to the terminology of the EU, I use in this chapter the term 'marine spatial planning' (not 'maritime spatial planning') which is consistent with the use of the term elsewhere in this book.

3 'An Integrated Maritime Policy for the European Union', p. 6. IMP includes policy areas such as renewable marine energy, fisheries, transportation and the protection of the marine environment. One of the operational objectives of the Regulation concerning a programme of support for the IMP (Regulation No 1255/2011 of the European Parliament and of the Council of 30 November 2011 establishing a Programme to support the further development of an Integrated Maritime Policy, OJ L 321, 5.12.2011, p. 1.) is to promote cross-sectoral tools, such as marine spatial planning (art. 2(b)). The importance of cooperation between member states is further emphasized in art. 3(2)(b) of the Regulation.

4 The Commission has emphasized that MSP as an implementation mechanism for Integrated Marine Policy requires taking into account the regional characteristics of the area that it is applied in. See also COM 2010 771, final. Communication from the Commission to the European Parliament, the Council, the European Economic and Social Committee and the Committee of the Regions. Maritime Spatial Planning in the EU – Achievements and Future Development, p. 7.

5 Directive 2014/89/EU of the European Parliament and of the Council of 23 July 2014 establishing a framework for maritime spatial planning, OJ L 25, 28.8.2014, p. 135. For those readers who are not familiar with the legal system of the EU it may be said that directives in general only set obligations to the member states in terms of their aims. National authorities have the obligation to adapt their legal system to facilitate these aims but are free to decide how this is done. Directives are used to bring national legislation in line with each other. See in a nutshell EC Commission website <http://ec.europa.eu/eu_law/directives/directives_en.htm>, accessed on 29.10.2014.
See on the concept of sustainability, Chapter 1 of this book.

6 In the drafting process the European Economic and Social Committee posed a question as to how the proposed MSP-directive would be coordinated with other EU-legislation, such as the Habitats Directive (Directive 92/43/EEC of the European Council of 21 May 1992 on the conservation of natural habitats and of wild fauna and flora, OJ L 206, 22.7.1992, p. 7). See Opinion of the European Economic and Social Committee on the 'Proposal of the Directive of the European Parliament and of the

Council establishing a framework for maritime spatial planning and integrated coastal management', OJ C 341, 21.11.2013, p. 69.

7 Directive 2008/56/EC of the European Parliament and of the Council of 17 June 2008 establishing a framework for community action in the field of marine environmental policy (Marine Strategy Framework Directive), OJ L 164, 25.6.2008, p. 19.

8 The MSFD is one further step in the EU Integrated Marine Policy. However, its implementation will show the successes and failures of the directive, see Juda, Lawrence (2010) 'The European Union and the Marine Strategy Framework Directive: Continuing the Development of European Ocean Use Management' *Ocean Development and International Law*, vol. 41, p. 45.

9 This point of view can partially be criticized in the sense that the MSP-directive can be seen as *deteriorating* the status of marine environmental protection by shifting the viewpoint from hard conception of sustainability to a weak one. The gist of the argument is that the adoption of multiple goals in MSP (environmental protection and economic development) at the same time will erode prior levels of environmental protection in the EU. See Qiu, Wanfei and Jones, Peter J.S. (2013) 'The emerging policy landscape for marine spatial planning in Europe' *Marine Policy*, vol. 39, pp. 182–89. Interestingly, similar argument was voiced in the Opinion of the European Economic and Social Committee on the 'Proposal of the Directive of the European Parliament and of the Council establishing a framework for maritime spatial planning and integrated coastal management', OJ C 341, 21.11.2013, p. 69. The Committee saw that it would be better to wait for the existing EU-legislation to reach its full potential before adding a new regulative layer in the form of an MSP-directive. While these arguments hold some merit, I would be inclined to argue that the MSP-directive places mostly procedural obligations for the implementation of the MSFD which do not *necessarily* convey in them the ability to weaken the level of marine environmental protection. It is up to the member states to deliberate, how different substantive sectoral policies will be made compatible with the overall aim of good marine environmental condition. In this sense, MSP is a blank tool for the implementation of other policies.

10 National security and defence issues are excluded from the planning process (art. 2(2)). Understandably, land-locked countries in the EU are excluded from the obligations set in the directive (art. 15(4)).

11 The problem of scale is further impeded by a very wide definition of MSP in art. 3(2) of the MSPD: '"maritime spatial planning" means a process by which the relevant Member State's authorities analyse and organise human activities in marine areas to achieve ecological, economic and social objectives –.'

12 See on these advantages Chapter 1 of this book.

13 MSPD does not alter the international legal framework forming the background of any MSP or effect national land-use planning which may include coastal areas (art. 2(3) and 2(4)). See on this international legal background, Chapters 4 and 5 of this book. The reason for leaving ICM out of the adopted directive was that legislating on ICM was seen to belong to the competence of the member states, see Opinion of the Committee of the Regions on Proposed directive for maritime spatial planning and integrated coastal management, OJ C 356, 5.12.2013, pp. 130–131. On the contrary the European Economic and Social Committee was of the opinion that integration of marine, coastal and even terrestrial planning would be a welcome development taking into consideration that a considerable amount of marine pollution is caused by land-based pollution, see Opinion of the European Economic and Social Committee on the

'Proposal of the Directive of the European Parliament and of the Council establishing a framework for maritime spatial planning and integrated coastal management', OJ C 341, 21.11.2013, p. 68.

14 See MSPD, preamble 9–11.

15 This provision sets a minimum requirement for adaptive management which is generally seen as an important characteristic of MSP, see Chapter 1 of this book. The provision does not prevent member states in adopting more frequently adapting MSPs. The interval for adaptivity was first set in the directive proposal to 6 years but was lengthened in the adopted directive to 10 years. One of the reasons for this can be seen in the Committee of the Regions' opinion which preferred to remove a strict timeline for adaptivity altogether, see Opinion of the Committee of the Regions on Proposed directive for maritime spatial planning and integrated coastal management, OJ C 356, 5.12.2013, pp. 129–130. European Economic and Social Committee on the other hand emphasized the importance of adaptivity of an MSP, see Opinion of the European Economic and Social Committee on the 'Proposal of the Directive of the European Parliament and of the Council establishing a framework for maritime spatial planning and integrated coastal management', OJ C 341, 21.11.2013, p. 68.

16 However, these requirements usually follow from other EU-level obligations.

17 In this sense it seems that the EU-level MSP-framework is still quite far from the ideal characteristics of MSP discussed in Chapter 1 of this book.

18 However, taking into account the preamble of the directive, one could argue that there are no substantive requirements in the directive. In the preamble of MSPD it is stated that the directive does not set substantive obligations on marine spatial planning as these issues are for the most part left to national discretion. See MSPD, preamble 9–11.

19 With regard to taking into consideration land sea interactions, the directive states the possibility of complementing MSP with Integrated Coastal Management, see art. 7 of MSPD.

20 In the legislative process, the European Economic and Social Committee was of the opinion that none of these requirements could be implemented '– in the absence of genuine cooperation the Member States and with third countries, given that maritime areas are, by their very nature, open and constantly interacting.' Opinion of the European Economic and Social Committee on the 'Proposal of the Directive of the European Parliament and of the Council establishing a framework for maritime spatial planning and integrated coastal management', OJ C 341, 21.11.2013, p. 69.

21 The Committee of the Regions in its opinion on the proposed MSP-directive stated that the directive should not include substantive elements and that in its suggested form it was in breach of the proportionality principle, see Opinion of the Committee of the Regions on Proposed directive for maritime spatial planning and integrated coastal management, OJ C 356, 5.12.2013, p. 124.

22 This was the opinion of the Committee of the Regions as well, see Opinion of the Committee of the Regions on Proposed directive for maritime spatial planning and integrated coastal management, OJ C 356, 5.12.2013, p. 126. The Committee 'underlines that MSP must be developed as a neutral planning tool which incorporates a certain level of flexibility to accommodate appropriate policy processes for diverse marine environments; further calls for clarity on the scope of the ecosystem-based approach of the draft Directive as there will need to be a balance between economic development and environmental protection; rejects therefore the setting of 'top-down'

priorities and minimum requirements for management plans and using MSP as an instrument to ensure implementation of sector specific policy objectives–.'

23 This was also the proposal of the Committee of the Regions, see Opinion of the Committee of the Regions on Proposed directive for maritime spatial planning and integrated coastal management, OJ C 356, 5.12.2013, p. 130.

24 However, the legal obligation is quite vague as to the exact mechanisms of transboundary cooperation. This vagueness is intentional, as modes of cooperation in EU-countries differ somewhat (Preamble 20 of the MSPD). This leaves room for adopting sub-regional approaches to transboundary MSP-cooperation. Within the context of the Baltic Sea, HELCOM-VASAB cooperation forms one of such sub-regional arrangement. In this context the HELCOM-VASAB roadmap for implementing transboundary MSP was adopted at the HELCOM Ministerial Meeting in 2013 and the VASAB ministerial Conference in 2014. The HELCOM-VASAB roadmap is available at <http://www.helcom.fi/Documents/Ministerial2013/Ministerial%20declaration/Adopted_endorsed%20documents/Regional%20Baltic%20MSP%20Roadmap.pdf>, accessed on 14.10.2014.

25 On a general level, the normative basis for the obligation to cooperate with regard to datasets can be traced to INSPIRE directive (Directive 2007/2/EC of the European Parliament and of the Council of 14 March 2007 establishing an Infrastructure for Spatial Information in the European Community (INSPIRE), OJ L 108, 25.4.2007, p. 1) and the directive on Environmental Information (Directive 2003/4/EC of the European Parliament and of the Council of 28 January 2003 on public access to environmental information and repealing council directive 90/313/EEC, OJ L 41, 14.2.2003, p. 26). The importance of interoperability of and access to data are emphasized also by Meiner, A. (2010) 'Integrated maritime policy for the European Union – consolidating coastal and marine information to support maritime spatial planning' *Journal of Coastal Conservation*, vol. 14, p. 9. See also the Opinion of the European Economic and Social Committee on the 'Proposal of the Directive of the European Parliament and of the Council establishing a framework for maritime spatial planning and integrated coastal management', OJ C 341, 21.11.2013, p. 68.

26 See also MSFD, preamble 17.

27 While the SEA-Directive (Directive 2001/42/EC of the European Parliament and of the Council of 27 June 2001 on the assessment of the effects of certain plans and programmes on the environment, OJ L 197, 21.7.2001, p. 30) sets the minimum level for transboundary cooperation in the context of plans and programmes, the MSP-Directive considerably strengthens the obligation for transboundary cooperation in planning as the SEA-Directive only requires transboundary consultations in the event of likely and significant effects on the environment of another state (art. 7(1) of SEA-Directive). In the MSPD this threshold is set considerably lower. Under art. 11(1) of the MSPD, member states shall cooperate without exception if the MSP deals with bordering marine waters of another member state.

28 One of the obligations of the directive to the member states is that they have to point a competent authority responsible for developing MSP in the member state (art. 13).

29 The obligation to cooperate in MSP with third countries is substantially weaker ('shall endeavour, where possible, to cooperate with third countries') compared to the obligation to cooperate among member states ('shall cooperate').

30 See on the criticism, Opinion of the Committee of the Regions on Proposed directive for maritime spatial planning and integrated coastal management, OJ C 356, 5.12.2013, p. 132.

31 However, this obligation has been narrowed down by stating that an MSP or a change thereof has to 'concern' other member states for the obligation to notify to apply. To obligation to notify the Commission remains regardless of the nature of MSP (art. 14(1) of MSPD).

32 This concern was also voiced in the legislative process of the MSP-directive in the Opinion of the European Economic and Social Committee on the 'Proposal of the Directive of the European Parliament and of the Council establishing a framework for maritime spatial planning and integrated coastal management', OJ C 341, 21.11.2013, p. 69.

33 See also on the problems of implementing a broad framework directive on MSP the Opinion of the European Economic and Social Committee on the 'Proposal of the Directive of the European Parliament and of the Council establishing a framework for maritime spatial planning and integrated coastal management', OJ C 341, 21.11.2013, p. 68.

References

COM (2006) 275, final, Volume II – Annex. Green Paper. 'Towards a future Maritime Policy for the Union: A European vision for the oceans and seas'.

COM (2007) 575, final, 'Communication from the Commission to the European Parliament, the Council, the European Economic and Social Committee and the Committee of the Regions'.

COM (2008) 791, final, 'Communication from the Commission. Roadmap for Maritime Spatial Planning: Achieving Common Principles in the EU'.

COM (2010) 461, final, 'Communication from the Commission to the European Parliament and the Council', Marine Knowledge 2020. 'Marine data and observation for smart and sustainable growth'.

COM (2010) 771, final, 'Communication from the Commission to the European Parliament, the Council, the European Economic and Social Committee and the Committee of the Regions. Maritime Spatial Planning in the EU – Achievements and Future Development'.

COM (2013) 133, final, 'Proposal for a directive of the European Parliament and of the Council establishing a framework for maritime spatial planning and integrated coastal management'.

European Commission (2011) 'Stakeholder consultation on MSP and ICZM', <http://ec.europa.eu/dgs/maritimeaffairs_fisheries/consultations/msp/summary-results-of-msp-questionnaire_en.pdf>, accessed on 14.10.2014.

Juda, Lawrence (2010) 'The European Union and the Marine Strategy Framework Directive: Continuing the Development of European Ocean Use Management', *Ocean Development and International Law*, vol. 41, p. 34–54.

Maes, Frank 'Maritime Spatial Planning: will there still be some space left for nature?' Presentation in the VVOR Conference – 20 years of Habitats Directive in Antwerp 13.12.2012. <http://www.omgevingsrecht.be/sites/default/files/habtitat1213122012/20121213-08.pdf>, accessed on 15.10.2014.

Markus, Till, Schlacke, Sabine and Maier, Nina (2010) 'Legal Implementation of Integrated Ocean Policies: The EU's Marine Strategy Framework Directive', *The International Journal of Marine and Coastal Law*, vol. 26, p. 59–90.

Meiner, A. (2010) 'Integrated maritime policy for the European Union – consolidating coastal and marine information to support maritime spatial planning' *Journal of Coastal Conservation*, vol. 14, p. 1–11.

Schäfer, Nicole (2009) 'Maritime Spatial Planning: The Roadmap' Presentation in the HELCOM MSP Workshop in Helsinki 27 – 29.1.2009.

Schäfer, Nicole and Barale, Vittorio (2011) 'Maritime spatial planning: opportunities & challenges in the framework of the EU integrated maritime policy', *Journal of Coastal Conservation*, vol. 15, p. 237–245.

Chapter 10

Marine spatial planning in the Bay of Bengal sub-region in South Asia

Daud Hassan and Emdadul Haque

Introduction

The Bay of Bengal is a lobe of the Indian Ocean that forms a roughly oval shape, measuring 1,800 km at its widest point and 1,500 km at its longest point, and covering an area of nearly 2.2 million km^2. The countries fronting the Bay of Bengal sub-region in South Asia (hereinafter 'the region') are Bangladesh, India and Myanmar.

The region is one of the least explored marine areas of the world (Bissinger, 2010, p. 113). It has remained unexplored mainly because of the non-settlement delimitation disputes among the three littoral states. The littoral states were also unwilling to exploit offshore resources because their land-based resources were in apex use. As a result of the settlement of the maritime boundaries disputes between Bangladesh and Myanmar in 2012 by the International Tribunal for the Law of the Sea (ITLOS), and because of increasing demands for energy to boost economic development, all the littoral states are now actively considering the exploration of their offshore resources, either on their own or by leasing to foreign oil and gas companies.

However, increased use of the Bay is having a negative impact on the marine environment, as evidenced in the loss of marine biodiversity, increased pollution and habitat depletion. An improved planning and management system, which emphasizes a balance between economic development and environmental conservation (not only conservation but also prevention of problems) are, therefore, urgent and imperative for the well-being of the region.

The settlement of maritime boundary delimitation between Bangladesh and Myanmar has brought to the forefront the need for transboundary marine spatial planning (MSP) between Bangladesh and Myanmar. A transboundary MSP for the region will provide for a holistic approach to sustainable sea use management, and for the sustainable development of the countries in the region.

This chapter explains MSP from socio-economic and environmental perspectives, and considers their legal aspects. It then examines the potential for a transboundary MSP for the region, and concludes with recommendations based on development of MSP as a useful instrument for the integrated and sustainable management of marine and coastal areas around the world, including the Great Barrier Reef in Australia.

MSP for sustainable ocean governance

President Dwight D. Eisenhower once said that a 'plan is nothing, planning is everything' (Backer and Frias, 2012). In that spirit, 'planning' is necessary for maritime spaces for the sake of the world's well-being. MSP has become an essential tool for identifying and utilizing marine spaces, and for drawing up plans for sustainable ocean governance.

MSP originated from two global trends in the development of ocean space: the utilization of marine energy resources and the declaration of marine protected areas to conserve marine ecosystems; the latter arising because of international concern over the loss of marine biodiversity (OTA, 2013). In general, MSP organizes the uses of the sea's resources in ways that will protect ecosystems for now and the future.

MSP relates to an improved planning and management system for protecting marine ecosystem health and services, which emphasizes a balance between economic development and marine environmental conservation (Hassan, 2013, p. 260), and provides an important framework for assessing biodiversity and ecosystem services, and for implementing potential responses (Douvere, 2008). It ensures that management or development decisions are taken coherently across sectors (European Commission, 2013). In fact, MSP is a significant departure from the sector-by-sector or use-by-use approaches; rather, it is an integrated approach that allows planners to consider various uses of oceans at the same time by way of providing accurate information and maps about the geography, environmental impacts and existing uses of the ocean spaces (Hassan, 2013, p. 260).

An effective MSP depends on effective marine space zoning as well as application of various environmental management principles. According to UNESCO, 'Marine spatial planning is one element of ocean or sea use management' while 'zoning plans and regulations are one of a set of management measures for implementing marine spatial planning' and thereby 'zoning plans guide the granting or denial of individuals permits for the use of marine space'.[1] In other words, zoning is a means of applying MSP to specific marine spaces: a toolkit for implementing the ecosystem approach with an aim of achieving a healthy marine ecosystem by separating potentially conflicting ocean uses, reducing conflicts and enabling economic and social benefits from various commercial and recreational activities (Hassan 2013, p. 261). Zoning actually defines what activities can occur in which locations.[2] There may be different types of zones in an MSP; zones may vary depending upon their geographical position, geological and geomorphological nature, stock of fish, mineral resources, and ecosystem.[3]

Thus, MSP together with integrated and sustainable coastal zone management are complementary tools: the MSP maps out existing human activities and identifies their most effective future spatial development; and zone management strategies ensure the integrated and sustainable management of the human activities. Basically, a balanced and explicit MSP includes both plans and management strategies that enable a state to comprehensively address the development of its marine and coastal areas (Backer and Frias, 2012, p. 14).

To be effective an MSP needs to be conducted as a continuous, interactive and adaptive process, consisting of at least three ongoing phases: planning and analysis, implementation, and monitoring and evaluation (Ehler and Douvere, 2009).

In order for an MSP to be formulated a coastal state must have a defined maritime boundary; the boundary enables a coastal state to exercise its sovereign rights and jurisdictions over the delimited maritime spaces and resources therein (The Nature Conservancy, 2009). Thus, the settlement of any maritime disputes between littoral states is an important precondition.

Rationale for the introduction of MSP in the region

The world's oceans are an important source of life, energy and food, as well as being important for commerce and recreation. Oceans are in demand as playgrounds for pleasure-seekers and nature lovers, as a highway for international commerce and as a home for unique communities of wildlife and people (Backer and Frias, 2012, p. 11). The ocean's resources of energy are also in high demand. As already noted, MSP has the potential to enable the varied demands on oceans to be met in an integrated and sustainable manner that ensures the protection and preservation of marine and coastal ecosystems.

Various marine uses such as shipping, fisheries, exploration of energy resources, coastal management and environmental protection have strong transboundary dimensions, as is the case in the Bay of Bengal sub-region. Although user pressures in the region are currently relatively low, they are expected to grow strongly in the future. In order to address and manage this likely future pressure, an MSP for the region should be developed now.

Geographical configuration

The mean depth of the Bay of Bengal is 2586 m (M Habibur Rahman, 1991) and the continental slope terminates at a depth less than 3000 m (ibid.). The configuration of the coast of Bangladesh is concave,[4] while the configuration of the coast of India and Myanmar adjoining the Bay of Bengal is convex.[5]

Bangladesh is situated at the north-eastern corner of the Bay of Bengal. Its entire coastline, which extends for approximately 310 miles (499 km) (Danzic, 1975) from the boundary with India in the west to the boundary with Myanmar in the south-east, is concave. The middle third of the coastline forms a second, even deeper concavity. To the east and south-east of Bangladesh lies Myanmar. The Naaf River forms the boundary between the two States. Myanmar's coastline along the Bay of Bengal runs in a relatively straight north-west-to-south-east direction, and is marked by a number of offshore islands. The portion of Myanmar's coastline that fronts the Bay of Bengal extends for approximately 595 km (Alexander, 1986) although not that entire coastline is relevant to the delimitation of the maritime boundary with Bangladesh. Completing the picture is India, situated to the west of Bangladesh, and separated from it by the Ichamati, Kalindi, Raimangal and Hariabhanga Rivers. The length of the Indian coastline is about 2,759 miles (4,440 km) (Alexander, 1967).

The need for MSP for the region

As noted earlier, the Bay of Bengal is one of the least explored marine areas of the world (Bissinger, 2010, p. 110), because of the conflicting claims between the littoral states and because they had little need to explore for offshore resources.

Because of increasing demands for energy to boost and stabilize economic development, all littoral states are currently actively considering the exploration of their offshore resources, either by their own means or in conjunction with foreign oil and gas companies. The need for setting boundaries has now become paramount. Bangladesh was the first country in the region to start negotiations to set its maritime boundary with its neighbouring states: India and Myanmar. Failing to settle such boundaries through peaceful negotiation, Bangladesh, in 2009, with the consent of counter states, lodged cases against India and Myanmar before the Arbitral Tribunal constituted in accordance with Annex VII of the 1982 United Nations Convention on the Law of the Sea (UNCLOS Convention).

Subsequently, the case between Bangladesh and Myanmar was transferred to the International Tribunal for the Law of the Sea (ITLOS) with mutual consent of both the countries. On 14 March 2012, the ITLOS pronounced its judgement by delimiting a maritime boundary between Bangladesh and Myanmar.[6] The arbitration between Bangladesh and India has been awarded by the Arbitral Tribunal constituted in accordance with Annex VII of the UNCLOS Convention on 7 July 2014.[7] These steps are positive signs for a resolution to definitions of maritime boundaries in the region.

The settlement of maritime boundary delimitation between Bangladesh and Myanmar has brought to the forefront the need for MSP for Bangladesh and, if possible, the creation of a transboundary MSP between Bangladesh, India and Myanmar. The history of MSP developments around the world at present is that most successful MSP have been those that are national initiatives. Given the uncertain relations and cooperation between the littoral states of the Bay of Bengal, it would be wise for Bangladesh to undertake national initiatives as a first step towards MSP.

Developing MSP is important for the region, not only because of the capacity of plans to formulate holistic approaches and integration of activities to ensure the sustainable use of the sea's resources, but also to provide for the long-term economic, social and environmental or ecological development of the countries of the region.

Economic development

After the discovery of gas, oil and other natural resource reserves in the region, it has become an important potential source for the further economic development of the littoral states. Surveys estimate that the Bay of Bengal has a probable reserve of 188 tcf gas in the offshore areas of the littoral states, with Bangladesh having a probable reserve of 38.8 tcf gas in its offshore areas (Bissinger, 2010, pp. 111–14). Recent gas discoveries in proximate waters and a promising geological make-up have led other governments and corporations to speculate that large reserves could lie in the region (ibid.). These reserves of natural gas are especially important to the economic development of Bangladesh because land-based reserves of gas and oil are running low,[8] and no significant new land-based oil and gas reserves have, as yet, been discovered.

Increased exploration and exploitation of oil and gas is likely to take place in the region in the near future to enable south-east Asian countries to keep pace with their rapid economic and population growth (Chellaney, 2009, p. 14). Bangladesh is considered the gateway to the Bay of Bengal. Its well-developed seaports are of enormous importance because India and land-locked states of south Asia, such as Nepal and Bhutan, depend on these port facilities to increase trade both nationally and internationally. China also uses these facilities to increase intra-regional and inter-regional economic cooperation (Saifuddin, 2009, pp. 12–13). The marine routes of the region are likely to experience significant growth in marine traffic in the near future.

Apart from oil and gas, and revenues from the utilization of port facilities by marine traffic from around the world, increased opportunities for offshore fishing offer important economic potential in the region. Bangladeshis rely on fish for more than 50 per cent of their animal protein intake (Maribus gGmbH, 2013). Bangladesh used to catch about two million tonnes of fish from the sea each year (Maribus gGmbH, 2010). At present it has a high dependency on aquaculture, which takes place inland (in fresh water) and in coastal areas.

Social development

The sea and coastal areas have a close nexus with urbanization, and the livelihood of people and their socio-cultural activities. From time immemorial people have dwelt on the coastal areas. Coastal zones cover 20 per cent of the earth space, and 45 per cent of Earth's human population live and work in coastal zones (Behnam, 2012). About 2.8 billion people (more than 40 per cent of global population) live and work in coastal cities (ibid.). Sixty million people now live within one meter of sea level; by the end of this century, that number is expected to jump to 130 million; and by 2025, about 75 per cent of the world's population could be living within 100 km off the sea (Ban Ki-moon, 2011). One-quarter of the world's population lives in the littoral States of the Bay of Bengal and 65 per cent of the region's urban population lives in the coast cities (Hassan, 2006, p. 150).

This data is crucial to Bangladesh. Bangladesh is the seventh most populous country in the world (Chellaney, 2009, p. 15) with a relatively small inhabitable area and is 'in the top ten in terms of percentage of population living in the low elevation coastal zone' (Pender, 2008, p. 38). According to the UNDP Human Development Indicators, the current population in Bangladesh is around 150 million (International Human Development Indicators, 2011) with the population density at 1,064 inhabitants per square km (Population Reference Bureau, 2008). More than 53 million of its people, 39 per cent of the total population of Bangladesh, reside in the coastal zones (Maribus gGmbH 2013, p. 69). Apart from this, in socio-economic terms, Bangladesh is one of the poorest nations in the world. Annual growth rates are slowly declining, currently at 1.8 per cent, and projected to fall to 0.56 per cent by 2045–50. The Human Development Index estimates that 56 million people (40 per cent of the population) live below the poverty line and the country was ranked 146th out of 187 in 2011 (United Nations Development Programme, 2011). According to the Population Reference Bureau (PRB), as much as 81 per cent of the Bangladeshi population live on less than US$2 per day (Population Reference Bureau, 2011). If the marine environment of the Bay of Bengal were to be degraded due to unsustainable human activities and unplanned use of marine resources, the implications, as will be shown below, will be catastrophic for a developing state like Bangladesh.

The marine area of Bangladesh is not only important for its significant economic role but also for its unparalleled natural panorama and aesthetic appeal. One-fourth of the total population of Bangladesh live along the coastline and many are directly dependent on the sea for their livelihood (Islam, 2004, p. 97).

The fisheries sector in the coastal zones provides an important source of income and employment for the local people (Ministry of Finance, 2003). From west to east, the coastal and marine area of Bangladesh possesses vast potential for tourism. Among the coastal and marine zones, Khulna, Kuakata (of Patuakhali district), Chittagong (Patenga beach), Cox's Bazar and St Martin's island (a coral island) are the major tourist spots with both domestic and foreign visitors, providing significant amounts of revenue to the government from this sector (Department of Environment, 2006).

Environmental development

The region has a huge coastline; the Bangladesh coastline alone is approximately 710 km long, and hosts a unique and diversified ecosystem (ibid., p. 1). Included among Bangladesh's most important ecosystems are the ecologically critical areas (ECAs) of Cox's Bazar Sea Beach, Sonadia Island, St Martin's Island and Sundarbans (Karim, 2009, p. 51).

Non-traditional security concerns, for example, the impacts of climate change, are a significant concern (Chellaney, 2009, p. 10). A climate crisis seems to be imminent, even though 'the science is immature and reasons for climate change are not completely understood' (ibid.). A study shows that, due to rising sea levels as a consequence of climate change, 17 per cent of Bangladesh will be flooded, and around 30 per cent of arable land will be lost by 2050 (Chellaney, 2009, p. 15.)

Again, the rising sea level is likely to have an impact on salt water intrusion, inundation, and coastal erosion. There are also likely to be more destructive storms and decreased freshwater availability (Warner *et al.*, 2009, p.iv; Bell, 2004, p. 135; Morton *et al.*, 2008, pp. 5–6). The evidence is strong that all of these impacts will undermine crop growth, destroy subsistence food resources, water supplies and vital infrastructure, as well as inundate low-lying coastal areas that are home to people (ibid.).

Due to the unregulated operation of a large number of domestic and foreign marine vessels within the inland and merchant shipping lanes, the country has been exposed to massive pollution that is causing a serious imbalance in the marine environment (Ministry of Environment and Forestry, 2001). The sea transportation route of the Bay of Bengal is becoming increasingly busy, and the likelihood is that marine pollution from marine vessels is likely to rise in the Bay. In addition, increasing over-fishing in the offshore area is a significant threat to the sustainability of the fisheries. According to a survey conducted from 1995/96 to 2002/03, the marine catch of Bangladesh has increased by about 65 per cent (Ministry of Finance, 2003). Over-extraction and unsustainable harvesting of marine fisheries have also been a major threat to the marine biodiversity of the region. However, land-based sources of marine pollution continue to be the most significant threat to the marine environment of the region. No control mechanisms have been established to protect the seas from this threat.

Regional initiatives for marine environmental protection

Evidence reveals that regional initiatives have been taken to protect the marine environment.

South Asian Seas Action Plan

The Governing Council of the UNEP initiated the South Asian Seas (hereinafter SAS) Action Plan eight years after the formation of UNEP's Regional Seas Plan (RSP). In May 1982, the Governing Council adopted Decision 10/20, which requested the Executive Director of the UNEP to enter into consultations with the concerned states of the South Asia Co-operative Environment Program (SACEP) to ascertain their views regarding development of the RSP in the SAS region. The states consulted agreed and those now involved in the SAS cooperative programme are Bangladesh, India, Maldives, Pakistan and Sri Lanka. Regional reports on the state of the marine environment were completed in 1985 and 1987, to be followed by an Action Plan (UNEP, 1987). The Action Plan for the Protection and Management of the Marine and Coastal Environment of the South Asian Seas Region was at last formally adopted on 24 March 1995, under the auspices of the UNEP (ibid.). The members of the Action Plan are the same as for the SACEP.

The overall objective of the SASAP is to protect and manage the marine environment and related coastal ecosystems of the region in an environmentally sound and sustainable manner. The objectives are: to establish and enhance consultations and technical co-operation among states within the region; highlight the economic and social importance of the resources of the marine and coastal environment and establish a regional co-operative network of activities concerning subjects/projects of mutual interest for the whole region (South Asia Co-Operative Environmental Program).

This Action Plan was designed to develop financial and institutional mechanisms for the protection of the marine and coastal environment from different activities. The Action Plan identified some priority areas. These included integrated coastal zone management (ICZM) for the protection of the marine environment from land-based activities (Status of the South Asian Regional Seas Program). Resolutions were adopted for the smooth implementation of this Plan. The existing regional inter-governmental organization, the SACEP, located in Colombo, Sri Lanka, was made responsible for facilitating the implementation of the Action Plan by organizing inter-governmental meetings of the member states; it was also given responsibility for administering the Action Plan. This Action Plan is now also supported by the Global Environment Facility (GEF), the World Bank's South Asia Development Triangle Initiative (SADTI), the Asian Development Bank (ADB), the United Nations Development Programme (UNDP), and various NGOs. In order to achieve socio economic goals for future generations and to reduce the rates of marine and coastal biodiversity loss and protect natural resources, currently, the SACEP and partners are working to implement a European Union funded project with the five maritime nations of South Asia: Bangladesh, India, Maldives, Pakistan and Sri Lanka (South Asia Co-Operative Environmental Program).

While the SAS Action Plan is an important positive development for regional management of marine related activities, including the review of national and regional problems and ICZM (UNEP 1996), the regime formation process has been very slow. This indicates that concerned states of this region are not ready to commit to the adoption of a co-operative regime for MSP. There was significant lack of political will to facilitate the consultation process for the adoption of this Action Plan. The reason seems to be that national actors and governments considered marine issues to be a low priority.

Coral Reef Task Force

South Asia is home to 6 per cent of the world's coral reefs, which provide a critical source of food and livelihoods to an estimated 400 million people.[9] In order to facilitate the implementation of regional and international initiatives in the management of coral reefs and associated ecosystems, and to promote collaborative action and transboundary responses to shared environments, the South Asia Coral Reef Task Force (SACRTF) was established in 2006 (South Asia Co-Operative Environmental Program). A number of regional resource coordination workshops, such as the Colombo workshop in 2007, have been held by the Task Force.

The Coral Reef Task Force project began in 2006, and work is underway in collaboration with country governments and coastal and marine stakeholders to improve management, communications, data management, and to promote awareness, improve the livelihoods of coastal communities, enhance resource capacity of personnel, improve regional cooperation and coordination of management and conservation efforts, and to assist participating countries to learn from each other's experiences.[10]

The Bay of Bengal Program (BOBP)

The Bay of Bengal Program (BOBP) is a regional fisheries project under the auspices of the Food and Agricultural Organization (FAO) that became operational in 1979. In its first two phases, the BOBP aimed to improve sub-regional socio-economic conditions through the use of new and innovative fishing techniques. The third phase of this project began to directly address the serious management problems facing the Bay's fisheries (Global Environment Facility, 1999, p. 5). Among other approaches, it includes ICZM, awareness raising and educational activities.

A proposal was made to develop a strategic action program (SAP) to enhance national and regional efforts under the BOBP to protect the health of the ecosystem and manage the living resources of the Bay of Bengal's large marine ecosystem on a sustainable basis (Global Environment Facility, 1999, p. 6). As a basis for the development of the SAP, important marine environmental issues, such as ecological and environmental analysis, systematic harmonised data collection, identification of opportunities (policy, institutional, technological, economic and legal options) and priority actions were considered (Global Environment Facility, 1999, p. 6). The SAP emphasized linkages between management of living resources and pollution, and regional cooperation. To effectively manage these issues it proposed a number of activities, including the establishment of national task forces to guide the preparation of the national reports, regional thematic papers on critical issues, regional and national workshops, regional studies on legal and legislative frameworks and opportunities for co-operation. Extensive consultation with a wide range of government and non-government organizations were also proposed to implement the SAP (Global Environment Facility, 1999, pp. 7–11).

The BOBP initially relied on support from the countries concerned, bilateral donor countries and the FAO. The advisory committee of the BOBP, at its nineteenth meeting, urged the FAO Secretariat to prepare a proposal and explore GEF as a possible funding source. This suggestion was endorsed by the Bay of Bengal Committee (BOBC) (Global Environment Facility, 1999, p. 13) and since then, the GEF has been supporting efforts to reduce coastal management problems in the Bay of Bengal, including fisheries management. For example, the GEF has funded an 'Aquatic Resources Development, Management and Conservation of Fisheries Project' in Bangladesh. It commenced work in October 2001, aiming to sustain growth in both inland and coastal fisheries through a number of interventions, including extension training and improvement of coastal shrimp culture (PDO-ICZM, 2001).

The aim of the BOBP was to assist countries of this sub-region to meet their obligations to manage and protect their marine and coastal environment. Although it was not directly related to MSP it is particularly relevant to the broader aims of the South Asian Seas Action Plan. However, it also includes activities directly related to the marine resources management, such as ICZM, and is therefore also directly relevant to LBSMP control.

There are sub-regional and regional initiatives on marine environmental protection. For the most part, they are not directly focused on MSP. Environmental management principles are grossly unused for the management of the marine resources in the region. Sustainable use of marine resources is very rare. In particular, the application of the precautionary principle, polluter pays principle and cleaner production is barely applied.

There are some laws to deal with marine and coastal zone management, such as the Territorial Waters and Maritime Zone Act 1974, Territorial Waters and Maritime Zones Rules 1977, in Bangladesh and the Coastal Zone Management Act in India.[11] Although they are not directly related to MSP, they encompass issues of marine environmental protection. However, their application is very broad as far as the concept of MSP is concerned. Ecosystem-based management is not sufficiently advocated in these legal and policy instruments.

A joint movement of both NGOs and the public has begun in relation to the degradation of the marine environment in the region.[12] Various workshops specifically focused on integrated water resources management. Various representatives from government and non-government organizations, and representatives from the public interested in environmental issues, participated. Although such research and education are not specifically directed to the development of a MSP, they could have an impact on broader awareness building on sustainable marine environmental protection. By promoting awareness on marine environmental issues, these activities could help to bring people together and provide the basis for a MSP in the region.

Experience sharing is a way forward for the region

The countries of the region have significant gaps between commitment and cooperative action to develop a transboundary MSP owing to inadequate legal approaches and lack of capacity. It is clear that present arrangements and mechanisms need to be revisited and strengthened to achieve an effective MSP in the region.

The region is occupied by developing countries with huge populations and few resources. But, in spite of resource and economic constraints, their economies are growing fast. Keeping pace with growing economies, rapid population growth and growing consumer demands has considerably increased the need for more food, more energy and more trade. Because of limited or diminishing resources on land, an increasingly larger share of goods and services need to come from coastal and marine areas. Resource extraction is expanding progressively into deeper waters and further offshore (Berkes *et al.*, 2006 pp. 1557–8.). Aquaculture, offshore energy, maritime transport and tourism are flourishing. The future outlook for offshore activities confirm that this trend will continue, and most likely accelerate, in the next decades.[13] All these activities have already considerably increased the demand for ocean space, and will continue to do so in future. If such multipurpose human activities cannot be shaped in a planned way, the implications, as mentioned above, may be more fatal and devastating than currently estimated.

Adding to these concerns, the predicted effects of climate change could tip the balance to disaster both in coastal area and marine spaces, affecting the social stability of the region. The geographic location, flat and low-lying topography, high population density, poverty incidence and dependence on natural resources render the counties of the region particularly vulnerable to climatic changes.[14] Bangladesh has already suffered economically, environmentally and socially as a result of climate change in the last decade, so threatening the country's stability. Hence in order to ensure an ecosystem based on sea-use management systems of the Bay of Bengal, the countries of the region have no alternative but to initiate activities for MSP. However, questions remain as to the scientific knowledge and institutional capacity for taking such initiatives by the countries of the region.

As noted, the importance of comprehensive management and planning systems for marine spaces have grown because of the increased use of oceans and their impact on marine and coastal environment. There has been an increasing interest in using the MSP implemented in the GBRMP in many parts of the world including the Baltic Sea Region (BSR).[15] In fact, the GBRMP has gained the state of a role model in the world for developing MSP as an instrument to ensure multipurpose use of the sea and its resources, and establishing a successful ecosystem-based management system in the marine and coastal area. In order to proceed with MSP in the Bay of Bengal, one of the most sensitive marine areas of the world, the littoral states such as Bangladesh, could learn lessons from the MSP experience of the GBRMP.

The overall goal of the GBRMP Authority is to provide for 'the long-term protection, ecologically sustainable use, understanding and enjoyment of the Great Barrier Reef through the care and development of the Great Barrier Reef Marine Park.'[16] The degradation of the Great Barrier Reef was a fundamental driver in the process of establishing the marine park in the late 1960s and early 1970s. The fundamental causes of degradation were oil drilling, limestone mining, pollution from shipping, land-based sources of pollution, and increased fishing and tourism activity.[17] The Great Barrier Reef's long-standing experience illustrates the need to conduct marine spatial management in a continuous manner, using monitoring and evaluation to guide continuous adaptation of plans to changing circumstances.

An analysis shows that the implementation process of any MSP depends on some prerequisites: adoption and implementation of adequate legal and policy bases; coordination and integration of complex political and economic elements, including national, regional and global institutions; improving measures for avoiding and settling marine environmental disputes; preventing and mitigating environmental damage; strengthening and developing marine environmental laws and compliance; and, over all, ensuring effective community participation (Hassan, 2013, p. 267). Stakeholder involvement and sustainable financing are critical to successful outcomes of marine spatial management over time.[18] The implementation process of the Great Barrier Reef seems to be relatively successful because of the inclusions of stakeholder concerns in the Marine Park Act (e.g. the inclusion of a new process for community participation by focusing on interactions between the public and private authorities, the role of the compliance committee, recognition of the independent role of the Marine Park Authority, necessary tools for measuring government accountability and transparency and responsiveness) along with development mechanisms, review procedures and public awareness mechanisms (Hassan, 2013, pp. 267–8.). Important lessons can be learned about the process of integrated sea use management and marine spatial planning from the experience of the GBRMP.[19]

Bangladesh is a new player in offshore marine activities. It lacks not only proper marine scientific and technical knowledge but also academics and institutions responsible for building national capacity in this aspect. Therefore, knowledge sharing is crucial to increase the country's capacity and ability to initiate the process of MSP adequately. The experience of the Great Barrier Reef Marine Park, not only for its successful implementation at a national level, but also for its international recognition as a pioneer project of MSP, can be very useful for knowledge sharing on the part of the region.

Conclusion

The world's oceans provide a range of benefits for human well-being and prosperity. However, various human activities have put the oceans at risk of irreversible damage by over-fishing, ocean acidification (from absorbed carbon emissions), increased pollution, unsustainable coastal area development, and unwanted impacts from resource extraction. These are also resulting in loss of biodiversity, decreased abundance of species, damage to habitats and loss of ecological diversity. In order to achieve a healthy and productive marine and coastal ecosystem, the importance of planned use of the ocean and its resources have been enunciated in the United Nations.

The goal of MSP is to enable better decisions about ocean uses and reduce potential conflicts. MSP is the first step towards ecosystem-based management of the sea and its resources. The Bay of Bengal sub-region in South Asia is one of the most sensitive and important marine and coastal ecosystems in the world. In order to enable the Bay's socio-economic and ecological potential to be realized, as well as achieve a balance between conservation and use of ocean resources, the region requires the integrated and sustainable management framework that an MSP process can provide, as well as technical supporting measures. Strengthening general science-based knowledge and building capacity for ocean management, along with providing coordinated global, regional and national mechanisms, is also important. Learning from the experiences of the GBRMP could be a way forward for enhancing capacity and putting the MSP commitments into practice in the region.

MSP should, ideally, be implemented in a spirit of cooperation. The current cooperative arrangements in the region are notional. They fall far short of optimal willingness for cooperative actions towards implementation of the objectives of the MSP process. There is a compelling need for a cooperative regime which will facilitate implementation by improving economic conditions, reducing the subregional conflicts among littoral states in the region, developing economic collaboration without contravening international obligations, and further encouraging in the participatory processes of MSP. Political will and partnership-building are essential to pave the way for an effective MSP in this region. Political negotiation, diplomatic conferences, and regional workshops on the development of an MSP to protect the region's marine environment, could also play an important role in enhancing a common understanding of the issues and lead to the achievement of a sustainable marine and coastal environment in the region.

Notes

1 See (http://www.unesco-ioc-marinesp.be/marine_spatial_planning_msp)

2 (http://www.gbrmpa.gov.au/visit-the-reef/zoning/about-zoning, accessed 25 December 2013)

3 For example, in Baltic Sea MSP, there are generally found four types of zones in MSP: (1) General Use Zones – where all activities permitted by law and policy are allowed; (2) Targeted Management Zones – where some restricted activities and uses are allowed; (3) Exclusive Use Zones – where only a specific type of use is allowed, although certain other activities, compatible with the main purpose of the zones, are allowed; and (4) Restricted access zones or single use zone – which is highly restricted for adequate protection of certain areas or issues, for example, unique ecological habitat, military use etc. See Hassan, Daud (2013) 'The Great Barrier Reef: Maritime spatial planning', *Environmental Policy and Law*, vol. 43, no. 4–5, p. 261. But the marine spaces in Australian Great Barrier Reef have been divided into eight zones namely: General Use Zone, Habitat Protection Zone, Conservation Park Zone, Buffer Zone, Scientific Research Zone, Marine National Park Zone, Commonwealth Islands Zone, and Preservation Zone. See Great Barrier Reef Marine Park Authority (2004).

4 Concave coast of a coastal state is a coast which is curved inward to the landmass of that state; as an example, the coast of Germany or Bangladesh.
5 Convex coast of a coastal state is a coast which is curved outward to the sea.
6 See(http://www.itlos.org/fileadmin/itlos/documents/cases/case_no_16/1-C16_Judgement_14_02_2012.pdf)
7 See (http://www.pca-cpa.org/showpage.asp?pag_id=1376)
8 Only 5 tcf proven gas reserved remain in the land ward part of Bangladesh. See Bissinger (2010, p. 112).
9 See South Asia Co-Operative Environmental Program' http://www.sacep.org/html/projects_ongoing_icran.htm, undated
10 See South Asia Co-Operative Environmental Program', http://www.sacep.org/html/sacrtf_abtsacrtf.htm
11 The Coastal Zone Management Act provides a framework for coastal zone management
12 For example, a workshop on 'Strengthening Governance and Communication in Bangladesh Water Sector' was organized in Dhaka by Environment and Geographic Information System (EGIS), Bangladesh, *The EGIS Newsletter*, Issue No 3, 2002, p. 1.
13 For example, the share of natural gas production derived from offshore exploitation is expected to grow to nearly 40 per cent by 2030 (compared to 20–25 per cent in 1990) as exploration and developments will shift to more lucrative offshore sites, a trend partly stimulated by ongoing high oil prices. A substantial contribution is expected from renewables (e.g., offshore wind farms) by 2030, mainly because of exploitation costs. See 'World energy outlook 2004', OECD/IEA International Energy Agency (IEA), 2004. Global future growth for the cruise business is estimated at an annual rate of 8 per cent, while eco-tourism, such as whale watching has grown to a multi-million dollar business in nearly 25 years, on an average growth rate of 12 per cent since 1990. See: 'Worldwide cruise ship activity', World Tourism Organization, 2003, p. 9; F. Kanji (2006) 'A Global perspective on the challenges of coastal tourism', Coastal Development Centre, Kasetsart University, Bangkok, Thailand, 16 November 2006. Aquaculture is expanding and intensifying in almost all regions of the world and has grown to about 43 per cent of global fish consumption (in comparison to only 9 per cent in 1980). See Delgado C. *et al.* (2003), 'Fish to 2020: Supply and demand in changing global markets', *International Food Policy Research Institute and World Fish Center*, p. 81; United Nations Food and Agriculture Organization (2004) The State of World Fisheries and Aquaculture (SOFIA).
14 See generally, Naser, Mostafa Mahmud, 'Climate Change, Environmental Degradation, and Migration: A Complex Nexus', *William & Mary Environmental Law & Policy Review*, vol. 36, p. 713 (2012), http://scholarship.law.wm.edu/wmelpr/vol36/iss3/4
15 This region encompasses Finland, Sweden, Denmark, Germany, Poland, Estonia, Latvia, Lithuania and part of Russia. See, 'The Baltic Sea Countries', http://www.baltic.com/countries.asp.
16 See The Great Barrier Reef Marine Park Authority, http://www.gbrmpa.gov.au/about-us/strategic-plans/statement-of-expectations.
17 See Marine Spatial Planning Initiative, http://www.unesco-ioc-marinesp.be/spatial_management_practice/australia_great_barrier_reef
18 See Marine Spatial Planning Initiative, http://www.unesco-ioc-marinesp.be/spatial_management_practice/australia_great_barrier_reef
19 See Marine Spatial Planning Initiative, http://www.unesco-ioc-marinesp.be/spatial_management_practice/australia_great_barrier_reef

References

Alexander, Lewis, M. (ed.) (1967) *The Law of the Sea: Offshore Boundaries and Zones*, p. 73, Ohio University Press.

Alexander, Lewis M. (1986) 'The delimitation of maritime boundaries', *Political Geography Quarterly*, vol. 5.

Backer, Hermanni and Frias, Manuel (2012) 'Foreword', in Hermanni Backer and Manuel Frias (eds.) *Planning the Bothnian Sea: Key Findings of the Plan Bothnia Project*, Finepress Turku, Finland.

Bell, Derek R. (2004) 'Environmental refugees: What rights? Which duties?', *Res Publica*, vol. 10, p. 135–152.

Berkes, F. *et al.* (2006) 'Globalization, Roving Bandits, and Marine Resources' *Science*, vol. 311, pp. 1557–8.

Ban Ki-moon (3 October 2011) 'United Nations Secretary-General's message on UN HABITAT Day'.

Behnam, Awni (2012) 'From UNCLOS to RIO+20 and the oceans compact', pp. 4–6, http://www.ioinst.org/index.php?option=com_phocadownload&view=category&download=319:1012-from-unclos-to-rio-20-and-the-ocean-compact-Behnam2012&id=47:ioinforma2012&Itemid=60, accessed 28 December, 2013

Bissinger, Jared (2010) 'The maritime boundary dispute between Bangladesh and Myanmar: Motivations, potential solutions, and implications', *Asian Policy*, vol. 10, p. 103–142.

Chellaney, Brahma (2009) 'Indian Ocean maritime security: Environmental security and climate change', proceedings from the Indian Ocean Maritime Security Symposium, Australian Defence College, Canberra, Australia, 15–17 April 2009.

Danzic, Aaron L. (1975) 'A funny thing happened to common heritage on the way to the sea', *The San Diego Law Review*, vol. 12, no. 3.

Department of Environment (2006), 'Bangladesh: National Programme of Action for Protection of the Coastal and Marine Environment from Land-Based Activities', Ministry of Environment and Forest, Government of the People's Republic of Bangladesh, p. 20, http://www.doe-bd.org/npa_draft.pdf, accessed 30 December, 2013.

Dispute Concerning Delimitation of the Maritime Boundary between Bangladesh and Myanmar in the Bay of Bengal (Bangladesh/Myanmar), International Tribunal for the Law of the Sea (ITLOS), Case no. 16, Judgement, 14 March 2012, http://www.itlos.org/fileadmin/itlos/documents/cases/case_no_16/1-C16_Judgement_14_02_2012.pdf, accessed 28 December 2013.

Douvere, Fanny (2008) 'The importance of marine spatial planning in advancing ecosystem-based sea use management', *Marine Policy*, vol. 32, pp. 762–771.

Ehler, Charles and Douvere, Fanny (2009) 'Marine spatial planning: A step-by-step approach toward ecosystem-based management', Intergovernmental Oceanographic Commission and Man and the Biosphere Programme, *IOC Manual and Guides* No. 53, ICAM Dossier No. 6, Paris, UNESCO. 2009, p. 18, http://www.unesco-ioc-marines.be/uploads/documentenbank/d87c0c421da4593fd93bbee1898e1d51.pdf accessed 27 December 2013.

European Commission (2013) 'Proposal for a directive of the European Parliament and of the Council: Establishing a framework for maritime spatial planning and integrated coastal management', EC Doc no. COM (2013) 133 final, p. 2, http://eur-lex.europa.eu/LexUriServ/LexUriServ.do?uri=COM:2013:0133:FIN:EN:PDF, accessed 27 December 2013.

Global Environment Facility (1999) 'Proposal for the Project Development and Preparation Facility Project entitled Preparation of a Trans-boundary Diagnostic Analysis and Preliminary Framework Strategic Action Program for the Bay of Bengal Large Ecosystem'.

Great Barrier Reef Marine Park Authority (2004) 'Marine park zoning', http://www.gbrmpa.gov.au/visit-the-reef/zoning/about-zoning, accessed 25 December 2013.

Hassan, Daud (2013) 'The Great Barrier Reef: Maritime spatial planning', *Environmental Policy and Law*, vol. 43, no. 4–5.

Hassan, Daud (2006) *Protecting the Marine Environment from the Land-Based Sources of Pollution*, Ashgate Publishing.

International Human Development Indicators (2011) 'Bangladesh: Country profile: Human development indicators', http://hdrstats.undp.org/en/countries/profiles/BGD.html, accessed 28 December 2013.

Islam, M. Rafiqul (ed.) (2004) *Where Lands Meets the Sea. A Profile of Coastal Zone of Bangladesh*, University Press.

Karim, M. Saiful (2009) 'Implementation of MARPOL Convention in Bangladesh', *Macquarie Journal of International and Comparative Environmental Law*, vol. 6, pp. 51–82.

Maribus gGmbH (2013) *World Ocean Review 2013*, series 2, Mareverlag Publisher, Germany, p. 37 (hereinafter WOR 2), http://worldoceanreview.com/en/, accessed 29 December 2013.

Maribus gGmbH (2010) *World Ocean Review 2010*, series 1, Mareverlag Publisher, Germany, p. 122 (hereinafter WOR 1), http://worldoceanreview.com/en/,accessed 29 December 2013.

M Habibur Rahman (1991) *Delimitation of Maritime Boundaries*, Rajshahi, Bangladesh.

Maritime Spatial Planning Initiative, 'MSP around the world', http://www.unesco-ioc-marinesp.be/marine_spatial_planning_msp, accessed 27 December 2013.

Ministry of Environment and Forestry (2001) 'Bangladesh: State of the environment', report, Government of Bangladesh, p. 44, http://www.moef.gov.bd/html/state_of_env/state_of_env.html

Ministry of Finance (2003) *Bangladesh Economic Survey 2003*, Government of Bangladesh.

Morton, Andrew *et al.* (2008) 'Human security policy challenges', *Forced Migration Review*, vol. 31.

OTA, Yoshitaka (2013) 'An overview of the international development of marine spatial planning and its policy application in Japan', *Ocean Policy Studies*, vol. 10.

PDO-ICZM, *Coast News*, Issue No. 4, Dhaka, October–December 2001, p. 4.

Pender, James S. (2008) 'What is climate change? And how it will affect Bangladesh', Briefing Paper, final draft, Church of Bangladesh Social Development Programme, p. 38.

Population Reference Bureau, '2008 World population datasheet', http://www.prb.org/pdf08/08wpds_eng.pdf, accessed 28 December 2013.

Population Reference Bureau (2011) 'World population data sheet 2011', http://www.prb.org/Publications/Datasheets/2011/world-population-data-sheet.aspx, accessed 27 December 2013.

Saifuddin, Shah Mohammed (2009) 'Indo-Bangla relations: India's regional ambition, Geopolitical Reality, and Strategic Options for Bangladesh', *Bangladesh Strategic & Development Forum*.

'South Asia Co-Operative Environmental Program', http://www.sacep.org/html/sas_objectives.htm undated.

Status of the South Asian Regional Seas Program, Annex IV, Colombo Workshop, p. 19.
The Nature Conservancy (2009) 'Best practices for maritime spatial planning: Executive summary', p. 3, http://www.marineplanning.org/pdf/msp_best_practices.pdf, accessed 30 December 2013.
The Territorial Waters and Maritime Zone Act 1974: aims to prevent and control marine pollution and also to preserve the quality and ecological balance in the marine environment in the high seas adjacent to territorial waters (Section 8).
The Territorial Waters and Maritime Zones Rules 1977: makes provision against serious marine pollution infringements (section 3(g)) and any contravention of rules is punishable by imprisonment of up to one year and a fine up to 5000 Taka (section 10).
United Nations Data (2012) 'Bangladesh', http://data.un.org/CountryProfile.aspx?crName=Bangladesh, accessed 28 December 2013.
United Nations Development Programme (2011), 'Human development report 2011', http://hdrstats.undp.org/images/explanations/BGD.pdf, accessed 29 December 2013. The HDI is a summary measure for assessing long-term progress in three basic dimensions of human development: a long and healthy life, access to knowledge and a decent standard of living.
United Nations Environmental Program (1987) South Asia Co-Operative Environmental Program' 1–2, http://www.sacep.org/html/sas_actionplan.htm; undated.
United Nations Environmental Program, 'Institutional Arrangements for Implementation of the Global Program of Action for the Protection of the Marine Environment from Land-based Activities', UNEP/GC.19/INF.4, 8 November 1996.
Warner, Koko *et al.* (2009) 'In search of shelter: Mapping the effects of climate change on human migration and displacement', report, p. iv, http://ciesin.columbia.edu/publications.html.

Part IV

Conclusions

Chapter 11

Comparative and forward-looking conclusions on transboundary MSP

Niko Soininen, Tuomas Kuokkanen and Daud Hassan

The perception of marine areas and resources has evolved over time from limitless to limited. The limitations are apparent in the face of a growing need for marine space, natural resources, and ecosystem services provided by the marine environment, in addition to the problems of marine pollution and overexploitation of resources. Marine spatial planning (MSP) is a brave attempt to address many of these issues. The world oceans are interconnected and have coastlines shared between many different states, making MSP transboundary by nature (Chapters 1 and 3). These transboundary aspects are discussed in the book through regional seas developments in Northern Europe and the EU MSP framework (Chapters 7, 8.1, 8.2 and 9) while Australia's Great Barrier Reef (Chapter 6) is portraying transboundary MSP within the context of a federal state. Finally, the Bay of Bengal in the Indian Ocean illustrates some of the problems of transboundary MSP from the perspective of a developing country (Chapter 10).

The problems of ocean governance can help in understanding the popularity of MSP. Despite the recent popularity, MSP still needs to prove its worth and added value compared to or in combination with existing instruments. As shown in Chapter 3, MSP does not hold intrinsic value on its own but provides a framework for a more integrated multi-level approach to ocean governance. This book has attempted to show that MSP provides a basis for achieving sustainable development and tries to mediate, *inter alia*, between legal instruments and institutions as well as branches of government and sectoral interests. MSP may provide a foundation for a more coherent and holistic way of addressing issues of ocean governance in order to sustainably use and protect the marine environment.

MSP may be a novel concept but has firm historical roots (Chapters 2 and 3), tracing its legal roots to the United Nations Convention on the Law of the Sea (UNCLOS), which seeks to bridge the gap between land-use and marine spatial planning. UNCLOS provides coastal states with legitimate ways of exercising their competence over planning and utilizing marine areas (Chapter 4). International law is on the one hand making MSP possible and on the other placing certain restrictions on it. There is no general obligation to undertake MSP nor are there any general rules to coordinate the scale, level or objects of planning (Chapters 4 and 5). Currently, only regional legal instruments are setting binding requirements on the marine environment, such as those developed by the European Union (EU). Nevertheless, those too lack substantive provisions regarding MSP (Chapter 9).

Despite the lack of global legal obligation to adopt and coordinate national MSPs with other coastal states, international law contains numerous procedural and substantive obligations that place limits on the contents of MSPs and related processes. For instance, coastal states have the legal obligation to conduct marine planning, in accordance with the freedom of navigation under UNCLOS, regulations and instruments on marine-protected areas formed, as well as requirements concerning transboundary communication, notification and cooperation for projects likely to cause significant transboundary harm. Transboundary elements have to be considered in national MSPs. The bulk of these obligations are scattered between international, regional and bi- and multi-lateral levels under a myriad of legal instruments and institutions (Chapters 2, 4, 5 and 9). As a consequence, the regulatory framework of MSP is highly fragmented which creates problems when trying to formulate an overall view on the legal obligations regarding MSP. At the same time as MSP is striving towards integration, it appears to suffer from fragmentation itself.

The fragmentation of the legal framework of MSP is not only a problem of scattered normative information but also a question of legal validity. While legal instruments on different levels are placing certain legal obligations on the coastal states regarding MSP, the legal framework is also being developed in several institutional contexts through soft law instruments. This means that the overall legal framework of MSP is complemented by legally non-binding management principles, good practices and recommendations (Chapter 5 and 8.2). A good example of this is the HELCOM-VASAB Working Group on Maritime Spatial Planning, which has developed MSP principles and institutional structures for transboundary MSP in the Baltic Sea (Chapters 5 and 7). Soft law documents produced in this and in similar processes may lack formal, legally binding status but their legitimacy and effectiveness through wide stakeholder participation, voluntary nature and open dialogue can have a great impact on the development and interpretation of the legal regime of MSP. As a consequence, a legal perspective on MSP necessarily means taking a broader governance perspective in which softer forms of regulation take centre stage in complementing legally binding obligations.

The lack of coherent and integrated legal framework on MSP and transboundary MSP alike contributes to the conceptual ambiguity of MSP. On a general level there seems to be a fairly clear understanding on the concept of MSP being a future-oriented and strategic process offering ways to minimize conflicts between users of the marine spaces and actively promoting synergies by way of spatial and temporal allocation. MSP, in all its forms, is a means of balancing sustainable development with the evolving and growing needs to sustainably develop marine economies (blue growth) and to protect the marine environment. As such, it is an instrument for sustainable ocean governance (Chapter 1), but this is where conceptual uniformity usually ends.

The uniformity of the concept of MSP seems to evaporate and conceptual fragmentation becomes visible as soon as one starts to discuss the specifics of the instrument and tries to analyse the different approaches to implementing MSP around the globe. In the Great Barrier Reef in Australia, MSP employs zoning along with legally binding restrictions on the uses within different zones. MSP operates on a very concrete level with clearly visible legal effect (Chapter 6). The importance of zoning for effective MSP was highlighted throughout the book, especially in Chapters 3 and 6. In contrast, the European Union seeks to coordinate and harmonize national approaches to MSP but this is being done without an obligation to use zoning as a part of MSP (Chapter 9). National MSPs are developed in the member states in a more general direction and function as overall strategic plans without a direct connection to the zoning of marine areas. Overall the scale and level of MSP, as well as its institutional and legal structures, appear to vary considerably between the three areas (Europe, Australia and Bay of Bengal), as discussed in more detail throughout the book. MSP means different things (legal and institutional arrangements, scales, management instruments etc.) in different contexts. It is for this reason that the legal frameworks associated with MSP vary according to location even though some of the basic legal rules governing the spatial jurisdiction of the coastal states, for instance, stay the same.

The institutional and conceptual fragmentation of MSP contributes to both its overall strengths and weaknesses. Fragmentation can be a weakness when trying to coordinate national approaches without a comprehensive and clear legal background. It may also be a curse, if transboundary MSP loses its valuable characteristics like predictability, its future-oriented visions and if it is only conducted on an ad hoc basis (Chapter 8.1). However, one has to keep in mind that to a large degree the success of MSP is a question of integration between different types of planning systems with different historical backgrounds. Chapters 6, 7, 8 and 10 show that the contexts of drafting and implementing MSP are quite different even for the limited selection of marine areas discussed in this book (Australia, Northern Europe and Bay of Bengal). One obvious difference that would present itself between developing and developed countries is the question of institutional context. In Europe, the regional seas convention organizations, such as HELCOM, have been active in developing transboundary cooperation in terms of MSP (Chapters 7 and 8.1). In this sense, many approaches discussed in the book may not be available everywhere in terms of institutional design. Without a similar institutional context, MSP becomes an issue of institution and capacity building between states and other actors, as can be seen in Chapter 10 on the Bay of Bengal in South Asia.

Due to the institutional differences, fragmentation of MSP may also become a strength – providing the freedom for coastal states to pursue the scope and form of planning, level of integration and sectoral involvement that they see most fitting for the context MSP is to be applied in. This freedom also allows for the coastal states to use discretion in choosing the most suitable legal instruments for implementing these requirements. As was emphasized in Chapter 8.1, the legal framework of MSP creates possibilities which in different situations might involve the use of existing institutions as a medium for transboundary cooperation, creating legally non-binding memorandums of understanding or binding bi- and multi-lateral agreements to facilitate further cooperation. Even though in the European Union (EU) there is an obligation for the member states to have legally binding MSP legislation and MSPs in place in the future, the directive sets primarily procedural minimum requirements, leaving questions of substance and its further coordination mainly to the discretion of the member states (Chapter 9).

While the fragmentation of the governance framework for MSP can be viewed as a strength in responding to the myriad of contexts in which MSP is applied, in the transboundary context, certain aspects of the framework require special attention *de lege ferenda*. There is a risk of the positive aspects of flexibility becoming a negative in terms of effective implementation of transboundary MSP. As realized in the Great Barrier Reef in Australia (Chapter 6), an effective MSP requires continued attention and some of the observations made in the book go to the heart of designing an effective governance framework for transboundary MSP.

Ideally, transboundary MSP can play a strategic and proactive role by increasing cross-border cooperation in marine spatial planning, setting out targets for spatial use and providing a future framework for action. In addition, it can ideally be implemented through a wide process of cooperation and negotiation between neighbouring jurisdictions, including fair representation of interests from the different jurisdictions involved, and establishing mechanisms for cooperation in MSP.

First and foremost, in order to achieve this, MSP requires accurate and comprehensive data regarding characteristics and interests of the marine area to be planned (Chapters 8.1 and 8.2). In the transboundary contexts, it is crucial to agree on the modalities for data gathering and analysis so that planners have at their disposal a coherent and accurate set of data. Therefore, data gathering and analysis should be well coordinated and harmonized among countries taking part in the MSP process. More often than not, in these situations, choices have to be made about how to prioritize between different sets of data. There should be a clear and coordinated view on which datasets are the most valuable for the successful execution of MSP. This, in turn, requires the establishment of a clear set of the goals and can have implications for designing stakeholder participation in the MSP process. Availability of data, comprehensive stakeholder participation and common goals of MSP can, therefore, be viewed as prerequisites for successful transboundary MSP. They also form the basis for discussions on the specific instruments to implementing MSP, such as zoning. Addressing these challenges requires patience as the evolution and implementation of an effective MSP framework takes a considerable amount of time in transboundary contexts (Chapters 7, 8.1, 8.2 and 9).

A second consideration to effectively implement transboundary MSP is to recognize the similarities and differences in the state parties regulatory framework to provide for more effective coordination, whether that is a legally binding or a softer form of coordination (Chapter 8.1). Transboundary MSP coordination can have an important effect on national legal arrangements for MSP. Countries lacking MSP legislation may have a regionally developed interest to take part in transboundary MSP activities. Such transboundary MSP cooperation can, in turn, facilitate and affect the development of a national MSP governance framework. Countries may wish to consider such solutions at the national level, which would best serve the transboundary context. In doing this, early transboundary developments on MSP may reduce the incompatibility of planning systems across borders.

A third component in achieving effective implementation of MSP is institutional facilitation. In transboundary contexts, regional seas convention organizations can function as facilitators for discussions in coordinating national MSP governance frameworks (Chapters 8.1, 8.2 and 9) and also provide assistance in the more concrete issues such as the gathering and storage of data (Chapter 8.2). Institutional facilitation may also take on further forms through coordinating a common understanding and education regarding MSP. Planners taking part in the MSP process often have different backgrounds and represent different expertise. In the MSP context, it would be important that they understand each other and that the collective expertise is combined to achieve integrated goals. For instance, joint MSP courses for planners coming from different fields would enhance mutual understanding and facilitate true integration between sectors. In transboundary contexts, emphasis can be put on the importance of human contacts and knowing the planners across borders. For example, cooperation under the auspices of the HELCOM-VASAB Working Group has led to networking between planners. Moreover, in order to facilitate transboundary MSP, 'good working relationships between stakeholders' are a prerequisite for planning (Chapter 8.2). Familiarity raises the effectiveness of transboundary cooperation (Chapter 8.1) and can also facilitate experience and knowledge sharing which is vital, especially in the developing countries (Chapter 10). The need for adequate institutional facilitation is also emphasized to ensure wide stakeholder participation with regard to transboundary MSP.

However, when it comes to coordination of national governance frameworks and institutional facilitation, the situation can be different between institutional settings. In an area where there are no strong regional seas organizations in place, such as the Bay of Bengal, MSP developments have to be taken first on a national level before coordination can occur. There may also be problems with the fragmentation of legal frameworks, lack of institutional capacity and a significant gap between commitment and cooperative action to develop a transboundary MSP (Chapter 10). While national approaches to MSP have been regular in Europe as well (Chapter 5 and 8.1), there have been parallel processes at play on the EU and the regional seas levels to develop transboundary approaches to MSP to facilitate future developments. When this kind of institutional facilitation is lacking altogether, the coordination and coherence of MSP across borders can face significant problems that differ from those in more developed settings. From this perspective there may be a need for an interlinking cooperative regime in regions where pre-existing institutional and legal frameworks in ocean governance are lacking. In these circumstances, MSP pilot projects and other informal means of initiating transboundary dialogue may gain considerable momentum and function as a stepping stone to start the process of formulating the institutional and legal frameworks required for transboundary MSP.

Without overly stringent legal constraints, MSP is able to roam relatively free and to adapt to the changing circumstances, which can be difficult to grasp with global and binding legal instruments. However, in order to be effective, the design of the governance framework of MSP should include coordination of instruments for transboundary cooperation to ensure comprehensive and accurate data, stakeholder participation and setting of common goals, to name but a few. In some aspects, the arrangements within the EU and the regional seas contexts in Europe can be considered as a success in facilitating the processes of transboundary MSP. However, further collaboration and increased participatory processes to enhance the common understanding of sustainable management of human activities in marine areas are crucial in order to achieve a substantively coordinated and coherent framework on MSP. Existing regional seas organizations are likely to play a big role in facilitating these developments.

In conclusion, the governance framework of MSP can be seen as facilitating the process and encouraging transboundary cooperation. The governance framework of MSP creates broad procedural and substantive boundaries for MSP cooperation, which are complemented by softer instruments, emphasizing the importance of voluntary MSP cooperation. The procedural nature of MSP makes it a continuing journey for sustainable and integrated ocean governance. MSP appears to share the same strengths and weaknesses as sustainable development, which it seeks to implement. As a consequence, MSP is not able to escape the problems of fragmentation but, at the same time, this is one of its strengths; countries can come together and adapt MSP to their needs to advance common goals. One of the central characteristics of both MSP and its governance framework is adaptivity.

Index

For Product Safety Concerns and Information please contact our EU representative GPSR@taylorandfrancis.com Taylor & Francis Verlag GmbH, Kaufingerstraße 24, 80331 München, Germany

"Rafael Outland and Thomas Noel, Jr. have produced a seminal work that sheds insights on a narrative of resistance that is not taught in schools, colleges and universities, until now. In fact, the current representatives of the corporate government seek to erase Black, Brown and Indigenous peoples' contribution to the history of this country. It is this paradigm of government that Outland and Noel challenges in The Impact of Police Killings on the Family and Community of Youth Victims: JUSTIFIED, by giving voice to those who have fought back, resisted and sought to end systems of state-sanctioned violence, mass incarceration and ethnic-cleansing despite the fact this country's foundation is based on the aberrant philosophy of white supremacy, the genocidal annihilation of the Indigenous population and the enslavement of Afrikan people. JUSTIFIED, exposes and reveals the devastation of U.S. government policy that is based on the aberrant philosophy of white supremacy, and how this philosophy and praxis, at heart, is violent and anti-human."

Baba Jalil Muntaqim, *Co-Founder, National Jericho Movement; Spirit of Mandela Coalition; Author of* We Are Our Own Liberators: Selected Prison Writings

"Black death is something not to be trifled with. Not something to be made about ourselves. Not something to be captured and made about our personal advancement. Not something to be exploited for other ends. Black death is something to be held sacred and with high regard, especially a Black life that resulted in Black death by actions of the State and its agents. The work of Outland and Noel is one of the few attempts to make Black death legible, coherent, and honorable by elevating the dead through the voices of those that are living that loved them."

Rasul Mowatt, *PhD, North Carolina State University* and **Too Black**, *Poet, Author, and Filmmaker (Pendleton 2); Co-Authors of* Laundering Black Rage: The Washing of Black Death, People, Property, and Profits

"Outland and Noel's book reminds us that policing in the U.S. holds steady as the permanent reflection of enslavement, genocide and settler colonialism. Simultaneously, they also alert us that knowing is not enough. Their unapologetic efforts to enhance our knowledge on the origins of police terror and its lethal results on the lives of young people provides the fuel for us to think, talk and act."

David Stovall, *PhD, University of Illinois at Chicago; Author of* Born Out of Struggle: Critical Race Theory, School Creation, and the Politics of Interruption

"As the whirlpool of violence and the police killings of Black and Brown people continues apace, becoming normalized and commonplace, Rafael Outland and Thomas Noel, Jr. refuse to turn away. They chronicle an unspeakable atrocity by any measure – the police murders of children and youth, their victims ranging from 4-months to 19-years old in a recent period – but they balk at merely documenting and archiving. They pursue the trauma to its outer limits, recording and illuminating the human cost of state terrorism and violence on mothers and fathers, siblings and friends, teachers and classmates, neighbors and indeed entire communities. They demonstrate that the state-sponsored brutality swirling through Black and Brown and poor communities, sweeping outward in a widening gyre with no end in sight, has devastating consequences on the entire society. And they offer a useful antidote to the pervasive and insidious copaganda that dehumanizes entire communities, presents petty crime in gaudy detail on the nightly news – car-jacking! shooting on the west side! – while down-playing or entirely disregarding other more serious crimes committed by the wealthy. This is an essential book for educators and organizers, for justice-seekers and freedom fighters, indeed for anyone who wants to understand the catastrophe unfolding before our eyes, and seeks a clear-sighted way forward."

Bill Ayers, *PhD, Educator, Author, and Activist; Author of* When Freedom Is the Question, Abolition Is the Answer: Reflections on Collective Liberation

"The precisely sniped children in Gaza are the brothers and sisters of the deliberately targeted U.S. Black and Brown youth Rafael Outland and Thomas Noel study the killings of. An interconnected genocide for which the authors give us a textbook of explicit intent."

Mama Julia Wright, *Poet, Author, Co-Founder/Member of the Mumia Health Committee; Editor of* The Man Who Lived Underground

"*The Impact of Police Killings on the Family* concludes its painstaking, powerful work with a warning: "Our youth are our future and we must protect them at all cost." This book outlines historical and contemporary protections and defenses against predatory police violence. Emphasizing young Indigenous, Black, Afro-Indigenous, Chicano/Latino working class and under-resourced children and teens, it details how state and society render racially-stigmatized youths as prey to predatory policing. Militarized police seek a "call to duty" that humiliates and disappears our young. This timely book calls us to resist and fight freedom battles that reject dystopia, and instead wages marronage – the Captive Maternal stage that emphasizes